HOSPITALITY MANAGEMENT

To the memory of Professor John O'Connor:
gentleman, mentor, friend

HOSPITALITY MANAGEMENT

a brief introduction

ROY C. WOOD

Los Angeles | London | New Delhi
Singapore | Washington DC | Boston

Los Angeles | London | New Delhi
Singapore | Washington DC

SAGE Publications Ltd
1 Oliver's Yard
55 City Road
London EC1Y 1SP

SAGE Publications Inc.
2455 Teller Road
Thousand Oaks, California 91320

SAGE Publications India Pvt Ltd
B 1/I 1 Mohan Cooperative Industrial Area
Mathura Road
New Delhi 110 044

SAGE Publications Asia-Pacific Pte Ltd
3 Church Street
#10-04 Samsung Hub
Singapore 049483

Editor: Chris Rojek
Assistant editor: Gemma Shields
Production editor: Katherine Haw
Copyeditor: Jane Fricker
Indexer: Charmian Parkin
Marketing manager: Michael Ainsley
Cover design: Wendy Scott
Typeset by: C&M Digitals (P) Ltd, Chennai, India

Library of Congress Control Number: 2014954699

British Library Cataloguing in Publication data

A catalogue record for this book is available from
the British Library

ISBN 978-1-4462-4694-8
ISBN 978-1-4462-4695-5 (pbk)

At SAGE we take sustainability seriously. Most of our products are printed in the UK using FSC papers and boards.
When we print overseas we ensure sustainable papers are used as measured by the Egmont grading system.
We undertake an annual audit to monitor our sustainability.

CONTENTS

1-5521

LIST OF FIGURES

LIST OF TABLES

ABOUT THE AUTHOR

 Dr Roy C. Wood FHEA, FIH, Hon. FCHME, has enjoyed a varied career in hospitality education and training. Amongst the positions he has held are: Professor of Hospitality Management at the Scottish Hotel School, University of Strathclyde, Glasgow; Principal and Managing Director of IMI Institute of Hotel and Tourism Management in Luzern, Switzerland, a private university college; Dean of the Oberoi Hotels Centre of Learning and Development (responsible for both the corporate management training centre and the corporate apprenticeship programme); and Chief Operating Officer of the Gulf Hospitality and Tourism Education Company in Bahrain. Since February 2010 Roy Wood has been Professor in International Hospitality Management at NHTV Breda University of Applied Sciences, The Netherlands.

Dr Wood is the author, co-author, editor or co-editor of 15 books and over 60 research papers in refereed journals as well as numerous other publications. His first book, *Working in Hotels and Catering* (Routledge, 1992; second edition 1997) remains a major reference point for the study of employment in the hospitality industry. He co-edited, with Dr Robert Brotherton, *The Sage Handbook of Hospitality Management* (2008), the current definitive reference work in the hospitality field, and is editor of *Key Concepts in Hospitality Management* (2013) also published by Sage.

ACKNOWLEDGEMENTS

I have never believed that any work of writing – least of all academic writing – is entirely an act of individual will or ability. The various positive influences I have enjoyed both on, and in, my career are numerous and, through discussion, encouragement and (dis)agreement, they have undoubtedly worked their way into both my thinking and writing, as has experience of the various employments I have been privileged to undertake. In this latter respect I owe debts that can never be repaid to Heinz Bürki, President of IMI University Centre, Luzern, Switzerland for trusting me with his School for five-and-a-half wonderful years; P R S Oberoi, Chairman of EIH Ltd for allowing me two equally fascinating years working at corporate level in one of the world's finest hotel companies; and Qutub Dadabhai, who gave me the opportunity to work in 'hands on' vocational education, thus filling a gap in both my CV and business experience. My current employer, NHTV Breda University of Applied Sciences, in the Netherlands, in the form of both Ms Gienke Osinga and Professor Frans Melissen PhD have been supportive of my position and work in a manner that no-one has the right to automatically expect, and I thank them sincerely for their personal and professional confidence.

Over a long period I have benefited from regular insights into management in the hospitality industry provided by those for whom it is, or has been, a daily reality. My thanks thus go to: Karan Berry, Major Rajesh Chauhan, Rohit Dar, Amanda Hayman, David Mathews, Gillian Rae, Susanne Reitz and Professor Dr Udo Schlentrich. The other constant social and intellectual influences in my life in recent times include Professor Michael Riley, Dr Bob Brotherton, Karan, Shivali and Mehek Berry, Gareth Currie, Juni Hidyat, Bryen Li, Henry Liu, Christian Lo, John Mackillop, Sandra Miller, Heather Robinson, Ashish Sachdeva, Stephen Taylor and Abhinav Ummat.

During the final stages of this book's preparation, its dedicatee – Professor John O'Connor – passed away. John O'Connor gave me my first full-time employment as a hospitality educator some 30-plus years ago and remained a constant and objective friend. In return, I hope I was a thankful one.

Finally, and somewhat more prosaically, I wish to thank, first, Sage Publications for permission to use edited and modified versions of my contributions to B Brotherton and R C Wood (Eds) (2008) *The Sage Handbook of Hospitality Management* and R C Wood (2013) *Key Concepts in Hospitality Management*; and, secondly, NHTV Breda University of Applied Science, the Netherlands, for similar permission in respect of my inaugural professorial lecture given in 2011 entitled 'The End of Hospitality?' I would also like to acknowledge the value of the critical insights of my colleague Rob van Ginneken. Finally, I wish to record my thanks to the staff of NHTV's Sibeliuslaan Library for their superb responsiveness to my requests during the preparation of this book.

Roy C. Wood
Breda, The Netherlands
May 2014

AUTHOR'S PREFACE

In any introductory textbook it is difficult to develop a central coherent argument or position. After all, the reader of such a book is, for the most part seeking an entrée into a field, subject or discipline, or, to continue the French culinary theme, a soupçon of the main ideas, issues and topics embraced by a particular area. They wish to acquire broad familiarity with topics rather than face a detailed and prosy treatise. Many existing introductory texts on the hospitality industry follow the worthy if sometimes over-descriptive approach of offering reviews of the various sectors making up the industry combining this with consideration of selected management topics. This book is somewhat different.

First, though the intention here is that the text will allow the reader to acquire a broad familiarity with the field of 'hospitality management', the approach taken is both descriptive and analytic, drawing on available research to illuminate and substantiate key themes and issues.

Secondly, this approach is underpinned by a pragmatically critical perspective on the hospitality industry. Many people equate the word 'critical' with 'negative' and it has, sadly, become increasingly common, even in academia, for those who hear an observation or opinion that does not correspond to their own world-view to respond by seeking to restrict or close down debate, often attempting to undermine the person articulating critical ideas by chiding them for being negative and/or 'cynical'. The underlying philosophy here is that any true loyalty to anyone or anything should be critical. Excessive conformity is the enemy of progress; reasoned critique is the wellspring of advancement. At the same time, to be critical for its own sake is to practise an art form with limited utility – hence the attempt to strive for pragmatism in this book. Most people are pragmatists: they recognize the value of idealism while understanding that the world is an imperfect place in which idealism faces a constant battle to flourish. Accordingly, this book presents a 'warts and all' view of hospitality and the hospitality industry. From one perspective, the hospitality industry can be wonderful to work in: exciting; offering fantastic rewards for those who progress to senior positions; and one which on occasion attracts extraordinary talent to its ranks. From another point of view, it is an industry which struggles to attract sufficient talent to make it a model or source of inspiration for other business sectors; where many people experience employment as demeaning, degrading and poorly paid; in which work–life balance is impossible to achieve; and in which conservatism and tradition often suffocate quality and innovation. This is the 'real world' of the hospitality industry – as with most aspects of life nothing is ever as good – or bad – as it seems.

Thirdly, and following from the above, it makes sense 'up front' to outline some of those overarching factors and themes that appear to give the hospitality industry its particular character. In preparing this text, and in addition to drawing on knowledge from my early academic career, some 600 research papers in academic journals and a further 30 or so textbooks and monographs covering the period 1999-2014 have been reviewed. In addition, a number of texts authored by industry figures, including biographies and autobiographies, have been trawled for useful insights. Regrettably, not all of the latter works offer up the wisdom that their covers invariably promise but some, at least, are useful and even valuable (see Venison, 1983, 2005; Meyer, 2006; Tomsky, 2012; http://waiterrant.net/). Inevitably, on this scale of coverage, obvious and sometimes less obvious commonalities and continuities are revealed. The majority of these will be touched upon again at various points in the text so only the briefest of summaries is advanced here.

The Contested Nature of Hospitality ... and Management

The terms 'hospitality industry' and 'hospitality management' have gained broad acceptance and legitimacy as descriptors of a range of economic activities, and their management, concerned with the public provision of accommodation, food and related services for those away from home. Yet as terms, they can be all of poorly defined, misleading, and, on occasion, the source of conflict, the latter not least because of a growing realization that 'hospitality' is a very broad social phenomenon that has meaning beyond the industry it purports to describe. These and related themes are discussed in Chapter 1, which is also concerned with the nature of management – both generally and in hospitality – and the reliability or otherwise of management knowledge.

An Economically Global, National and Local Industry

Those, usually representative-composed organizations that lobby on behalf of the hospitality industry at local, national and global level tend to suggest that the importance of the industry is underestimated, and that it can, given the correct support, be a major source of jobs and wealth creation. Similar claims are often made for the tourism industry more widely. Yet, as we shall see in Chapters 1 and 2, anyone who dispassionately reviews the available evidence is certain to come up with a more nuanced view. Many businesses in hospitality, being small in nature, operate at what may politely be called the economic margins. Many are what are – equally politely – called 'lifestyle' businesses where the provision of services is not made in pursuit of some abstract entrepreneurial wish fulfilment but simply to make a 'living'. In the corporate sector, differences between hotels and restaurants emerge. Even large internationally branded hotel chains possess many features of economic marginality – albeit different in nature and scope to those of small and medium sized enterprises (SMEs). Branded restaurant chains, operating in higher demand markets, look more like an international business in any other industry, a fact perhaps reflected in McDonald's Restaurants being the highest ranked hospitality company in 2013 (at 51st position) in the well-regarded Financial Times Global 500.

A further observation here is that, though rarely stated in so many words, there is a pride among those involved in the hospitality industry that it was the first, truly global industry (for many it remains so). Global presence does not always, however, mean global scope. Most hospitality businesses serve the needs of their local, national and regional communities more than they do those of visitors. The industry is dominated by the aforementioned SMEs. In many countries, product and labour markets are predominantly local. There are parts of the world where an indigenous population possesses values that limit the ability of some or all of that population to work in hospitality occupations and this means that labour must be imported. In other parts of the globe, similar values combined with economic and social inequality lead to many hospitality jobs being taken by nationals who have origins elsewhere.

People, People, People

The hospitality industry is essentially a people industry. This egregious cliché forms the basis for the investigation of hospitality industry employment in Chapter 3, and for an examination of hospitality managers and management in Chapter 7 and hospitality education in Chapter 8. At this juncture it is only necessary to note two points. The first will become evident in Chapter 2, namely that the capital investment requirements for new hospitality businesses is considerable, not least in the case of large and professionally managed – and usually internationally branded – hotels and in the chain restaurant industry. Many hospitality businesses are capital *and* labour intensive although the latter is much more variable than people think, largely because we allow ourselves to succumb to the romanticized image of the 'luxury-plus' hotel invariably peopled with countless employees. At best, however, establishments of this nature account for only a tiny proportion of the total market supply. The second point here is that in many countries, and certainly the UK, almost all forms of hospitality labour carry a degree of social stigma. This was well captured in an early study of the UK industry by Saunders (1981) and continues as a recurring theme in both academic and public discourse on the industry. A report in *The Independent* newspaper by Wynne-Jones (1996: 11), commenting on the preference of young craftspeople entering the industry for a career as chef rather than waiter, quoted a member of the British House of Lords, Lady Parkes, as saying 'We've got to get away from this stupid pre-war attitude that waiting tables is in some way demeaning. On the continent, you see waiters take a pride in their work: it's considered a profession. In this country, people hark back to the days of domestic service and it's seen as a stigma.' Some 16 years later, Harris (2012a: 30) wrote: 'Unlike in Italy, France or elsewhere in Europe, where waiters are regarded as skilled professionals, in Britain the job is hardly regarded as a profession at all.

At best, it is seen as a necessary station on the way to more glamorous destinations …
it is regarded as a holiday job or a temporary berth before something more prestigious
in another sector comes along.'

Stigma has many practical implications and not only for operative level workers
in hospitality. Although in many countries it is possible to attain well-paid general
manager positions at a young age, in terms of career development, graduates rarely
enjoy preferment advantages compared to non-graduates entering the sector (Riley
and Turam, 1988). This raises important questions about both the value of formal
hospitality education and the human resource practices of the industry – both issues
we shall examine in this book.

The Product and Service Mix

The distinctive features of the hospitality industry's product and service mix are
the provision of accommodation and food which are the subjects of Chapters 4
and 5 respectively. This provision comes in myriad, but not infinite, forms. In large
organizations offering both products, and their related services, specialist managers
are called into being to deal with them, and this specialization has implications for
the structure and operation of hospitality organizations.

There is a growing tension in both the academic and 'real' worlds of hospitality
between those who regard the provision of services as the main focus of hospitality
management and those who argue for a more instrumental approach emphasizing
the primary objective of hospitality provision – the creation of profit. Thus, in the
case of the first, we frequently hear that the hospitality industry's success depends
primarily on delivering guest and customer satisfaction, creating 'customer delight',
and in the case of one international hotel company at least, fulfilling 'even the unex-
pressed wishes and needs of our guests', which is a very neat trick when one thinks
about it. A report in *The Economist* (2013d) described the modern corporate hotel
as 'industrial' and points to how companies have sought to 'engineer "emotional
touch points" and "wow moments" with guests' in order to compensate for physical soullessness. Somewhat dryly, *The Economist* notes, approaches of this kind may
be counterproductive as 'many people do not want to be touched, emotionally or
otherwise' – a surely accurate diagnosis.

Indeed, one problem experienced by the hospitality as well as many other industries is a periodic obsession with 'innovation', not always easy in an industry that
must cater to basic and familiar human needs. On occasions, the pressure to innovate, which can be perceived by managements as arising from the need to gain
competitive advantage, has led the hospitality sector to succumb to, or overindulge
the whims of specialists including chefs, interior designers and marketing executives.
The results from the point of view of the effective provision of the industry's basic
products and services have not always been positive, a point considered in Chapters
4 and 5, and further in Chapter 6. Indeed, there is a good case for arguing that
managerial obsessing at the margins of customer and guest concerns detracts from

the hospitality industry – and especially the hotel sector – fulfilling the more basic requirements of their business – clean and well-designed and -equipped rooms; and honest, effective service.

Conservatism, Exceptionalism and Operational Bias

Throughout this text, as opposed to in specific chapters, we shall encounter certain recurring themes concerning the conservatism, exceptionalism and operational bias of the hospitality sector.

The hospitality industry is a conservative industry in the sense of being seemingly all of traditional, cautious, insular and averse to change. This is hardly surprising since, although the purchase of hospitality products and services is an economically discretionary activity (very few people *have* to buy them), the core products and services of the industry relate to fundamental human needs for shelter and nourishment. It is, Pizam and Shani (2009: 141) state in a fascinating study, 'a business that has been providing essentially the same basic services throughout history', noting that many of the managers they interviewed believed that: 'Although technological developments have definitely impacted the industry … the industry is not as technologically astute as other industries, nor does it need to be. Yet technology does allow for a slightly higher degree of sophistication in providing the service, especially in regard to catering to specific needs of individual guests.'

The phrase 'nor does it need to be' is suggestive here, if only because it encourages us to consider the strong tradition of insularity and related exceptionalism that imbues the values of hospitality management and its practice. There is a long tradition in the industry and its associated institutions (particularly the edifice of hospitality education) of insisting that both the industry and management practice differ significantly, if not uniquely, from other forms of industry and management in terms of the products and service they offer – notably accommodation and food and beverage – and thus require separate and distinctive forms of management. Similar views have, until fairly recently at least, arguably dominated approaches to hospitality management education and research. Since all industries have their distinctive features, this claim to uniqueness has always seemed somewhat improbable. The hospitality industry has many features in common with other sectors. That it is a sector with low barriers to entry, numerically dominated as we have seen by small and medium sized enterprises, many owned and operated by those without prior management experience or professional qualifications (albeit with variable success) is certainly not suggestive of the existence of a unique managerial skill set.

In a highly perceptive commentary, Mars et al. (1979) described internships and placements that figure in most formal hospitality education programmes as part of the 'pre-entry' (to industry) socialisation' of students. The socialization entailed is one that embraces a managerially operational bias and world-view – emphasizing the importance of day-to-day operational control, rather than the skills of long-term planning and any number of other techniques that usually fall under the heading of 'strategy'. This operational bias has implications not only for managers themselves in terms of career development possibilities, but also for those they manage and indeed, it permeates the culture of the hospitality industry to an extent that we have only recently begun to thoroughly understand. For example, it has implications for managerial turnover in the industry (which is considerable); for helping to explain why so few graduates in hospitality management are found in senior corporate positions within the sector; and for why certain 'traditional' and generally disadvantageous human resource practices (to employees and the organization) endure for no obvious reason.

Concluding Remarks

We shall touch upon the above themes on a number of occasions in the various chapters of this text. In adopting a critically pragmatic approach to our subject matter the main hope here is to stimulate prospective 'hospitality managers' and others to reflect upon this fascinating industry and their own relationships, as owners, employers and consumers, to it. Despite its centrality to our lives, the hospitality industry is still little understood (and occasionally misunderstood). It is the intention of this text to give a little solidity to the base from which future, and broader, narratives might hopefully emerge.

1

WHERE ARE WE GOING? THE NATURE OF HOSPITALITY MANAGEMENT

After reading this chapter, you should:

(a) better understand the nature of hospitality and hospitality management and the difficulties associated with these terms;

(b) have gained insight into a variety of ways in which researchers have theorized about the nature of hospitality and the hospitality industry, including 'hospitality studies' perspectives; and

(c) have developed sensitivity to the limitations of management knowledge and its applications to the study of hospitality and the hospitality industry.

Introduction: What is Hospitality Management?

The original intention for the title of this book was *Hotel Management: A Brief Introduction*. A person who studies the nature and character of hotel management is pretty much prepared for managing not only hotels, but restaurants and other types of business that provide food and/or temporary accommodation for the purposes of business or pleasure. This is because the study of hotel management embraces all (or most) of the basic knowledge sets required in preparation for an operational career in the many diverse businesses that make up a fascinating industry. Furthermore, most people know what a hotel or restaurant or accommodation manager is – or at least can make an educated guess. However, in this second decade of the twenty-first century, most students in the field to which this book is addressed are (in the UK at least) likely to be studying a course in *hospitality* management, a term which has a nice, warm, inclusive feel to it. But what is 'hospitality management'?

Ideally, hospitality management implies the management of hospitality but the concept of hospitality is a somewhat abstract and fluid one: it can mean different things to different people. Even if we could engineer a definition of hospitality on which most could agree, it would still leave open the question of whether it was possible to 'manage' so complex a phenomenon, whereas to talk of hotel management or restaurant management or food and beverage or lodging management is to 'pin' management practices to a specific form or function of particular kinds of organization. In reality, the term hospitality management as it is generally employed is of relatively recent origin and has few intellectual anchors. Its use began to grow in popularity among educationalists from the 1980s onwards and came to replace, though not universally, various descriptors like 'hotel management', 'hotel and catering management', 'hotel and restaurant management', 'food and accommodation management', and 'lodging and food service management' (the term 'lodging management' is principally North American and its use persists). Subsequently, the term has attracted more widespread adoption, so much so that we now refer unselfconsciously to the 'hospitality industry', on the use of which Lashley (2008: 69) notes: 'It appears that the description of hotel, restaurant and bar business as "hospitality" was an early attempt at *spin*, that is, adapting the name of the sector to create a more favourable impression of commercial activities.' The attraction of the term hospitality management has been explained by some in terms of the extent to which in the English-speaking world the hotel, catering, restaurant and associated industry sectors are held in low social esteem. In this view, adoption of the term has been an attempt by the academic world at creating a respectable cover to deflect these negative associations (Wood, 1997; Brotherton and Wood, 2008a).

Whatever the case, the terms 'hospitality management' and 'hospitality industry' are, in essence, flags of convenience which are at best vague and suspiciously pretentious and at worse, unnecessarily confusing in incorporating related but different industries under a single umbrella. As Lashley (2000) among others has shown, the many distinct sectors that are taken to comprise the hospitality industry all arguably share *some* production and service elements in common as well as having affinities with business models found in other industries – notably, but not exclusively, the retail sector. This is an important observation because before we focus on current thinking about the nature of the hospitality industry (and what this implies about the nature of hospitality more generally and the quality of hospitality management) it is necessary to recognize that there are numerous ways in which academics, business analysts and others have sought to *theoretically* characterize the sector. In an industry which prides itself on its practical and operational nature, the very mention of the word 'theory' is likely to raise blood pressure. For one writer, Hemmington (2007: 747, emphasis added):

> The schizophrenia of the hospitality industry, and the 'fragmentation' of hospitality academia … is a potentially limiting factor in the industry's drive for growth and development. This schizophrenia is illustrated *by questions about whether the hospitality industry is a service industry, whether it is entertainment, or art, or theatre, or retailing, or whether it is no more than another form of business.*

Far from being evidence of schizophrenia, a perhaps unfortunate choice of word, the questions noted by Hemmington arise from legitimate theorizing about the nature of the hospitality industry. Theorizing about the nature of any phenomenon (even if sometimes unsuccessful) is not some abstract exercise in unreality but rather the opposite: it is crucial to understanding what we can accept as 'real' and plausible about a phenomenon, in this case, the hospitality industry.

Theorizing Hospitality and the Hospitality Industry

Following from the final comment in the preceding section, we shall consider here several different attempts to theoretically define and characterize the hospitality industry under the following headings: hospitality as part of the tourism industry; hospitality as a service industry; the 'McDonaldized' hospitality industry; the hospitality industry as an 'experience' industry; and hospitality as a social phenomenon.

Hospitality as part of the tourism industry

The idea that the hospitality industry is a sub-set or function of the tourism industry is so well established in academic discourse that to challenge the notion is to invite ridicule. Yet not only *can* the notion be challenged, there are good reasons for arguing that it *should* be. The fields of tourism studies and tourism management have increasingly adopted (or at least not critically challenged) ever more expansive definitions of the tourist and tourism, as have various international organizations. The United Nations World Tourism Organization (UNWTO) defines tourists as people: 'traveling to and staying in places outside their usual environment for not more than one consecutive year for leisure, business and other purposes', and the 'tourism sector' as:

> the cluster of production units in different industries that provide consumption goods and services demanded by visitors. Such industries are called *tourism industries* because visitor acquisition represents such a significant share of their supply that, in the absence of visitors, their production of these would cease to exist in meaningful quantity. (http://media.unwto.org/en/content/understanding-tourism-basic-glossary, last accessed 31.03.13)

This definition is in many ways quite peculiar – what for example are we to call 'tourism industries' in areas where visitor acquisition does not constitute a significant element of the demand for the goods and services they supply? The UNWTO view is good enough when applied to those parts of the world where tourism is the dominant industry (or one of the dominant industries) and where hospitality business activity is substantially dependent on tourist arrivals. In harsh reality and most parts of the globe, however, parts of the hospitality industry at least are not called into existence because of tourism and travel but rather exist to serve the needs of local, regional and national communities for food, drink and shelter. The UNWTO recognizes that there are numerous different types of tourism industry although a more accurate description might be 'industries' involved in the servicing of tourism and travel. This approach is consistent with the analysis of Leiper (2008: 238), who argues that:

> the concept of 'the tourism industry' as a single entity directly linked with all tourists is unrealistic, stemming from flawed perceptions and defective understanding of business and industries. Clearer vision, alongside deeper knowledge of business theories and practices, recognises multiple tourism industries.

(Bernini and Guizzardi, 2012, offer a similar take on accommodation industries.) The hospitality sector should not be viewed unequivocally as part of some agglomeration of tourism industries. Clearly, as already noted, there are many economies dependent on international tourism arrivals. Equally, there are places with a plentiful supply of certain hospitality businesses (restaurants, bars) and a restricted supply of others (e.g. hotels and other accommodation businesses) that do not see an international tourist/traveller from one end of the year to the next (in the UK, recent statistics suggest that London alone accounts for 53% of international visitors' expenditure; see *The Economist*, 2013c). Of course, in terms of the UNWTO definition cited above, and in terms of academic tourism studies more generally, a tourist is a tourist. Thus a business person travelling within their own country and stopping one night away from home is a tourist. If this seems absurd it is because the definition invites incredulity. Our business person is certainly a traveller, but a tourist? This is a much more contentious point. Tourism scholars have so accustomed us to many different 'types' of tourism (health tourism, educational tourism, business tourism, shopping tourism) that the word has been robbed of any real meaning.

To summarize, in parts of the world the existence of hospitality businesses is heavily dependent on various forms of travel and tourism but in many, if not the majority of cases, much of the core hospitality industry – or more appropriately 'industries' – exists to serve local and regional populations in their daily needs for the products and services offered by the sector. In theorizing that the hospitality sector is *simply* part of the tourism industry we obscure this fact and draw attention away from those parts of the hospitality industry involved in the servicing of needs that are categorically *not* tourism dependent – as in, for example, many forms of business-to-business catering, schools, prisons and hospitals.

Hospitality as a service industry

Just as the relationship of the hospitality to the tourism industries appears at first sight to be unproblematic, then so does the question as to whether the hospitality industry is a service industry – indeed, in some American academic hospitality writing it is not unusual to refer, in error, to the hospitality industry as *the* service industry. Everybody knows, or thinks they know, that the hospitality industry is a service industry. A service industry is normally defined in contrast to a manufacturing industry, the latter primarily being involved in the production of physical, tangible goods, the former focused upon the provision of some service or services that are not physically tangible.

It is now regarded as a simple truth that we live in a 'post-industrial' or 'service' society. Daniel Bell (1973) and subsequently many others predicted the coming of 'post-industrial society', the three most important features of which were: (a) a change from a goods producing to a service economy; (b) the growth in pre-eminence of white collar workers within the occupational structure, and within this category the growth in importance of what would today be called 'knowledge workers'; and (c) increasing mastery and use of technology, and the incorporation of technology into increasing aspects of life. Bell's views have been hotly disputed. Kumar (1978, 2004) argues that so-called post-industrial society characteristics can be traced back to the nineteenth century with service employment being a normal feature of early industrialization in most economies. In this respect, the UK was anomalous in having, albeit only for a short period in its history, the majority of its workforce engaged in manufacturing.

Gershuny (1978, 1979) maintains that Bell (1973) confuses definitions of services based on service 'products' and those based on service employment. For Gershuny, services are consumable at the instant of production, being always consumed 'once and for all'. Goods in contrast are material things that maintain an existence after the production process. Gershuny found no increase in the percentage of household expenditure on services between 1954 and 1974 but did find evidence of patterns of substitution where needs previously met externally to the household were now met by the purchase of capital goods. Entertainment needs previously met by cinemas or theatres were replaced by television; domestic help in the form of human labour by domestic appliances; public transport by private transport – in each case a good substituting for a service. Gershuny suggests that definitions of service *employment* should be constrained to describing employment in industries whose final product is a service in the 'once and for all' sense. The apparent growth in services employment noted by proponents of post-industrial society theories is, Gershuny suggests, a problem of misclassification. He notes that a large proportion of service workers are closely connected with the production of goods in the widest sense, thus workers employed in financial services are associated with the production or purchase of goods. Therefore, though service workers may constitute a majority of the workforce this does not imply that the production of services predominates over that of goods. This view accords with those of a number of economists, for example Greenfield (2002: 21), who pursue the somewhat purist notion that demand for services is always subordinate to demand for goods – that is 'no services can be produced without a prior investment in capital goods having been made'.

Gershuny's contribution to our understanding of services is paralleled in one strand of largely unrelated academic Marxism. At a time when service industries were still largely ignored by academic social scientists, not least by those of a leftist persuasion, Harry Braverman (1974: 360) argued that much service work is similar to manufacturing work. He instances chefs and cooks preparing a meal to illustrate his point, reinforcing this by considering chambermaids, who, though classed as service employees, produce in their work, a tangible good (a clean room for sale). It is fairly straightforward to accept the chef as a producer of manufactured goods rather than a service worker but do we regard the outcome of a chambermaid's efforts – a clean room – as a product or a service? In Gershuny's terms, a service is consumed once and for all: a hotel bedroom is not consumed once and for all, it endures. Gershuny and Braverman (and many others besides – see Miles, 2001, for a useful review) indirectly highlight the reductionism entailed in simply classifying hospitality as a service industry. The co-presence of goods and services within the hospitality sector is self-evident. Advances in science and technology have allowed development of food production and service systems that permit the separation of production from service/consumption thus furnishing operators with a wider range of choices as to the models of hospitality and hospitality management that can be developed in contrast to the traditional model of same-site production, service and consumption. This has implications for the type, cost of production and service, and the nature of the consumer experience, and for the quantity and skill levels of the employees required to operate particular production and service configurations.

A similar point is made in more general terms by Unvala and Donaldson (1988: 468), who distinguish between emerging 'economic' and 'marketing' traditions in discussions of the nature of services, maintaining that: 'new employment and continued employment in services cannot be safely predicted without a detailed analysis of (a) criteria for characterising services … . This needs (c) detailed research on the similarities and differences between services at company, industry and unit level.' In point of fact, the 'marketing tradition' has in many ways come to dominate contemporary discourse on services with the development of a whole field devoted to services marketing (e.g. Gronroos, 2007; Palmer, 2007). One consequence of this has been that relative to services in general and hospitality in particular, the wider economic and social issues raised by Gershuny, Braverman and other, similar, writers remain largely unresolved, indeed they have been marginalized, letting matters rest with the view that the sector combines both production and service elements or, as has become somewhat ironically commonplace in many nominally service industries, referring to 'service products' as if in some way this removes questions relating to the conceptualization of services.

To summarize, theorizing about the nature of services, together with the study of hard data, suggest that the obvious truth that hospitality is a service industry (blanketing all hospitality processes, products, services and forms of employment under the 'service' heading) is not actually very obvious at all. Both theory and observation tell us, again, that reality is more complex, not simply because the hospitality industry offers a mix of products and services (and then often within the same business unit) but because products *and* services can be delivered in diverse ways.

The 'McDonaldized' hospitality industry

The McDonaldization thesis of the distinguished American sociologist George Ritzer was first outlined in his 1993 book *The McDonaldization of Society* (currently in its seventh edition). Ritzer's ideas both parallel and to some extent duplicate those of Braverman (1974) whose views on services were briefly mentioned in the preceding section. However, instead of using Marx and Marxism as his source of inspiration, Ritzer relies on the work of Max Weber, another founding father of sociological theory who is more widely known for evolving the concept of bureaucracy. Ritzer interprets Weber as proposing bureaucracy (or more accurately bureaucratic organizations) to be the paramount model of a rational system, a rational system being defined in terms of the pursuit of efficiency, predictability, calculability and control (the last often through technology). His central argument is that these four 'principles' of production rationalization have dominated much of western manufacturing industry since the onset of industrialization, being extended during the latter part of the twentieth century to service industries. The archetypal rational bureaucratic organization of the modern age is, for Ritzer, McDonald's, hence the coining of the clumsy term 'McDonaldization', a phenomenon which embraces 'notably homogeneous products, rigid technologies, standardized work routines, deskilling, homogenization of labour (and customer), the mass worker, and homogenization of consumption' (Ritzer, 1993: 1), phenomena not confined to hospitality but widely present in most aspects of production and consumption in social life including education, banking and retail.

Over the 20 or so years since the initial publication of Ritzer's book, many commentators have noted that there is nothing especially novel or innovative about his thesis (Levitt (1972), for instance, evolved the 'industrialization of service' thesis advocating the reduction of inefficiencies in service industries through the application of manufacturing techniques to service production). One early critic savaged *The McDonaldization of Society* noting that it 'is too simplistic and sloppy to have much educational value. It is not sociology and it would certainly not teach students how to reason' (Gilling, 1996: 24). More recently Roberts (2005: 58) has commented on the 'Ritzerization' of academic management texts, remarking: 'there is a formula present in Ritzer's book, which can be found in many academic texts. Such formulae are not primarily designed to create a highly effective tool for learning and developing the knowledge of readers, but, rather, to maximize the commercial success of the book.' Timo and Littler (1996: 20) suggest that McDonaldization is the application of the principles of Taylorism/scientific management to work organization in services (for more on scientific management and related matters in a hospitality context, see Wood, 1994a, 1997, 1998). Lyon et al. (1994, 1995) assert not only that the process of McDonaldization is neither ubiquitous nor inevitable, but that it fails to take account of product differentiation and varied styles of producer choice in creating and satisfying market demands.

In sum, Ritzer views the effects of McDonaldization as irretrievably detrimental to modern social life, dehumanizing and degrading people. In arguing thus, Ritzer does little more than articulate a standard sociological critique of work and employment. What is distinctive about the McDonaldization thesis is the populist and accessible manner in which it is advanced. In terms of its capacity to provide a framework for the analysis of contemporary hospitality, its utility is more questionable.

The hospitality industry as an 'experience' industry

An extension of the discussion as to whether the hospitality industry is a service industry is of more recent origin and relates to its status as part of the so-called experience economy. This debate derives from the work of Pine and Gilmore (1999), who have famously posited that certain creative and service industries are principally involved in the creation and sale of experiences. Thus, in the context of the hospitality industry, Hemmington (2007: 749) asserts that: 'customers do not buy service delivery, they buy experiences; they do not buy service quality, they buy memories; they do not buy food and drink, they buy meal experiences.' Pine and Gilmore (1999: 97, cited in Smith et al., 2010: 62) themselves state that 'customers unquestionably desire experiences'. The singular lack of widespread hard evidence for assertions of this kind, and for the 'experience economy' concept more generally, has not been an obstacle to a bandwagon effect in tourism studies and research, and in scholarship relating to the so-called creative industries. The conceptual problem with the 'experience economy' idea is exemplified by Smith et al. (2010: 63), who write: 'The tourism industry, traditionally concerned with the provision of standardised travel, accommodation and catering services, is of course embracing the contemporary experience economy and providing more and more tailored and unique experiences for visitors.' The questions, simply put (and ignoring the historical inaccuracy attendant on the assertion of what the tourism industry has been *traditionally* involved with), are how can each tourist's experience be made unique and, more pointedly, without a command of each individual's personal psychology, how can experiences be optimally customized?

In the context of hospitality and especially in the light of Hemmington's comment cited above, Stierand and Wood (2012) conducted a review of the evidence pertaining to the experience economy in general and the 'meal experience', a well-established concept in hospitality management (see Chapter 5), more specifically. A survey of the key academic literature confirmed the relative absence of research on the experience economy and that which did exist either was reminiscent of one of the criticisms of the McDonaldization thesis, i.e. that there is little new in the experience economy concept that cannot be traced to earlier managerial and social scientific theories (e.g. Kociatkiewicz and Kostera, 2009), or focused on problems inherent in developing effective measures of the underlying dimensions of the experience economy model (Hosany and Witham, 2010).

Almost all facets of human existence involve experiences and in this sense it is difficult to understand why a commonplace concept embodied in an idea like the 'experience economy' should be elevated to a special status. The test of the integrity of any concept is its empirical veracity – the extent to which data can be generated to support the core of that concept. If we accept that all human existence entails experience then the idea of an experience economy is unexceptional. Of course, there are industries and business types that consciously set out to create specific forms of experience – e.g. theme parks. Intentionality is thus an important factor in determining whether a business or organization is seeking to offer 'an experience'. However, the intention to provide a particular type of experience is not a guarantee that a consumer will have the experience intended. Given the number and variety of factors entailed, it is simply impossible to guarantee any *particular* experience. To summarize, the idea – or assumption – that people are forever seeking experiences is (so far) empirically questionable and as a concept appears at least mildly absurd. It belongs to that category of social theorizing that borders on favouring a view of (in this case) consumers as essentially passive and easily malleable. As a perspective for analysing the hospitality industry, the experience economy concept remains unproved.

Theorizing hospitality as a social phenomenon

We noted in the introduction to this chapter that the terms 'hospitality management' and 'hospitality industry' have been adopted to replace other labels for reasons unrelated to both reflection on the nature of hospitality itself and, if there is indeed a 'hospitality industry', what it is that is being managed. One consequence of the widespread adoption of these terms has been a growth of interest in the nature of hospitality as a generalized social phenomenon and recognition of the fact that the 'management' of hospitality can take place in a variety of contexts – in the home, in commercial organizations and in not-for-profit organizations. Put another way, just as we can assume the phenomenon of hospitality to be complex, diverse and heterogeneous then management practices can be similarly characterized and need not always be conceived in terms of the *formal* management of commercial organizations.

In recent years, a small but vociferous group of hospitality management academics have argued, correctly, that hospitality is a distinct social phenomenon that can be studied on its own terms. They see the management of public hospitality (whether commercial hospitality or not-for-profit) as but one instance of the study of the wider nature of the phenomenon. The origins of this approach are to be found in work by Brotherton (1999), Wood (1994a) and Brotherton and Wood (2000). Brotherton (1999) in contrast was centrally concerned with the relationships of concepts of hospitality to hospitality management. While both writers have remained active contributors to the debate over the nature of hospitality (see Brotherton and Wood, 2008a), a range of complementary and sometimes competing perspectives have, and continue, to be generated, including the notable contributions of Lashley (e.g. Lashley and Morrison, 2000; Lashley, 2007a, 2007b, 2008), who, with other writers, have been labelled as advocates of what has become known as the 'hospitality studies' approach. This term is misleading because there is evidence of not one hospitality studies approach but several. Some writers (e.g. Brotherton and Wood, 2008b) are motivated by interest in the question of whether it is possible to clearly define something called 'hospitality management', and if so, what it is that we need to know about the nature of hospitality that will usefully or otherwise impact on management theory and practice in the sector. Others, Lashley arguably among them, seem to define hospitality studies in distinction from, if not outright opposition to, the study of the commercial management of hospitality, leading some contributors to the field to imply that hospitality studies and hospitality management are in fact two distinct subject areas or disciplines (Morrison and O'Gorman, 2008). At least five differing if complementary 'hospitality studies' approaches can be identified, and all utilize knowledge and research from disciplines as diverse as history, sociology, social anthropology, philosophy and economics. They are as follows:

1. A focus on pre-industrial and early industrial hospitality centred on the general social duty to protect travellers and strangers (Muhlmann, 1932; Heal, 1990); recent years have also seen a growing but thus far inconclusive interest in the wider history of hospitality (see Durie, 2011).

2. Examination of the economic and social dimensions to the idea that hospitality is based on principles of gift giving and reciprocity (Mauss, 2000 [1924]; Burgess, 1982; Telfer, 1996; Davis, 2000).

3. Analysis of hospitality as an element of the structure of spatial and social control in society (Wood, 1994a; Bell, 2007; Lugosi, 2009).

4. The economic analysis of hospitality as an exemplar of rational exchange theory (e.g. Bell and Henry, 2001).

5. A focus on the management of hospitality broadly defined as a concept that should not, evidentially, be restricted to corporate entities, that is, hospitality can be managed in different contexts and different ways (as in the earlier-noted suggestion that one can speak of the management of hospitality in the home) (Brotherton and Wood, 2008b; Lashley, 2008).

To many observers outside the hospitality research and education field, these intellectual endeavours are largely uncontroversial, appearing at worst as characteristically self-indulgent academic preoccupations and at best as a serious effort to engage with a range of issues that might illuminate understanding of a complex phenomenon. Certainly, 'hospitality studies' approaches raise legitimate and interesting questions, made all the more interesting because of the comparatively limited interest in the concept of hospitality shown by social scientists more generally. This has largely been limited to consideration, on the one hand, of the sociological implications of the role of hospitality in global migration and the implications thereof for localized patterns of migrant adaptation and integration, and patterns of resistance by receiving communities, on the other. Bauman (1990) and Molz and Gibson (2007) offer useful insights into this perspective although it is the more high profile French theorist Derrida (2000) who has surprisingly attracted the attention of some proponents of the hospitality studies approach (e.g. O'Gorman, 2006) (because Derrida's views on hospitality add little of originality on the topic of hospitality to prior commentaries). Equally certain is the fact that hospitality studies approaches have not (yet) had any notably extensive impact on research, learning and teaching in the area of hospitality *management*, or for that matter on the way in which the hospitality industry operates.

Whereas the reaction among hospitality researchers in general to the first four perspectives described in this section has been to ignore, sidestep or accept uncritically their content, in the case of theorizing about hospitality as a social phenomenon the reaction has been somewhat more lively, if not, in more extreme cases, highly combative. Put simply, there has been some resistance to the ideas embodied in hospitality studies approaches. Slattery (2002: 23) accuses proponents of the hospitality studies approach of offering 'a denuded and sterile conception of commercial hospitality and hospitality management'. Jones and Lockwood (2008: 27) are somewhat more emollient, but no less sceptical, writing that:

> We would accept that the hospitality studies perspective most certainly provides insights into the phenomenon of hospitality and may even provide relevant insights for managers in the industry. What we do not agree with is the advocacy of this approach at the expense of management-based research.

Jones and Lockwood suggest that the key to developing hospitality management research is to do (management) research 'better'. In traditional higher education institutions where research is the central component of the academic reward system, their view represents current orthodoxy, the established wisdom and way of doing things. Accordingly, there is no obvious career incentive for researchers to experiment with approaches alternate to this dominant management research paradigm. Indeed, current debates initiated by the growth of hospitality studies perspectives reveal an enduring truth about hospitality management research, namely a resistance to theorizing in general, and to theorizing beyond the boundaries of management knowledge in particular. This phenomenon was captured in the 2002 UK Research Assessment Exercise (RAE) (a periodic government sponsored assessment of the quality of higher education research which determines the allocation of research resources to universities) which in assessing hospitality research (as a sub-division of management research) commented that: 'The sub-area relies heavily on theory developed in the management field, with only application to the hospitality industry, and in some cases work lags a number of years behind theory development in mainstream management' (http://www.hero.ac.uk/rae/overview/docs/UoA43.pdf).

We shall briefly examine this statement further in Chapter 8. For the purposes of this discussion it is sufficient to be aware that in opposing hospitality studies approaches and advocating 'better' management research, critics in the vein of Jones and Lockwood (2008) can draw on the apparently supportive observations of influential bodies as exemplified by the RAE panel. Does any of this matter? The answer is a resounding 'yes' for two reasons. First, as we have seen, the term 'hospitality management' is largely meaningless: there is hotel management, food service management, events management and so on but if there is something called hospitality management it must surely be about the management of hospitality and thus we require good theoretical and practical models of what hospitality 'is'. Secondly, underpinning the claims of those who oppose hospitality studies approaches is an assumption about the superiority – or at least privileged position – of management knowledge. In order to fully understand the various ways in which hospitality and the hospitality industry are conceived and studied, as discussed in this section, it is necessary to take a small detour to examine how much reliance we can place on management research as a model for hospitality research.

The Naked Emperor – the Problem of Management Knowledge

In an ideal world, management knowledge should really enlighten us as to the nature and practices of management. In reality, the study of what managers do, how they manage, what skills and competencies they employ and so on represents (an albeit significant) minority research interest in contemporary business and management studies. As is partially signalled in the title of Henry Mintzberg's book *Managers Not MBAs* (2004), academic business and management studies tends to favour the mastery of relatively abstract knowledge over acquisition and command of those skills that are believed to make for effective managers and management. Indeed, most business and management degrees are not about business or management at all in any integrated sense, rather they involve the study of distinct subjects often with their own strong research traditions (think marketing, human resource management, operations research, accounting, finance and so on).

Nevertheless, business and management education and research has been the big higher education success story of the last 30 years or so. Few universities now operate without a business/management school and the postgraduate Master of Business Administration (MBA) qualification has gained 'must have' status for those ambitious for a high level business career. But what if, as in the Hans Christian Andersen story, the Emperor has no clothes? Or put another way, what if most academically generated management knowledge is of no, or marginal, significance in terms of both intrinsic content and relevance to the business world? Many academics might regard the latter situation as virtuous, pointing out that research scholarship should not favour relevance but instead focus on truth. Yet, though business and management studies remains the youngest of all the social science disciplines, its growth as a field has been largely predicated on its claimed relevance for business and the wider economic success of nation-states. Business and management educationalists within and beyond the university exercise increasing power and influence. Yet, one can argue that the claims made for the field by its academic practitioners are rarely challenged in any systematic manner – at least outside the subject area itself.

There are, however, growing critiques of management knowledge and research from within the business/management field, though they are rarely studied in any depth on degree courses. Further, researchers and writers critical of the nature of management knowledge usually have to record their dissent in specialist rather than mainstream academic journals, or in books. Thus the *Academy of Management Journal*, widely regarded as the 'best' academic management journal, proudly announces that 'Purely conceptual papers should be submitted to the *Academy of Management Review*. Papers focusing on management education should be sent to *Academy of Management Learning and Education*' (two sister publications) (see http://aom.org/Publications/

AMJ/Information-for-Contributors.aspx, last accessed 02.03.14). Current criticisms of management knowledge and research can, for the sake of convenience, be seen as falling into one of two categories. The first is termed here the liberal-idealist approach, signalling that writers in this tradition though articulating criticisms of management and business knowledge and research generally accept the political and economic assumptions that inform most management thinking. Many commentators in this tradition seek ways to make the academic study of management more relevant to the actual experiences and practices of managers 'in the field'. The second approach manifests itself in the so-called 'critical management' movement, comprising scholars who adopt a broadly leftist approach to the study of management and often challenge the capitalist foundations of management theory and practice. We shall consider each approach in turn.

Liberal-idealist critiques of business and management education

Widely considered to be one of the most insightful contemporary management thinkers, the late Sumantra Ghoshal (2005: 75) remarked that: 'Many of the worst excesses of recent management practices have their roots in a set of ideas that have emerged from business school academics over the last 30 years.' Ghoshal was, and a significant minority of other business and management academics remain, sceptical of the narrow intellectual base and focus of academic management studies (see Durand and Dameron, 2011, for a review). Ghoshal argued against what he saw as academic management's 'pretence of knowledge', highlighting *inter alia* the need for management to be understood in its social context. Stewart (2009: 12) also sees business and management research in terms of a pretence to natural scientific integrity and status. He writes that management has 'sent us on a mistaken quest to seek scientific answers to unscientific questions. It offers pretended technological solutions to what are, at bottom, moral and political problems. … It induces us to devote formative years to training in subjects that do not exist.' For Stewart (2009: 11), a new approach to management is required:

> management is … a neglected branch of the humanities … the study of management belongs, if anywhere, to the history of philosophy. Management theorists lack depth … because they have been doing for only a century what philosophers and creative thinkers have been doing for millennia. This explains why future business leaders are better off reading histories, philosophical essays, or just a good novel than pursuing degrees in business.

Charles Handy (2007: 184), doyen of British management gurus, criticizes unnecessary obfuscation in the language of management, writing that: 'Management has, however, often gone over the top in its exaggerated language, which has either become a cliché, meaning nothing much anymore, or is so gobbledegook that only a few initiates can decipher it.' He goes on (Handy, 2007: 185, emphasis added) to argue that:

'Re-engineering, Core Competences, JIT, Six Sigma, 360-degree Feedback, CRM, Social Network Analysis, Globalisation, Format Competition and ROI Marketing are just some of the *pseudo-technical terms that make the obvious seem clever.*'

Griseri et al. (2010: 80) in examining the philosophical basis to management argue that: 'academic scholarship in business and management is inherently problematic. There are just so many variables, so many different fields and factors, all interacting, that it is for all practical purposes impossible to generate conclusions that carry any significant weight.' Griseri et al. go as far as to argue that populist books on management and business – what they call the 'railway station' literature – may have little to commend them in terms of advancing hard evidence for the diverse claims made but often appeal to managers because of their pragmatic qualities. Pragmatism is, by definition, not something that one automatically views as theoretically (or at least systematically) informed, but Griseri et al. (2010) are surely correct in arguing that it could form the basis for an understanding of how managerial thought becomes action. Views of this nature are rarely welcome and often regarded with scepticism in the academic management community: pragmatism, together with 'common sense' represent a dangerous challenge threatening to undermine the power, expertise and standing of the academic specialist.

The UK *Financial Times* newspaper is a regular commentator on business education. Schiller (2011) points to the problem business schools face in terms of their relevance to the constituency they serve. A central problem identified was the emphasis placed in the academic reward system on research published in academic journals as opposed to the relevance or uptake of that research and its impact on the external world. Some business schools were reported to be assessing both the research output of their faculty and the relevance of their school's work to industry as measured by consultancy contracts won and requests for academics to participate in advisory boards. Schiller's article struck a chord with the newspaper's correspondents, one of whom wrote, somewhat colourfully:

> It is time to see BE [business education] for what it is. Lacking a fundamental question that drives research and teaching, it is, apparently unknowingly, a subsidiary area in the social sciences and mainly a vocational/technical field that only provides techniques for getting a job done. This is a good thing to do. But, it is the height of vanity, envy and egotism to think that this is anything more than technical training … business education is just vocational jibber-jabber. (Johnson, 2011: 10)

We might further observe that the idea that consultancy contracts and corporate advisory board memberships obtained by business school academics may be some magical guarantor, or indicator, of the quality and/or relevance of management knowledge and practice and of the capabilities of business school academics is little short of bizarre. Many business school academics may possess some operational management experience but many (almost certainly the majority) lack experience of senior corporate and strategic management whether in commercial or other kinds of organization. There is an enormous difference between the senior company executive – even in small and medium sized enterprises, who has to constantly worry about whether s/he is going to be able to pay their staff this month, or whether they will meet their monthly budget targets (a point made by Chia and Holt, 2008, in an excellent if challenging article on the nature of business school knowledge) – and the managerially inexperienced academic whose vacuous nostrums are rendered as part of a consultancy assignment.

A potentially more embracing critique of management education, knowledge and practice is to be found in an emerging evidence-based management 'movement'. Popularized by Pfeffer and Sutton (2006: 13) and derived from a medical/health care model of investigation, it is defined as follows:

> Evidence-based management proceeds from the premise that using better, deeper logic and employing facts to the extent possible permits leaders to do their jobs better. Evidence-based management is based on the belief that facing the hard facts about what works and what doesn't, understanding the dangerous half-truths that constitute so much conventional wisdom about management, and rejecting the total nonsense that too often passes for sound advice will help organizations perform better.

Attractive though all this may sound, the implication is depressingly clear – namely that much of what currently passes for management knowledge and its application in practice is *not* evidence based. A further consideration here is that while evidence-based management sounds plausible, the approach implied is still one based on the aspirations to *scientific* veracity so effectively critiqued by Stewart (2009; see additionally Hodgkinson and Starkey, 2011). Similarly, as any legal scholar will aver, not all evidence is factually neutral; but subject to interpretation and reinterpretation. Nevertheless, if the goals of evidence-based management are to clarify the useful content of management knowledge and encourage less abstraction in management practice then it can be cautiously welcomed as a support to critical reflection.

Many of the observations considered thus far in this section contain implicit or explicit indicators as to how business and management research and education might be conducted, and how business and management knowledge might be evaluated. In 2009, the 'Schumpeter' columnist of *The Economist* magazine engaged in some chest beating over business education, in light of the beginning of the West's current economic problems in 2008. Pointing out that many of those nominally responsible for some of the worst aspects of the financial crisis were MBAs, the writer speculated on what needed to change in business schools noting that a popular argument was that 'management education needs to start again from scratch. On this view, these institutions [business schools] are little more than con-tricks … built on the illusion that you can turn management into a science and dedicated to the unedifying goal of teaching greedy people how to satisfy their appetites' ('Schumpeter', *The Economist*, 2009: 72). Five years later, 'Schumpeter' (*The Economist*, 2014a) was at it again, lamenting that:

Professors ... will perish unless they publish in the right journals. And they have too little incentive to produce usable research. Oceans of papers with little genuine insight are published in obscure periodicals that no manager would ever dream of reading.

In the first of the two articles cited above, 'Schumpeter' rejects the argument that business schools are little more than 'con-tricks', citing a single study purporting to show that companies deploying the management techniques commonly taught in business schools outperform their peers. Instead the advice offered is that business schools need to place more emphasis on teaching economic and financial history, and that the tone of their education should encourage greater cynicism and scepticism. Some cynicism and considerable scepticism are at the heart of critical management approaches to business knowledge.

The critical management studies approach

Critical management studies (CMS) has evolved since the 1990s as a set of Marxist and other perspectives that focus on challenging the fundamental ideological dimensions to management theory and practice, specifically the discipline of management's pretension to offer 'scientific', 'unbiased', 'objective' and 'neutral' insights and techniques that allow for 'better', 'improved' or 'more effective' organizational and societal administration (Marx and Marxism is not often extensively studied on business and management degrees: those seeking a painless short introduction to the subject in the context of employment could do worse than consult Hyman's (2006) beautifully limpid account; a longer but valuable introduction is offered by Seed (2010)). The essential difference between those pursuing a CMS approach and those critics of management considered in the previous section is that the latter accept the broad orientation of management knowledge and education towards supporting existing predominantly capitalistic, economic systems. The problems of management knowledge and its limitations are to be resolved within this framework. Followers of a CMS approach in contrast entertain the possibility of economic arrangements alternative to capitalism. More significantly, CMS writers are particularly alert to what they perceive as the limitations of capitalism.

According to Tadajewski et al. (2011: 1-6; see additionally Alvesson et al., 2009: 1-26) CMS *is not*: (a) concerned with helping managers to run better businesses; (b) is not interested in developing and implementing strategies for increasing the quiescence of employees; or (c) is not motivated to support organizations and managers in product and service development and delivery. Instead, CMS stands, *inter alia*, for critical evaluation of the (a) predominantly capitalist ideology that underpins business and management education; (b) the effects that this ideology and associated managerial practices have on the wider social environment; (c) the structures of social and economic inequality created by capitalist ideology as mediated by management practice; and (d) the design and effectiveness of management techniques.

An obvious response to CMS, and one anticipated by its exponents, is that if the effect of critique is exaggerated it not only courts the possibility of being unfair and unbalanced with regard to the role of managers and management in organizations but also represents an unhelpful negativity concerned only with the diagnosis of the perceived disease's symptoms, not with possible cures. 'Normal' management studies in contrast are, as we have established, at least always implicitly concerned with the relevance of knowledge for practice. Most CMS practitioners reject the first notion, pointing out that while the actions of managers might be the subject of particular critical focus, they too are affected, often negatively, by the prevailing models of economics and management. Forget the so-called 'fat cat' bankers and their bonuses, the management class is large and differentiated and often far from well paid: many people classed as managers bear unwelcome responsibilities often for very little formal power or reward. As Burrell (2009: 554) points out in a characteristically insightful article, the bestselling management texts of the 2000s were Scott Adams's *Dilbert* cartoon strip collections which deal with the frustrations of middle managers in large organizations.

The second criticism, that CMS is essentially a negative enterprise that eschews responsibility for identifying and promoting solutions to the problems it identifies, has a certain resonance. However, as we observed in the Preface to this book, there is a contemporary trend for any critical challenge to poor reasoning and 'group think' to be instantly derided, often because they simultaneously represent challenges to power and authority. CMS is integrally concerned with analysing the power relations of management and the ways in which management knowledge is used to support powerful interests. Accordingly it is reluctant to engage in encouraging a model of knowledge, the primary end product of which is the evolution of practical and possibly deleterious applications of that knowledge. Many people will view this as an unsatisfactory stance but this is, perhaps, more an indicator of how a superficial bias for action in the development and use of management knowledge has obscured the social scientific tradition of systematic and self-critical theory building where the consequences for action are pluralistic. Put another way, CMS upholds values intrinsically unfashionable in the dominant business and management studies paradigm – it takes nothing for granted and certainly does not accept that the dominant system of management knowledge and practice is neutral and unbiased.

Critical management studies approaches have so far had limited impact in the hospitality field with one notable exception. Lugosi et al. (2009: 1468) reference much of the material discussed above. However, they stop short of embracing the core agenda at the heart of CMS, instead positioning what they call critical hospitality management research as the intersection of a Venn diagram the two sets of which are 'hospitality management research' and 'hospitality studies research'. As a model for framing discussion of what remains an emergent debate, the model has its uses, but it contains an unnecessary degree of caricature (particularly of the so-called hospitality management position). The authors appear to appreciate, as we have argued here, that there is no single 'hospitality studies' approach but a history of social scientific writing on hospitality, some or all of which may or may not bear on one aspect of that phenomenon – hospitality management – or, more precisely, the management of materials, procedures and processes attendant on the provision of accommodation and food and beverage services in diverse organizations. The question thus arises, where does this discussion of the nature of management knowledge finally lead us *vis-à-vis* our understanding of management research as a model for conceptualizing and studying hospitality and the hospitality industry?

Concluding Remarks: And the Result Is ...

The relevance of the foregoing discussion of management knowledge to debates about the nature of hospitality, hospitality management and hospitality studies is as follows. *First*, it is clear from the criticisms examined that we cannot accept management knowledge as unproblematic or as enjoying some privileged intellectual position *vis-à-vis* other forms of knowledge. Business and management knowledge is produced within specific ideological frameworks that in general are 'biased' towards particular political and economic models, usually some variant of capitalism. *Secondly*, one cannot easily, if at all, conduct management research according to natural scientific principles and methodologies when the central focus of that research is human variability. Academic business and management studies is *not* a science, indeed it is not even a unified, distinct, systematic body of knowledge – but rather, as we noted earlier, a portmanteau term embracing numerous distinct subjects. It follows that if we accept this point then, *thirdly*, the traditions of hospitality management research and practice as advocated by commentators like Jones and Lockwood (2008) and noted earlier are fully a variant part of management 'in general' and should be subjected to the same critical scepticism that was illustrated in the previous sections.

The origins of management knowledge are to be found in the social sciences and it is to an understanding of the strengths and limitations of social scientific knowledge that we must look if we are to stand the smallest chance of comprehending the nature of human behaviour. This does not mean automatically endorsing the various 'hospitality studies' approaches that prompted this discussion. At present these amount to little more than a loose protest movement dedicated to the rather obvious proposition that hospitality can be detected in social contexts other than management. Furthermore, the earlier-noticed tendency of some strands of the hospitality studies approach to appear to wilfully reject or at least sidestep the implications of different perspectives on hospitality for conceptualizing management in the hospitality industry has the appearance of an exercise in futility. One cannot simply wish existing hospitality management research away – nor should one. The practice of management in the hospitality industry is itself a rich source of varying concepts of hospitality that have potentially more widespread applications (for efforts by some members of the hospitality studies approach to reconcile the study of hospitality with the established subject of hospitality management, see Morrison and O'Mahoney, 2003; Morrison and O'Gorman, 2008).

This marginalization of hospitality management research and practice is paralleled by an apparent reluctance of hospitality studies approaches to engage with other perspectives from the social sciences that have been brought to bear on hospitality, several of which were considered in the earlier section 'Theorizing hospitality and the hospitality industry'. Indeed, in one sense at least, hospitality studies perspectives can be seen as the latest in a series of atomized approaches derived from analysing hospitality and related industries, approaches momentarily modish, rarely followed through and frequently discarded. To this we can add that whereas some strands in the hospitality studies approach embody the study of the *nature* of hospitality in some form, the major thrust of research seems to be more about establishing the diversity of contexts in which hospitality and hospitable behaviour appear. One consequence of this is that rather than focusing on changing historical narratives about the nature of hospitality and from this generating alternative conceptual/theoretical perspectives on the phenomenon that can be explored in diverse contexts (essentially a deductive approach to research), what is being created is a body of largely inductive research that offers multiple perspectives on the contexts in which hospitality figures but leave us little the wiser as to how the nature of hospitality has been, and can be, conceived and constructed.

Despite substantial research efforts over time, our conceptual and theoretical understanding of the hospitality industry is both patchy and very limited. The absence of even competing, yet alone complementary, frameworks for interpreting and understanding the structures of the hospitality industry limits opportunities to develop systematic and coherent accounts of the sector. It may even be that use of the insubstantial term 'hospitality' is itself partly responsible for this state of affairs, seeking as it does to impose vague uniformity on a number of related but distinct businesses that share many features but also differ in key respects. As we progress through this book, readers may note further instances of these differences and commonalities, not least in the next chapter which examines structural and economic issues in the hospitality industry.

Further Reading

Brotherton, B and Wood, R C (2008) 'The nature and meanings of hospitality', in B Brotherton and R C Wood (Eds) *The Sage Handbook of Hospitality Management*, London: Sage, 37–61.

Lashley, C and Morrison, A J (Eds) (2000) *In Search of Hospitality: Historical and Sociological Perspectives*, Oxford: Butterworth-Heinemann.

Miles, S (2001) *Social Theory in the Real World*, London: Sage.

Tadajewski, M, MacLaran, P, Parsons, E and Parker, M (2011) *Key Concepts in Critical Management Studies*, London: Sage.

2

WHAT KIND OF INDUSTRY? STRUCTURE, STRATEGY AND THE NATURE OF THE HOSPITALITY INDUSTRY

After reading this chapter, you should:

(a) have acquired familiarity with perspectives on the size, structure and scope of the hospitality industry, including corporate entities and small and medium sized enterprises;

(b) understand key current trends in hospitality business ownership and operation; and

(c) be able to relate (a) and (b) above to specific considerations of strategy and strategic management in the hospitality industry, including political dimensions to these phenomena.

Introduction

When reading about the tourism and hospitality industry in books, journal articles, industry reports or the popular media we persistently encounter messages on how *it is one of the largest economic activities employing millions of people worldwide … . Throughout the globe, policy-makers in various localities enthusiastically embrace tourism and hospitality activities, touting these as the panacea for the widespread malaise accompanying industrial restructuring and decline.* Concurrently, in many communities, especially those in peripheral regions, the tourism and hospitality industry emerges as one of limited, if not the sole, options for engineering economic growth and diversification. (Zampoukos and Ioannides, 2011: 26, emphasis added)

As implied by Zampoukos and Ioannides (2011) in the quotation above, the significance of the hospitality and wider tourism industries needs to be understood in the context of the trend of recent decades whereby many – particularly industrial 'first world' – countries have sought to develop tourism products and services in order to compensate for the decline of economic wealth derived from extractive and manufacturing industries. In developing and less developed countries, opportunities to grow tourism have proved attractive because of the relative ease of exploiting various aspects of natural and cultural heritage in a manner that generates hard foreign currency earnings. In this chapter, we shall: (a) seek to make a broad assessment of the general economic 'importance' of the hospitality industry engaging with the sector's rhetoric and probing some of the statistical and other evidence that bears on the issue; (b) as part of this, explore the relative roles of the small and medium sized enterprise and corporate sub-sectors of the hotel and restaurant industry; and (c) briefly explore the relevance of an understanding of strategy and strategic management to the hospitality manager.

How Important is Important?

The claims made for the economic significance of the hospitality and tourism indus-tries come mainly from self-interested advocacy groups, not least representative bodies and trade associations in pursuit of their lobbying of governments and international regulatory bodies for (usually) various self-serving forms of privileged treatment. Consider the following examples of promotional reportage:

- The World Travel and Tourism Council (WTTC) states it is 'the forum for busi-ness leaders in the Travel & Tourism industry. With Chief Executives of some one hundred of the world's leading Travel & Tourism companies as its Members, WTTC has a unique mandate and overview on all matters related to Travel & Tourism' (http://www.wttc.org/our-mission/, last accessed 31.03.13). One of WTTC's pri-mary objectives is to campaign for governments to recognize tourism and travel as a 'top priority' on the basis that 'Travel & Tourism is one of the world's largest industries, supporting 255 million jobs and generating 9 per cent of world GDP' (http://www.wttc.org/our-mission/last accessed 31.03.13).

- According to the European Commission, 'Europe is the **world's no. 1 tourist destination**, with the highest density and diversity of tourist attractions. As a result, the tourist industry has become a **key sector of the European economy**, gener-ating over **10% of EU GDP** (directly or indirectly) and employing 9.7m citizens in 1.8m businesses' (http://ec.europa.eu/enterprise/sectors/tourism/background/index_en.htm, last accessed 07.04.13, bold-faced emphasis in original).

- HOTREC (a European umbrella association of national hospitality trade asso-ciations) states that between 2003 and 2007, employment growth was over 21% in the hospitality industry compared to about only 6% in the whole economy. It estimates that total EU employment in the hospitality industry is 9.5 mil-lion workers in 1.7 million enterprises, representing 4.4% of total employment in Europe (http://www.hotrec.eu/about-us/facts-figures.aspx, last accessed 07.04.13). It is worth noting that, given the similarities, HOTREC appears to use the European Commission statistics cited in the previous bullet point – both are similar. However, the European Commission's figures embrace the whole tourism industry. Both cannot be correct unless one is meant to infer from HOTREC's presentation that only 0.2 million citizens are employed in sectors other than hospitality but within the tourism industry.

- The British Hospitality Association (BHA) (2010: 2) estimated that the hospitality industry was the fifth largest in the UK, directly employing 2.4 million people, and accounting for 8% of all employment, the last statistic apparently confirmed by the UK Office for National Statistics (2013). Elsewhere, and in 2012, the UK Office for National Statistics suggested that accommodation and food services employed around 5% of the workforce; retrieved from http://www.ons.gov.uk/ons/dcp171778_276985.pdf, last accessed 22.05.14. The BHA further claimed (a) that an additional 1.2 million jobs were created as a result of the multiplier effect, of which 700,000 were via supply chain purchases in food and beverage manufacture and related sectors, and (b) that there was the possibility of creating 236,000 net additional jobs across the UK by 2015 (British Hospitality Association, 2010: 2-3).

A warning on statistics

The above examples are 'promotional' because the statistics involved are not reported neutrally but with a smattering of inflationary language presumably intended to elicit a 'wow!' reaction. In addition, as we saw in the HOTREC instance (the third bullet above) statistics are not always presented with precision and clarity. In the case of the hospitality industry and the wider tourism sector, statistical data are collected by diverse organizations: governments, government bodies (e.g. tourism ministries), government-related organizations (e.g. tourism marketing and promotion bodies), supra-government bodies (e.g. the European Union), national and international trade associations (e.g. the aforementioned World Tourism and Travel Council, and national and international hotel and restaurateur associations), international public organizations (e.g. the International Labour Organization [ILO] and United Nations World Tourism Organization [UNWTO]), private consultancy companies and certain international foundations (e.g. the World Economic Forum). There are, inevitably, many difficulties with statistical information derived from these sources. Rarely is any one set of data comparable to any other. Original data are gathered according to varying standards and interests and no common framework is employed in describing or measuring particular variables. Secondary data are often used selectively and sometimes subjected to forecasting and extrapolation techniques yielding barely credible conclusions. Furthermore, there is often a time lag in the collection of data, especially by 'official' organizations (notably governments), which means (as with many of the data discussed later in this chapter) that when the information becomes available in the public domain, it is already out of date. However, one advantage of statistical data on the hospitality industry is that there are many instances of evidence both contemporary and reaching back into time, allowing the painstaking analyst the possibility of establishing at least plausible assertions about quantitative aspects of the sector.

Shape and form

The issue of the hospitality industry's economic importance is essentially one of definition and is therefore highly subjective in nature. It could plausibly be argued that the importance of an industry should be measured in terms of the representation of companies in that industry among all of the 'top' companies (by some measurement) in the world. In this case we might turn to the well-regarded Financial Times Global 500 companies list (http://www.ft.com/intl/indepth/ft500, last accessed 20.06.14), which ranks companies according to their market capitalization. If we extract the top companies in the Travel and Leisure sub-category for 2013 we find the data shown in Table 2.1, where only one company of interest – McDonald's – figures in the global top 100. Employment is another criterion that can indicate economic importance (the capacity to employ and to grow employment is not infrequently advanced by advocacy groups as a sign of the hospitality industry's economic significance). Here, interpreting statistical data becomes very hard indeed. However, as we noted earlier, at a European level, HOTREC (http://www.hotrec.eu/about-us/facts-figures.aspx, last accessed 07.04.13) estimates that across the European Union, hospitality (mainly hotels and restaurants) accounts for around 4.4% of total employment, although there are some issues with the accuracy of this calculation. Assuming the data to be correct, they suggest a worthy but hardly exceptional economic role for the hospitality sector in European industrial activity. Thus far, then, two factors (the representation of hospitality companies among the world's leading firms in terms of market value and the proportion of employment – at least in the EU – accounted for by the sector) do not immediately suggest that the hospitality sector is the industrial powerhouse that some of its advocates claim.

Table 2.1 Top travel and leisure companies in the Financial Times Global 500, 2013

Rank	Rank in FT 500 (2013)	Company	Business
1	58	McDonald's	Restaurants
2	167	Las Vegas Sands	Hotels, resorts and gaming
3	197	Starbucks	Coffee shops
4	203	Sands China	Multiple, including casinos and hotels
5	250	Priceline.com	Global online travel reservations
6	272	East Japan Railway	Transport and other, multiple, businesses
7	274	Yum! Brands	Restaurants
8	354	Carnival	Cruise liners
9	416	Compass Group	Contract catering
10	420	MTR (Hong Kong)	Transport

Strategy as Growth

Strategy and/or strategic management are subjects that have become fixed points in the business, management and hospitality curriculum. Yet, for most hospitality management graduates, strategic management and marketing (see Chapter 6) are disciplines they will have little reason to call upon. As we shall shortly see, at the corporate level, hospitality industry 'strategy' might not be as complex as some of the subject's academic practitioners appear to sometimes pretend. Of the many people who own and manage the vast number of small and medium sized businesses that populate the hospitality industry, legions have no prior education or training in hospitality management, let alone exposure to strategic management.

In the beginning: small and medium sized enterprises

It is oft remarked that the hospitality industry is numerically dominated by small and medium sized enterprises (SMEs). The International Labour Organization (2010: 8) records that more than 2.5 million SMEs are estimated to be involved in the European industry. HOTREC estimated that in Europe, 99% of hospitality enterprises had fewer than 50 employees and as many as 92% fewer than 10 workers on their payroll (http://www.hotrec.eu/about-us/facts-figures.aspx, last accessed 07.04.13). The European Foundation for the Improvement of Living and Working Conditions (Eurofound) a European Union agency (2009: 1; see in addition Eurofound, 2004) noted that: 'half of all [hospitality] workers were employed in organizations of 2–9 employees compared to 27.5% in all sectors.' Numerical domination is not, however, always the same as significance. Interest in this facet of the hospitality industry has generated a rich research literature exploring entrepreneurial and other motivations to establish hotel and restaurant businesses. A 'state of the art' review by Thomas et al. (2011) summarizing research into SMEs in tourism is enlightening as to some of the myths and challenges attendant on the sub-sector. The authors make a number of interesting observations:

1. Describing tourism industries as being dominated by SMEs disguises the fact that large firms play a disproportionately important role in terms of the numbers of people employed.

2. In respect of the predominance of SMEs the tourism industry may not be all that different to other sectors of the economy. The authors point to the work of Smith (2006: 56), who suggests that tourism is less dominated by SMEs than 'agriculture, forestry, fishing, and hunting; construction; real estate, and rental and leasing services; and professional, scientific, and technical services'.

3. It is easy to confuse the dominance of the sector by SMEs as evidence of entrepreneurship but evidence suggests that many operators are 'lifestyle' owners with little interest in growing their business.

4. Public policy initiatives, e.g. those designed to encourage collective marketing, collective quality assurance and provision of training to small tourism businesses, may be less effective if they do not meet the aspirations of lifestyle owners.

5. The objectives of lifestyle owners of tourism businesses may not be in accord with local tourism policy (as, for instance, in cases where tourism has been iden- tified as a mechanism for economic regeneration).

6. Some evidence suggests that many small firms are being squeezed out of the UK market by budget hotel chains including, *inter alia*, Holiday Inn Express, Premier Inn and Travelodge (this process may be in partial reverse as a result of the growth of the 'sharing economy' – see Chapter 9).

People have different reasons for entering into ownership in the hospitality industry but the message of the above list is that many of those who make up the owners and managers of SMEs have no prior knowledge or experience of hospitality, may have no real interest in entrepreneurship but are drawn to the industry for 'lifestyle' reasons, and are thus often operating businesses at the economic margins. In respect of the last, Heller (2011) reports data showing that since the beginning of the 2008 economic recession up to August 2011 some 4854 UK hospitality businesses have failed, equal to 6% of all insolvencies in the period. Barriers to entry to the SME hospitality sector are comparatively low, and exit is easy (for more specific consideration of business failure in the restaurant sub-sector see Chapter 5). That an important part of the overall industry may be construed as operating in the economic twilight zone is, once again, hardly compatible with the view of those representative and advocacy organizations who promote an idea of the industry as dynamically entrepreneurial and of major industrial importance.

The international chain/branded hotel industry – the move to 'asset light'

Most hotels are managed by brands or independent operators – not their own- ers. The owner is generally responsible for providing funding for the operation of the hotel when necessary while the operator manages the hotel's day-to-day operation. The agreement between the two parties is often structured with the operator as a contractor using a contract that specifies duties, obligations, and liabilities. (Detlefsen and Glodz, 2013: 2)

Over the past 15 years the major multinational hotel companies have imp- lemented an asset-light or 'virtual-hotel' business model which involves them divesting of owned and leased hotel properties and growing by franchising and managing hotels … . The major companies have developed into multi- segmented and multi-branded chains in order to meet differing customer needs, to get around territorial exclusions and to adapt to country-level con- ditions. (Roper, 2013: 1)

Continuing the theme from the previous section that numerical dominance is not the same as significance, the sixth point drawn from the work of Thomas et al. (2011) discussed there resonates with the views of those who assert that in the hotel sector, corporations provide more rooms than the SME sub-sector (Slattery, 2010). Langston and Livingstone (2010: 14) estimated that in 2009 nearly 40% of all UK hotels were branded. Slattery (2010: 11) suggests that chain hotels hold 60% of UK room stock and there has been a decline of 35% in independent hotel rooms. *The Economist* (2010b: 71) reported that Marriott owns only 6 of the 3400 hotels carrying its brand and InterContinental owns 15 hotels, manages 628 and has around 3800 franchises over various brands (see Brookes and Roper, 2012: 584; Sohn et al., 2013 for complementary information). The international hotel industry, in both domestic and international markets, has grown significantly in numerical terms in the last 30–40 years through mechanisms among which the management contract and the franchise are pre-eminent (see Cunill and Forteza, 2010; Alon et al., 2012; other than direct ownership, hotel leases have enjoyed some more limited success – see Ielacqua and Smith, 2012). According to deRoos (2010: 68) American Hotel and Lodging Association statistics estimated that there were 800 management companies managing 12,000 hotels worldwide with (in 2006) a total of 4370 managed by the nine largest companies. Table 2.2 shows the leading 10 hotel companies in 2013 presented in a 'traditional' way that is, inviting the inference that these numbers of hotels are owned by the firms concerned. Nothing could be further from the truth. The majority of these rooms are 'managed' by the named companies.

Most international hotel companies have pursued an 'asset light' strategy to become management companies 'selling' their brand and management expertise to investors who wish to enter the hotel business. Cunill and Forteza (2010: 505) suggest that franchising is the main and preferred method of expansion for hotel companies in economy and middle brand markets while the management contract is more popular in the luxury brand market, though Payne and Perret (2014) detect a widespread increase in hotel franchising in Europe (readers uncertain as to the nature of franchising could do worse than consult Cunill and Forteza's and Payne and Perret's articles; for the basics on management contracts Detlefsen and Glodz, 2013, offer a short, clear introduction; see also van Ginneken, 2011). This has been the core of corporations' strategy – growth in brand representation and management

Table 2.2 Top 10 hotel companies, 2013, by number of rooms

Rank	Company	Country	No. of hotels	No. of rooms
1	IHG	UK	4602	675,982
2	Hilton Hotels	USA	3992	652,378
3	Marriott International	USA	3672	638,793
4	Wyndham Hotel Group	USA	7342	627,437
5	Choice	USA	6198	497,023
6	Accor	France	3515	450,199
7	Starwood Hotels and Resorts	USA	1121	328,055
8	Best Western	USA	4024	311,611
9	Home Inns	PRC	1772	214,070
10	Carlson Rezidor Hotel Group	USA	1077	166,245

Source: Retrieved from http://www.hospitalitynet.org/news/4060119.html, last accessed 12.05.14.

around the world via contractual arrangements of one kind or another. It is a strategy that appears to have been highly successful. Sohn et al. (2013: 276; see also Aliouche et al., 2012, for insights into the financial advantages of franchising) sought to empirically verify the efficacy of asset light strategy and found that:

> our results indicate that the capital market assign premiums to hotel firms that go asset-light. The results show that decreasing fixed–asset ratio mitigates operating risk and elevates firm value, suggesting that investors' concerns about the firms going asset-heavy outweigh benefits provided by fixed assets. In the meantime, our analysis also shows that fee-business is effective in improving operating profitability, earnings stability, and eventually the firm value. In sum, the results suggest the two sides of the ALFO [asset light and fee-oriented] strategy have worked in sync to create value for investors.

In other ways too, the asset light strategy has been visibly effective. As the quotation from Roper (2013: 1) above implies, the management contract and franchise are very simple and broadly accepted vehicles for achieving market presence in economies where there are many local restrictions on foreign ownership of assets – not least restrictions on foreign direct investment (FDI). Panvisavas and Taylor (2006: 232) record that: 'Due to FDI restrictions, the use of management contracts and franchises is widespread as a form of doing hotel business in Thailand and in other countries where similar restrictions to foreign ownership apply.' Further, as Detlefsen and Glodz (2013: 2) point out, the relative simplicity of the management contract can encourage investors who might not otherwise be attracted to the hotel industry because of limited knowledge and experience of the sector.

Bloody owners and other irritations

One of the main challenges facing hotel brand owners entering into a franchise arrangement and/or management contract is the dynamics of the relationships that then exist between them and investors and owners. Much of the research literature in this area tends to posit, no doubt for reasons of narrative convenience, a single hotel owner. However, it is often the case that the building of a new hotel will involve several partners/investors and it is quite conceivable that in some cases a third party will be involved at least peripherally in the form of the owner(s) of the land on which a hotel is built. Owners are not always passive – many are activists. As part of the arrangement with the brand contractor, owners may live in the hotel and seek to engage themselves in its day-to-day management. Gannon et al. (2010: 641) report research that suggests many owners involve themselves in personnel and budgeting matters. In their own survey, the phenomenon of 'interfering' own-ers was more apparent in the luxury than the mid- or budget market. In some locations, owners may have more than one hotel with the same brand contractor, or more than one hotel with different brands from a single contractor. According to Detlefsen and Glodz (2013: 9) a potentially inherent difficulty in owner–operator relationships is attitudes to spending. Managers in general want to maximize spending from contractually agreed reserve-fund balances to ensure brand conformity and local competitiveness through ensuring their property is in the best possible physical condition. In contrast, owners want to minimize spending because (a) they are usually contractually responsible for funding expenditure that exceeds that in reserve-fund balances and (b) unspent reserve funds can be distributed to the owner and equity partners if and when the former sells the hotel.

Harris (2013: 28) notes that while most hoteliers want to concentrate on guest care, a property asset that is under pressure can lead senior managers to spend more time with those responsible for the management of that asset. These 'representatives' or 'asset managers' are often members of a hotel's investment team or owners' families but increasingly the pursuit of an asset light strategy has, since the 1980s, called into being a professional international hotel asset management profession (deRoos, 2010; Singh et al., 2012).

Motivations and consequences

Whitla et al. (2007: 781) found that market drivers are most important to hotel companies' international expansion. Broad coverage/presence in multiple regions was a common goal as was ensuring the provision of a common range of services as a minimum requirement for functioning in a market while simultaneously ensuring a degree of local responsiveness and differentiation. Responsiveness can involve deviation from brand standards. Hotels that in their countries of origin and elsewhere are devised as budget/limited service may not be acceptable in that form in certain other locations where they become full-service brands (this is often the case in South and Southeast Asia). Similarly, whereas in the West revenue from accommodation is normally the mainstay of a hotel, in other parts of the world, revenue from food and beverage services can be as important and sometimes more important, requiring companies to address considerable resources to this area. When Whitla et al. (2007) comment on the need for broad coverage and presence in multiple areas as a motivator of international growth, we may speculate that there is a 'me too' element in international hotel chain expansion that is facilitated by the asset light management contract/franchising model. On the 'Why should the devil have all the best tunes?' principle, hotel chains view the activities of their competitors in towns and cities around the world and often feel the need to establish a competitive presence in order not to 'lose out'. An arguable advantage of this is that in growth economies or economies where there is an observable lack of capacity in hotel rooms, hotels spring up not only in primary locations but in secondary and even third-level towns and cities – as in China (Liu et al., 2014) and India (Vardharajan and Mobar, 2013). A potential disadvantage of a 'me too' approach to strategic expansion is what will be termed here 'spoiling' or collective levelling. Seul Ki and SooCheong (2012: 1050) note that the 'deteriorating profitability of the US lodging industry has been repeatedly attributed to overcapacity'. In many international markets where hotel expansion has been relatively rapid a familiar pattern is that a city begins with too little hotel room capacity, often provided by indigenous companies and/or a handful of internationals, then it moves to, and past, a point of equilibrium to a situation of overcapacity. The financial impact of this overcapacity is felt in declining average room rate.

An interesting case in this regard is India where, between 2007 and 2013 (six years) the number of branded hotel rooms more than doubled and the 2013 average room rate was 66% of its 2007 level (Vardharajan and Mobar, 2013; see Table 2.3). In India, where relatively strict controls on FDI exist together with other barriers to market entry by overseas companies, of the top 10 branded hotel companies in the country in 2013, four were national firms (Taj, ITC, Sarovar – linked with Carlson Hospitality – and Oberoi; see Table 2.4). Of course, in interpreting this information it is necessary to bear in mind that while the data are highly suggestive, they pertain to a period of global economic difficulty and thus other factors may have played a role in producing these trends. Interestingly, however, the contemporary economic circumstances are barely alluded to in a related report on the Indian hotel industry. Thadani and Mobar (2013) identify four kinds of challenges facing the sector (see Figure 2.1).

Table 2.3 Average room rate and number of branded hotel rooms, Indian hotels, major cities, 2005–2013, various years

Year	Average rate in US$	Number of branded rooms
2005	95.97	22,400
2007	162.27	39,285
2008	187.12	46,982
2010	135.00	61,795
2012	130.00	84,313
2013	107.00	93,479

Source: Vardharajan and Mobar, 2013, and others.

Table 2.4 Top 10 Indian hotel companies, 2013, by existing room inventory and country of origin

Rank	Company	Country of origin
1	Taj Hotels and Resorts (including Ginger)	India
2	ITC Hotels (including Fortune)	India
3	Carlson Hospitality	USA
4	Starwood Hotels and Resorts	USA
5	Hyatt Hotels Corporation	USA
6	Marriott International	USA
7	Sarovar Hotels and Resorts	India
8	Accor Hospitality	France
9	Oberoi Hotels and Resorts	India
10	Intercontinental Hotel Group	UK

Source: Vardharajan and Mobar, 2013.

OPERATOR-RELATED CHALLENGES	FUNDING-RELATED CHALLENGES
• Management contracts often biased towards protecting the brand • Owners rarely briefed or involved on/in ongoing hotel operations • Management contracts are less favourable to owners compared to their western counterparts	• Owner egos are difficult to control often leading to vanity-driven excess in development costs, making loan repayment difficult • Bank loan terms are discouraging to investment • Traditional methods of structuring capital requirements predominate
DEVELOPMENT-RELATED CHALLENGES	HUMAN CAPITAL-RELATED CHALLENGES
• Multiple government approval and licensing schemes are numerous and inconsistent leading to a loss of time in development as well as money • The high cost of land is such that hotel developments are faced with the challenge of creating more revenue-generating space within properties • Absence of infrastructure status	• A failure of international brands entering India to invest in hotel education • Operators fail to exert sufficient control of the quality of training processes • For most employees in hotels, career development opportunities are fairly limited

Figure 2.1   Challenges facing the Indian hotel industry

Source: Thadani and Mobar, 2013.

Finally in this section, it is worth pointing out that the chain hotel sector apparently sees strategic expansion in a very limited way, as evidenced by the dominance of the asset light model. Such strategic behaviour is a far cry from the numerous complex considerations outlined in academic research as necessary to developing and implementing a strategy. Some writers persist in conducting more nuanced research into corporations' strategic choice. Dev et al. (2008) consider how in global brand expansion, hotel companies select a market entry strategy (market entry strategy being one of the pillars of the conventional approach to strategic planning and management). Yet, their research immediately has to contend with a model of strategic growth and entry that is, in concept, very simple, even if in practice it is difficult to manage. Put another way, the sector is the strategy and the strategy is the sector: the asset light model may be complex in terms of execution and management, but the core strategic concept is simplicity itself. More importantly, and once again, the wider transformation of the chain hotel sector to owners and managers of brands as opposed to owners and managers of hotels gives a sense of an industry that owes much for its survival to the cautious minimization or-transfer (to the actual property owners) of financial and capital risk.

The chain restaurant sector

The top 10 global chain restaurants are shown in Table 2.5. They all originate in the USA. Other popular franchises include Wimpy (South Africa), Costa Coffee

(UK – owned by brewers Whitbread), Esquires Coffee Houses (Canada) and Hardee's (USA) among many others. The majority of chains listed in Table 2.5 are fast food/ quick service restaurants – there are, further, a good many (again US dominated) midscale/family dining chain restaurants grown through franchising. The website statista.com (2014) reports that in the spring of 2013 the total number of restaurants in the USA was 617,505 (retrieved from http://www.statista.com/statistics/ 244616/number-of-qsr-fsr-chain-independent-restaurants-in-the-us/, last accessed 08.06.14). The equivalent number for the UK was, according to the Horizons (2014) food service research organization (2013 figures) 61,443 (http://www.hrzns. com/mint/pepper/tillkruess/downloads/tracker.php?url=http://www.hrzns.com/ files/UK_Foodservice_Industry_in_2013.pdf&force&inline, last accessed 09.06.14). The most franchised business is the fast food restaurant and, of course, McDonald's is the market leader here with, in 2012, nearly three times the sales of its nearest rival (http://www.azfranchises.com/franchisefacts.htm and http://www.statisticbrain. com/restaurant-franchise-sales-statistics/, last accessed 09.06.14).

Chain restaurant brands are usually stronger than is the case for hotels, supported by intensely defined and managed systems covering equipment, marketing and sales, standard operating procedures and human resource practices. Franchisees essentially buy into a system that they, as opposed to the franchisor, manage, or have managed by franchisor-trained personnel. In many companies, project management techniques support potential franchisees in determining suitable locations for businesses based on well-tried algorithms that cover, *inter alia*, footfall, conversion of footfall into custom, dine-in and dine-out demographics and other similar factors. Restaurant franchisors usually engage in much more vigorous and wide-ranging marketing campaigns as volume is important to revenue because the products on offer are relatively inexpensive and purchase is discretionary.

Table 2.5 Top 10 global chain restaurants, 2013

Rank	Global top 10 (all US)
1	McDonald's
2	KFC (Yum! Brands)
3	Subway
4	Pizza Hut (Yum! Brands)
5	Starbucks
6	Burger King
7	Domino's Pizza
8	Dunkin' Donuts
9	Dairy Queen
10	Papa John's

The subtleties of the operation of chain restaurant franchises are not well researched although there are a number of useful general studies of the macro-implications and implementation of franchise agreements in the sector (Hsu et al., 2010; Aliouche and Schlentrich, 2013; IHS Global Insight, 2014). The most important thing we can probably note here is that business format franchising in the chain restaurant sector is a relatively (compared to hotels) long-standing arrangement that has facilitated the rapid expansion of brands across the globe, thereby expanding numerous businesses while at the same time enhancing the value of the brand (see Chapter 6). As a business model, franchising defrays a good deal of the mother company's risk, transferring it to franchisees. At the same time, the capital requirements of these businesses are considerable as are the systems required for monitoring and maintaining quality across the brand.

Strategy as Politics

One of the dangers inherent to conventional models of strategic management is that strategy and its management are seen solely in terms of economics and markets and less attention is paid to political factors. Politics – that is political values and political orientations as opposed to the political ideologies underpinning the development and application of public policy – has not been much researched in hospitality. Investigations of voting intentions, party affiliations and policy preferences unsurprisingly reveal a significant orientation towards formal conservatism and, in the UK, the policies of the Conservative Party among hospitality employers, managers and other industry leaders (Kerr and Wood, 2000; Kerr, 2003). The conservatism of the hospitality industry tends rhetorically towards the 'right-wing' libertarian kind, but as with many industries, its representative bodies and other advocacy groups are primarily involved in promoting the specific interests of the sector, not least the development and maintenance of certain 'privileges' (Wood, 1996). As we shall see in Chapter 3, the British Hospitality Association throughout the early 1990s vigorously lobbied the then Conservative government in a campaign in favour of the abolition of the sector's wages councils and, with other industries' representative organizations, contributed to an often foolishly hysterical lobbying effort to discourage the introduction of a national minimum wage which was the opposition Labour Party's policy. To hear some of the arguments of the time one would think that the introduction of a national minimum wage would lead to economic Armageddon and the end of life on Earth (or at least the British part of it). At that time, as today, the academic research into extant systems of wage regulation was ambiguous, broadly balanced between those who claimed it had little effect on overall economic performance and those who detected more negative consequences. The fact is that for the UK at least, the Labour Party's victory at the 1997 General Election and the subsequent introduction of a statutory minimum wage has had little apparent negative effect and indeed the hospitality sector at least has continued to grow healthily.

There are numerous instances of how the hospitality and wider tourism industries through their representative organizations lobby government, normally for some kind of special economic status that would achieve one or more of reducing corporations' costs and/or as a corollary, and crudely put, improve the probability of increased profits. Away from minimum wages, the British Hospitality Association has in recent years campaigned for a lower rate of value added tax (VAT) for the industry. The argument advanced is that industry VAT rates are lower in other countries (the UK apparently has the third highest VAT rate in Europe) placing the hotel sector at a competitive disadvantage. Ufi Ibrahim (2012: 28), Chief Executive of the BHA, has argued that the UK's tourism balance of payments has been steadily declining for 30 years and that the World Economic Forum placed the nation in the last five of 139 countries for competitiveness. She points to reports that suggest a reduction in VAT would create a substantial quantity of new jobs in the industry, writing:

> A reduction in VAT would lead to lower prices … . Some of the reduction would be used for investment, or for training and increased wages, thereby improving quality standards. All of this will lead to a virtuous cycle of increased demand, quality and employment.

A cynic's response to this would be to believe that any reduction in VAT would be more likely to see bottom lines and shareholders' dividends rise without any of the 'virtuous' consequences suggested by Ibrahim. Even though the VAT burden may be greater in Britain than in other European countries, we can see from annual tourist arrival figures that if accommodation prices are higher in the UK they do not seem to be a disincentive to tourists visiting. Withnall (2014) reports that in 2013 London received more visitors than at any time in its history. Other topics on which the global hospitality industry lobbies governments include the intro-duction/abolition/level of bed taxes (this has been a particular issue in the USA over the years) and luxury taxes (which in some countries, e.g. India, can, relatively speaking, be quite ferocious). In 2014, *The Jakarta Post* newspaper reported that the Bali chapter of the Indonesian Tourism Industry Association was urging local governments to impose a moratorium on hotel building on the island (already with 90,000 rooms) on the grounds of both overcapacity and environmental des-poliation – budget accommodation was particularly singled out as a problem (see Erviani, 2014: 5).

Of course, one must expect and regard as wholly legitimate the right of cor-porations and other organizations to employ as part of their strategies an ongoing process of lobbying for their own interests. At the same time we need to be alert to the contradictions often inherent to lobbying processes. While the hospitality and tourism (and of course many other industries) often use – and use very crudely – the language of economic liberty and free markets in lobbying for their interests, the underlying, and ironic, reality is that often they are arguing for privileges which run contrary to 'free market' values. There are few, if any, examples of the unfettered totality of the operation of free markets. In a recent book on modern economic oligarchs and the economic crisis that began in 2007/2008, Mount (2013) reminds us that Adam Smith, the doughty advocate of the invisible hand of the free market, cautioned (in his book *The Wealth of Nations*, 1776) against monopolies and cartels. 'People of the same trade', Smith wrote, 'seldom meet together, even for merriment and diversion, but the conversation ends in a conspiracy against the public or in some contrivance to raise prices.' Indeed, the capitalist world is one in which diverse industries enjoy various forms of 'subsidy' that effectively stymie or partially thwart the operation of 'free' markets. In the hospitality and wider tourism context, instances of hidden and not so hidden subsidies include the global convention of tax exemption on aviation fuel, and funding taken from general taxation or hypothecated revenues and used in the marketing of a country via central and local government institutions, and national, regional and local tourist boards (thus relieving hospitality and tourism companies of having to fund destination promotion themselves). Strategy is thus not simply about economics, business organization and product/service promotion but about the manipulation of sentiment and the lobbying of (in particular) governments for privileges that in reality corrupt markets and act in opposition to market freedom.

Concluding Remarks: A Question Answered?

It should be clear from the foregoing discussions that defining and circumscribing the hospitality industry (as well as hospitality itself, see Chapter 1) is a complex matter in terms of all of theoretical perspectives, conceptualization and practice. From what we have learned so far then, how can we create meaningful propositions that more or less accurately describe the subject of interest? What kind of industry *is* hospitality?

First, in its breadth and range the hospitality industry provides a varied range of products *and* services to guests. *Secondly*, these products and services are principally generated in response to demand from two kinds of 'market': (a) local/regional/national populations and (b) travellers and tourists. *Thirdly*, hospitality is an industry, the economic importance of which is in danger of being exaggerated by its practitioners. The reliability of statistical data across a range of indicators is highly suspect and there is little in the way of global agreement as to how statistics should be produced. The egregious habit of including the hospitality industry as part of tourism and travel, statistically speaking, further confuses the issue. Insofar as categorical statements are possible, however, it appears that the tourism sector, including hospitality, accounts for no more than 8% of employment and 9–10% of GDP globally, in which case we can infer that the contribution of hospitality will be somewhat less than this. *Fourthly*, and as we shall further briefly consider in Chapter 3, while nearly every introductory textbook on hospitality management points up the industry's supposedly labour intensive character very few draw attention to its capital intensive nature. While it is the case that hospitality firms are labour intensive relative to their manufacturing counterparts (restaurants less so than either hotels or man-ufacturing entities; see Guillet and Mattila, 2010: 679), their capital intensiveness is frequently forgotten in terms of investment in land, buildings and equipment. In many ways, the risks (and indeed the benefits) associated with the extensive ownership of land and property are now effaced by hotel companies as a result of employing the 'asset light' model but the risks and benefits remain to those who hold those two resources. In chain restaurants a similar degree of amelioration of risk can be achieved through the rental, rather than purchase, of premises on which to conduct business. Of course, while the asset light model has certainly changed the nature of the hotel sector in terms of reducing the range and number of some risks, we must maintain an open mind as to the exposure of the industry to other kinds of risk associated with that particular business model. As the industry's domi-nant strategy for global expansion, the use of franchising and management contracts has, as we have seen, greatly simplified the means of expansion but at the same time introduced arguably greater complexity into the longer term operation of hotels and other hospitality businesses. The *final* point to be made here is that we must be careful not to accept too readily the industry's own assessment of its importance as a global powerhouse. This will be a controversial view but as has been asserted in this chapter many hospitality businesses – whether small and independently owned and managed, or part of the corporate 'chain' sector – exhibit characteristics of economic marginality rather than entrepreneurial dynamism and innovation. With these general factors in mind we can now turn our attention to some more detailed aspects of operations and management in the hospitality industry.

Further Reading

Aliouche, E H and Schlentrich, U (2013) 'Franchising', in R C Wood (Ed) *Key Concepts in Hospitality Management*, London: Sage, 41–45.

deRoos, J A (2010) 'Hotel management contracts – past and present', *Cornell Hospitality Quarterly*, 51, 1: 68–80.

Detlefsen, H and Glodz, M (2013) *Historical Trends: Hotel Management Contracts*, Chicago: HVS.

Thomas, R, Shaw, G and Page, S J (2011) 'Understanding small firms in tourism: a per-spective on research trends and challenges', *Tourism Management*, 32, 5: 963–976.

3

A PEOPLE BUSINESS?
HUMAN RESOURCES IN THE
HOSPITALITY SECTOR

After reading this chapter, you should:

(a) having also read Chapter 2, be familiar with the relative importance of people in delivering hospitality services, including awareness of the limitations of describing hospitality in clichéd terms as a 'people industry';

(b) understand concerns over the 'quality' of hospitality jobs, notably in terms of the skill content perceived as intrinsic to hospitality employment in both domestic and international contexts;

(c) be familiar with debates about payment and reward in the hospitality sector; and

(d) have gained insight into the marginal nature of much hospitality employment and its consequences for labour stability in the industry.

Introduction

We observed in Chapter 2 that many representational and promotional organizations in the tourism and hospitality industries would have us believe that these sectors are the 'fastest growing', among the globe's largest employers and hold potential salvation for countries struggling to generate greater wealth. The hospitality industry is frequently presented and perceived as a 'people industry', a cliché but as with most clichés, partly true – although only partly true for as Chapter 2 sought to demonstrate, one of the most egregious errors we can make in analysing the sector is to ignore the huge amounts of capital (especially land and buildings) often tied up in hospitality businesses. The assertion that hospitality is a people industry implies that it is in some way unusual, whereas a brief pause to consider all the businesses that rely on people to deliver front line services should instead invite the response 'so what?'. Being a 'people business' is neither novel nor distinctive in a world where services of various kinds – and broadly defined – are the norm rather than the exception. At one level, we tend to think of the hospitality industry as labour intensive, largely because of an idealized notion of the delivery of personal service in grand hotels, with guests attended by countless flunkies catering to their every whim. Some grand hotels and other hospitality organizations do indeed aspire to, and achieve this ambience, and not only in countries where labour is relatively cheap (past research has shown that in five star hotels it is not unusual for the staff–guest ratio to be 1:1 but the number of five star hotels is, globally, relatively small (see Johnson, 1985)). For the most part, however, labour cost in the hospitality industry is one of the biggest costs – if not the biggest – for most organizations, and considerable effort is thus directed towards keeping it as low as possible.

The 'people industry' cliché has been somewhat reinforced by developments in human resource management (HRM) rhetoric over the past 40 years not least the oft-articulated views (a) that people are an organization's most important resource and (b) that customer satisfaction and the development and maintenance of business (and thus financial success) is dependent on working 'through' people, motivating and rewarding them appropriately. In respect of (a) we can remind ourselves of management guru Charles Handy's (2007: 184) view that 'Every organization proclaims that their employees are their most precious asset, even while making swathes of them redundant.' In other words we can and should be justly sceptical about the claims of any organization in regard to its people policies. In respect of (b) we need to be aware that laudable though the sentiments expressed are, the general picture painted by research into employment in the hospitality industry is a largely negative one. Employment and HRM are among the most systematically studied aspects of the hospitality sector attracting periodic interest from researchers in the social sciences as well as those rooted in the hospitality management subject area. Among the most useful extended reviews of the field are studies by Baum (2006), Christensen Hughes (2008), Gabriel (1987), Guerrier (1999, 2008), Lucas (1995, 2004), Riley et al. (2002) and Wood (1994b, 1997).

In a single chapter it is not possible to do justice to the full range of employment and HRM issues prevalent in the industry. For managers and potential managers it is arguably vital to understand how the largely negative image of the hospitality industry has come about and to make some assessment of how reliable this image is. Accordingly, the remainder of this discussion will address the following three often-aired 'concerns' about the nature of hospitality employment:

1. The question of the (supposedly poor) quality of hospitality jobs, including the conceptualization of hospitality work as low-skilled and involving little training.

2. The question of the (supposedly poor) remuneration of hospitality jobs.

3. The employment of large numbers of 'marginal' workers that is often said to be a major cause of labour instability in the industry.

The majority of illustrations employed will focus on UK experience simply because the majority of academic research into hospitality employment conducted to date originates from the USA and UK and other Anglosphere countries. Following this there is a brief consideration of what is known about cultural and regional variations in employment experience across the globe. The chapter concludes by considering reasons for the persistence of current employment practices in the industry.

The Quality of Hospitality Jobs

When we say the image of hospitality employment is largely negative we have to enter an immediate caveat, differentiating between negativity of perspective and negativity of outcome. Mainstream HRM research, for the most part informed by sociological perspectives, has, until comparatively recently, largely ignored service industries. Growth of interest in research in the field has been marked in many cases by *a priori* views of service employment as, variously, inferior to other kinds of employment, intrinsically routine in content and invariably poorly paid. One example of this phenomenon can be seen in the concept of the 'McJob', a term with sneering and snobbish overtones coined (allegedly by sociologist Amitai Etzioni in 1986) to describe employment in the sector and beyond.

In its plural form, according to Gould (2010: 780), the term 'McJobs' alludes to all jobs that are 'boring and tedious, low-paid and with few career prospects'. Indeed, Gould, in an enormously subtle argument attendant on reportage of a study into employees' experiences of working in McDonald's, makes it apparent that many negative sociological and other commentaries on 'McJobs' (and particularly those in the fast food industry) are characterized by frequent condescension and often specu-lative reasoning on the part of their authors. Gould's (2010) important contribution to the debate about 'McJobs' does not argue that everything in the fast food garden is rosy, but rather suggests that in analysing this kind of employment, it would be wise to have fewer preconceptions about the nature of the work while paying greater attention to how the work is experienced at the individual level (Gould, 2010: 799). He is undoubtedly correct. As *The Economist* (2013b) noted (but see the critical responses of some of the magazine's readers, http://www.economist.com/news/international/21576656-degree-burgerologyand-job-too-fries/comments?page=2, last accessed 11.01.14):

> British universities can be depressing. The dons moan about their pay and students worry they will end up frying burgers – or jobless. Perhaps they should try visiting McDonald's University in London's East Finchley. Students are often 'rough and ready', with poor qualifications and low self-esteem. ... McDonald's is one of Britain's biggest trainers. It gets about 1m applicants a year, accepting only one in 15, and spends £40m ($61m) a year on training. The Finchley campus ... is one of the biggest training centres in Europe ... . A year-long apprenticeship programme emphasising English and maths leads

to a nationally recognised qualification. McDonald's has paid for almost 100 people to get degrees from Manchester Metropolitan University. The company professes to be unfazed by the fact that many alumni will end up working elsewhere. It needs to train people who might be managing a business with a £5m turnover by their mid-20s.

There are plausible reasons for arguing that *some* authors of research studies in both mainstream human resource research and the hospitality field have in *some* cases fallen foul of their own unexamined biases. If 'McJobs' are objectively boring and tedious, this presupposes the existence of jobs that are not objectively boring and tedious, the latter presumably including university researchers in HRM. It requires only a moment's reflection to establish how difficult it is to talk of objectivity in this regard. So much employment experience is subjective. Critics of the growth in the number of 'McJobs' in particular and the quality of hospitality, and other perceived 'lowly' forms of service employment, often operate, implicitly or explicitly, with a hazy hierarchical view of the 'quality' of particular kinds of job. The degree to which comfortably off middle-class social scientists tend to romanticize the nature of work – and particularly manual work – has, over the years been much criticized from within that professional community (not least in the context over debates about the work of Braverman as briefly discussed in Chapter 1: see Littler, 1982; Rose, 1988: 317-320).

Questions of skill

All of the above said, we cannot avoid the fact that, despite its seemingly infantile construction, the term 'McJobs' retains some descriptive accuracy of many employees' experiences of hospitality (and other) work – service industries in general and hospitality in particular are often associated with low-skilled, poorly paid jobs and generally poor conditions of employment. This is the negativity of outcome referred to earlier – the empirical evidence base as opposed to the perspectives adopted in approaching the study of service employment. However, at least with regard to hospitality, this caricature disguises both the character and diversity of work in the hospitality industry not least in the contrast between relatively skilled and relatively well-paid jobs on the one hand (manager, hotel engineer, senior chefs and cooks), medium-skilled and -paid work (most supervisors in whatever department) and low-skill and low-paid jobs on the other (food service, routine front desk positions and cleaning jobs).

Skill is an inherently problematic concept because, as with the experience of employment, its definition is largely subjective. Many HRM specialists and sociologists of work view skill not as an objective category but as being *socially constructed*. Skill is thus defined as the outcome of interaction between social convention and political and industrial power, a view that comes in two forms. The strong version of the social-construction-of-skill thesis asserts that definitions of skill may be created and sustained for reasons other than the technical content of jobs: most jobs therefore unnecessarily bear skill labels and might, theoretically, be performed by anybody who gains access to a particular occupation. The weak version of the thesis is that nearly all skilled jobs can be said to have some objective skill content but that it is the collective strength and action of workers that lead some occupations to be regarded as skilled and other jobs as semi- or unskilled (Littler, 1982: 9–10). Applications of the social-construction-of-skill thesis during the 1970s and 1980s were mainly directed towards examining the claims of writers like Braverman (1974, see Chapter 1) that over the course of the twentieth century all forms of work were degraded as a result of deskilling. Critics systematically undermined this thesis pointing out that while deskilling had undoubtedly taken place, so had reskilling and 'enskilling' (the creation of jobs around new skills or the addition to existing jobs of skill elements that did not previously exist). Others suggested, in the manner described at the end of the previous section, that Braverman and others romanticized the nature of pre-industrial labour, pointing out that relatively few workers, pre-industrialization, were engaged in skilled craft work (see Littler, 1982; Rose, 1988; Thompson, 1989; and for an extended review of the nature and extent of deskilling in the hospitality industry, Wood, 1997).

The application of the social-construction-of-skill thesis to hospitality employment raises interesting issues. Work typified as low- semi- or unskilled, e.g. the work of housekeeping and waiting staff, does not, upon close scrutiny, appear to deserve such labels in terms of the range and complexity of technical and other knowledge and practitioner abilities required. To perform a housekeeping (and more fundamentally, cleaning) job, one needs to know how to use chemicals, materials and machinery, and how to apply these appropriately so as not to cause damage to property. One needs to know optimal ways of cleaning (e.g. from the farthest wall to the door in a guest room, and from the ceiling to the floor). One needs to know how to make a bed, clean an easy chair, and how to operate safely in order to avoid injury to the self and others. No doubt there are elements missing from this list. Why is work of this nature classified as, at best, semi-skilled? One explanation is found in feminist explorations of work. Because housekeeping work is domestically (and in the UK at least) publicly performed mainly by women it does not conform to what Beechey (1982: 64) has called the 'male artisan/mechanic' conception of skill. Indeed, most definitions of skill have evolved in the context of male labour performed in non-service industries. As Beechey (1982: 64) writes: 'There are, for instance, forms of labour which involve complex competencies and control over the labour process, such as cooking, which are not conventionally defined as skilled (unless performed by chefs within capitalist commodity production).' The argument that flows from this observation is that work traditionally performed by women as part of 'their' domestic responsibilities is regarded as trivial and only regarded as possessing a serious skill element when transferred to a public organizational setting and performed or controlled by men.

A more recent extension of the social-construction-of-skill thesis associated with Baum and others (e.g. Baum, 1995, 2008; Duncan et al., 2013) but rooted more widely in discussions of the nature of human mobility (e.g. Molz and Gibson, 2007) should be noted here. It has two elements. The first broadly follows the central tenets of the social-construction-of-skill thesis, arguing that conventional definitions of skill in hospitality are essentially western-centric and cannot automatically be assumed to accurately describe the nature, acquisition and practice of skill in the hospitality industry in other countries. The second element argues that in many (in particular) service industries the definition of skill needs to be widened to include emotional and aesthetic components. This approach is not unproblematic. Discussion is often couched in somewhat obscure language with a heavy serving of jargon and this does not always facilitate easy understanding. Further, as Baum (2008: 82) himself notes, these two propositions are largely conceptual in nature and require greater evidential support.

Turning to the second of the elements first, the notion that certain service workers are required to labour emotionally derives from Hochschild's (1983) classic study (see Bolton, 2005, for an overview of the field). Emotional labour embraces, *inter alia*, skills of empathy and nurturing that in some occupations (nursing, teaching, flight attendant and so on) are required to be articulated as part of job performance and which employers institutionalize through recruitment, selection and training. So-called aesthetic labour is most associated with Warhurst and Nickson (see Warhurst and Nickson, 2007; Nickson and Warhurst, 2007; and Harris and Small, 2013, on the related area of 'lookism') and refers to the physical attributes (looks, body size and voice/accent) that employers supposedly employ as a basis for discrimination in hiring decisions and similarly institutionalize as part of human resource practice. As Warhurst and Nickson (2007: 107) write: 'in aesthetic labouring employees contribute to the production and portrayal of a distinct and defined corporate image or, more prosaically, are simply (perceived by employers to be) attractive to customers and so likely to enhance initial and repeat custom'. Although it is sometimes hard to discern (especially in the aesthetic labour literature), both these approaches have firm roots in established theoretical and applied social psychology research (e.g. Dion et al., 1972; Elmer and Houran, 2008) and, in the case of 'emotional' labour, both general and feminist sociology. In the context of hospitality (and doubtless other) employment, there is little doubt that elements of what are embraced by the concept of emotional labour – not least the notion of (customer) care – have been made concrete in behavioural training models, standard operating procedures, and marketing and advertising materials. Aesthetic labour is somewhat more problematic as a concept. As the quotation from Warhurst and Nickson above suggests, in matters of aesthetics, perception is, perhaps, all. Advocates of the 'aesthetic labour' thesis have thus far failed to address or successfully reconcile relativist/ absolutist (or, if preferred, subjective/objective) dilemmas at the heart of the study of aesthetics itself (see the collection of essays in Craige, 2010). Much more needs to be done to operationalize the concept, thus allowing greater dissection of the role aesthetics plays in employment, and moving it beyond a set of minor insights putatively challenging the notion that beauty is in the eye of the beholder.

Addressing now Baum's first point concerning the western-centric nature of definitions of skill employed in discussing hospitality work, he argues (Baum, 2008: 77-78) that official (usually government) skill constructions can differ between countries, leading to substantial variations in what work is classified as skilled, and in what proportion. In western countries, Baum (2008: 76–77) asserts that there is a 'cultural and experiential proximity' shared by workers whereby:

> Employees, in this sense, have shared experience in both delivering and receiving services, they have 'stood in the shoes' of the guests they are serving. By contrast, there are significant cultural and experiential gaps between, on the one hand, in similar international hospitality operations in less developed or westernised countries and, on the other, the employees who deliver their products and services to guests.

For Baum (2008: 80–81) the dominant concept of (at least commercial) hospitality is of western origin and the assumptions underlying its construction when exported to non-western cultures need not be entirely familiar in, or to, those cultures. He writes:

> In less developed countries … employees join tourism and hospitality businesses without western acculturation, without knowledge of the implements and ingredients of western cookery and service for example. Learning at a technical level … is considerably more demanding than it might be in western communities … work that may be deemed unskilled in Australasia, Europe and the USA requires significant investment in terms of education and training elsewhere and cannot, therefore, be universally described as 'low skilled'.

Baum (2008: 77) suggests that non-western employees will less certainly have 'stood in the shoes' of their guests and thus 'where exposure to this … model … is not widespread among those working in the industry, there is the potential for a skills gap in the delivery of services and experiences.'

We can agree with Baum that globally, official and unofficial definitions of skill vary. It is perfectly possible for a job in the UK to be classified as unskilled whereas, say, in Indonesia, it is classified as skilled. This, after all, almost certainly reflects reality as well as being the essence of the social-construction-of-skill thesis. However, the notion that skill might be further defined in terms of a lack of exposure to western cultural models of hospitality generated at the interface of production (inexperience of working in an industry cast in western cultural terms) and consumption (inexperience of consumption of the products and services of a westernized hospitality industry) suggests a mildly patronizing view of less developed countries. Large international and hotel restaurant chains expanding overseas normally start in large urban conurbations and/or resort areas. In these locations at least there is more than a passing familiarity of local populations with the nature, culture and conventions of western hospitality. Of course, there are many parts of the world which the 'western' hospitality industry does not reach but following Baum's arguments, by definition they have very limited or no need for workers with 'western' hospitality skills.

Training

One of the characterizations of hospitality work is its supposed failure to offer a significant quantity and quality of training, thus contributing to the image of hospitality employment as low- or unskilled. It is indeed the case that in some cultural contexts and in certain occupations researchers have identified a reliance by employers on skills assumed to be already present in employees and thus requiring limited or no further development. The classic instance is housekeeping/cleaning where the sexist assumption is that women learn to clean 'naturally' as part of gendered domestic roles and that these skills can be easily transferred to diverse working contexts (a UK hospitality organization found that housekeepers, room attendants and cleaning staff were least likely to receive training, see People1st, 2010). There are problems with this view, however. In certain countries for reasons of religious belief and/or convention and/or social control and/or the indigenous wealth of the local population, male labour, often imported from other countries, dominates occupational categories like housekeeping, which are seen as unsuitable for women. The sheer variety of occupations present in the hospitality industry means that there is a fairly wide skills mix. In the case of highly skilled professional cookery, many chain hotels, wherever they may be in the world, persist in the tradition of recruiting and training local apprentice labour. In front office, some employees come to the work already trained in necessary IT skills (at hotel school or in previous jobs) but yet others have to undergo training. Hotel engineering personnel, customer-facing IT professionals responsible for Wi-Fi and other services, business centre operatives – all require certain skills and sometimes organization-provided basic and higher level training in order to both perform at an elementary level and acquire skills in new and developing technologies.

A further difficulty in discussing training in the hospitality industry is that despite the assumptions of critics of 'McJobs', relatively little is actually known about the topic. That research which does exist undoubtedly suggests that training in the hospitality sector is of suspect quality. In a study of 94 US restaurants Berger and Ferguson (1986: 19; see, further, Harris and Bonn, 2000) found that the most favoured approach to training was the unstructured apprenticeship during which 'a new employee simply observes an experienced, trusted employee until the trainee is ready to try the job alone'. Go and Pine (1995: 206-210) reflect the findings of many studies when they suggest that 'on-the-job' training is the most frequently used method of preparing new employees for work (see Wood, 1997, for a fuller review of the literature). An interesting development in recent research has been a focus on measuring the value of training – the rate of return of investment on training specifically. Kline and Harris (2008: 49; see additionally Harris, 2008) point out that the rate of return on investment (ROI) in training within the hospitality industry is rarely calculated: 'Accountants, revenue managers, and chief financial officers can track money, time, product, and the value of real estate, but the challenge with tracing the variables related to the impact of training is, inherently, subjective to a great degree.' The authors note that it is certainly true that existing techniques for calculating the cost of training and ROI are imperfect, but they find it extraordinary that so few hospitality organizations do not insist on some attempt at measurement given the implied costs of training. Reasons given by hoteliers for not doing so invariably pertain to perceived barriers to obtaining valid and reliable information (including the labour intensive nature of data gathering) and a lack of interest in the process (Harris, 2008: 486).

The latter may, of course, be indicative of how little 'real' training actually takes place, or, equally, that it is routine, conventional and minimalist in character. There is evidence of relatively isolated innovation in hospitality training. Levere (2010: 20) reports that two hotels in the USA employed improvisational comedians for coaching and training and that other companies, including some hospitality organizations, are increasingly using PSP and iPod devices to deliver elements of training. A 20-minute training video for iPod costs in the range of US$30,000–50,000, and is a form of delivery appealing in particular to young people thus having the potential to reinforce training more readily.

Payment: Wages and Salaries in the UK

Sturman (2001: 75) writes, on hospitality employment in the USA:

> My analysis supports the long-held anecdotal belief that jobs in the hospitality industry pay less than do comparable jobs in other industries. More important … disparities in pay expand with the jobs' level of complexity. It seems reasonable to argue that such a gap makes it difficult for the hospitality industry to attract the most-skilled employees. Pay disparities may also increase turnover among midlevel employees (who eventually leave for greener pastures) and affect the success of internal promotion and employee-development systems.

In many countries the hospitality sector is a 'minimum wage' industry: that is with hourly rates set by government or some agency of government in order to ensure they do not fall below a level deemed to be socially fair. In the UK during the 1980s and 1990s the then Conservative government received much support from industry in general and the hospitality industry in particular (in the guise of its representative organization, the British Hospitality Association, or BHA) for limiting the extent of wage regulation in hospitality and other industries and, ultimately, removing wage protection (Wood, 1995a). As indicated in the previous chapter, when the opposition Labour Party indicated that if elected to government (which it duly was in 1997) they would introduce a global minimum wage for the British economy there was much wailing and gnashing of teeth with many employer organizations, the BHA included, predicting that this measure would lead to a reduction in the capacity of industries to create jobs because of excessive wage bills. Of course, when the minimum wage was introduced very little happened. In the early 2000s, Williams et al. (2004: 177), citing UK Low Pay Commission reports, found that: 'Overall, it has been estimated that the NMW has increased the hospitality wages bill by approximately two per cent ... the NMW does not appear to have caused significant, if any, job losses in the hospitality sector. Indeed, since the minimum wage came into effect, employment in the industry has grown.' It has grown so well that in 2013 the BHA's Chief Executive was able to claim that in 2012 the hospitality industry accounted for one-third of all new jobs created in the UK economy (Walker, 2013a: 13).

In truth, research into the impact of minimum wages has itself generated considerable ambiguity, studies showing, variably, all of positive, negative and neutral impacts upon the implementation of baseline rates. If rates are set at a reasonably low level then, in general, impact appears to be neutral or at worst marginally negative. To take a judicious academic perspective is, however, too easy. In 1993 when the then Conservative government abolished the wages councils that regulated payment in selected industries, three councils covered different sub-sections of the commercial hospitality industry and the mean hourly rate of pay set by these councils was £2.97 per hour, £115.83 for a 39-hour week or £6023.16 per annum (Goldsmith et al., 1997). In 2012, the hourly rates for the UK economy globally were (under a coalition government consisting of the Conservative and Liberal Democrat parties and assuming entitlement to receive the minimum wage): £6.19 for those aged 21+; £4.98 for those aged 18–20 years; £3.68 for those under 18 and above the school leaving age of 16; and £2.65 for those on certain apprentice schemes (https://www.gov. uk/national-minimum-wage-rates, last accessed 27.03.13). Crude computation and comparison of the figures for the two years 1993 and 2012 therefore suggest that the 1993 mean hourly rate of pay was 68% of the 2012 mean of £4.38, hardly a growth that can be described in terms of a prince's ransom. Even worse, one might think, is the fact that in 2012 the median gross weekly earnings for all UK jobs (full-time and part-time) was £405, which assuming a 40-hour working week yields an hourly rate of £10.12 (Office for National Statistics, 2012). For a worker who is 21 or older earning the minimum wage of £6.19 per hour the equivalent weekly wage is £247.60. Of course, one cannot assume a 40-hour working week, nor is it entirely reasonable to compute an hourly rate from median earnings and compare it to a mean hourly rate. Nevertheless, in reality, it is fair to assume that there is *some* discrepancy between earnings based on the hourly minimum wage and earnings overall and it is possible that this discrepancy is, relatively speaking, quite large. In the case of one specific occupational group – waiters – Harris (2012a: 30) asserts that average gross full-time earnings are £12,975 per annum.

Now of course, much of the above discussion rests on the assumption that employers in certain industries – including hospitality – pay *only* the minimum hourly rate and not more. In the days of the old wages councils, many employers used to frequently claim that they paid more than the minimum rates set by the councils. Many were lying. Most research of the time shows that in wages-council industries the minimum rate set by the council was the going rate, that is, employers used the officially sanctioned rate and rarely paid above it (see Wood, 1997). As employers were represented on the wages councils they further had the opportunity to influence what those rates would be. Another line of employer argument was that wages were *supplemented* by tips but, dependent on the system employed for the distribution of gratuities, it is not always the case that all workers receive them – they are often restricted only to those in customer-facing roles, particularly food and beverage service. Furthermore, in the days of the wages councils, many employers robbed tips of their supplemental value using them to subsidize the basic pay of employees. As recently as 2008, UK newspaper *The Independent* found practices of this kind persisting as employers exploited loopholes in minimum wage legislation. The following extract from an article by Hickman et al. (2008) gives an insight into alleged employer behaviour:

> Gondola Holdings, Britain's largest casual dining giant with annual sales of £228m, deducts an 8 per cent administration charge from tips to staff at PizzaExpress. A waiter at PizzaExpress, Nabil Guirguis, was allegedly dismissed for talking to the media about the practice, which the private equity company insists is fair. The British Hospitality Association, which represents restaurants, denied that its members were mean – and blamed the Inland Revenue for failing to provide a clear lead. Its deputy chief executive, Martin Couchman, said that there were 'legitimate' costs involved in distributing service charges and credit card tips.

The situation is even worse elsewhere. According to Lin and Namasivayam (2011: 924) tips can make up more than half the incomes of restaurant workers in the USA and they suggest that tipping in restaurants exceeds US$40 billion per year. Further, they note, 'In many US organizations, tipped employees are (legally and in compliance with Federal laws) paid below the mandated minimum wage levels; it is assumed that tips will make up the gap' (Lin and Namasivayam, 2011: 926). Tipped employees are usually front of house (particularly waiters); back of house (BOH) employees are usually compensated at the federal minimum wage rate.

In summary, we have considered here only wages within the hospitality industry. Broader comparisons reveal just how poorly paid hospitality work is despite employers frequently complaining (in hospitality businesses and beyond) that the costs of labour are too high in the UK. The UK minimum wage for those aged 21+ is, as we have seen, £6.19 per hour (2012 figure). The respected German organization Destatis (2013) calculated that in 2012 the European Union average hourly pay rate (27 countries) was €23.50 and for the euro-currency area €28.20. The UK ranked 12 out of 27 countries with an average hourly rate of €21.90: the top rate was Sweden, with €41.90. The UK minimum wage is thus 28% of the average hourly rate for the nation as a whole. Growing interest in the UK in the concept of a living wage (a wage that reflects the cost of living, see http://www.livingwage.org.uk/, last accessed 20.11.14), which some companies already pay on a voluntary basis, suggests that in London the hourly rate should be £9.15 per hour and for the rest of the UK £7.85 (2014 figures). These represent 40% and 35% of the 2012 figure for the average hourly rate.

Marginal Workers and Hospitality

In discussions of hospitality industry labour markets, the term 'marginal workers' has been used in two distinct ways. Early, qualitative, studies of hospitality industry employment (see Mars et al., 1979; Shamir, 1978, 1981; and, for much more recent commentary, Pritchard and Morgan, 2006) focused on hotels in particular as organizations that could facilitate various kinds of 'deviant' behaviours, and which were attractive to employees who themselves bore some social stigma. In respect of the latter, one of the respondents to Mars et al.'s (1979: 79) study famously observed that the hotel industry attracted 'all kinds of crooks, queers [male homosexuals], men on the run, alcoholics' and a general manager characterized the working population as 'misfits'. With regard to the former, the hotel, and to a lesser extent restaurant, has attracted social scientific interest as a location for diverse 'illicit' activities, not least of a sexual kind. That hotels persist as locations for activities of this nature was confirmed in the wake of the Dominique Strauss-Kahn scandal in 2011 when the then head of the International Monetary Fund was accused of sexually assaulting a female hotel worker – a room attendant/cleaner – in New York. Thus surfaced an example of what for many hotel workers – female and male – can be a routine, frightening and degrading hazard.

Following this event, Bernstein and Ellison (2011: 48-49; see Fineman, 2012: 84-85 for a more clinical overview) in *Newsweek* reported the outcomes of a specially commissioned survey of 400 married men who travelled regularly. They found that:

- 8% of men reported cheating on their spouse during a business trip;

- 3% said they had made a pass at a member of hotel staff with 55% of those approached rejecting the advance and 27% accepting; and

- 11% of those who booked a massage through their hotel said it led to sexual contact.

The authors note that hotels officially do not condone guests' behaviour but add that: 'many business travellers know they can get almost any extracurricular activity they want without ever leaving the hotel', adding that 'In an industry where the customer is always right, hotels can't afford to be puritanical about their guests' peccadilloes … so the customers' desires can trump almost anything else – including safety and basic decency' (Bernstein and Ellison, 2011: 49). The article as a whole can be interpreted as reaffirming a view of 'extracurricular' activity as a normative feature of hotels; it contains, depressingly, a number of comments from workers who have endured unwanted experiences of harassment and experienced inaction on the part of hotel employers in response to their complaints (for an altogether more sobering view of sexual harassment in hotels, see Guerrier and Adib, 2000; and for an insightful re-evaluation of the marginal worker thesis, Robinson, 2008).

HOSPITALITY MANAGEMENT

Figure 3.1   Selected statistics on UK and European hospitality employment

*Source:*Various, as cited

General

'Tourism … allows for quick entry into the workforce for youth, women and migrant workers. … In 2010, the sector's global economy will account for more than 235 million jobs, equivalent to about 8 per cent of the overall number of jobs' (ILO, 2010: 11).

Age structure

'In contrast to other industries, employment tends to be oriented towards people under 35 years of age, half of which are 25 or under, and a large number of this percentage are women' (ILO, 2010: 13–14).

'Hotels and restaurants are major employers of young people: about half of the work force is below 35 years of age' (HOTREC, http://www.hotrec.eu/about-us/facts-figures.aspx, last accessed 07.04.13).

European hotels and restaurants are a 'young' sector with around one-third of workers aged 24 or less compared to an average of 12% for all sectors (Eurofound, 2009: 1).

The average age of UK waiting staff is 26, and 77% of all waiting and bar staff are under 30 (Harris, 2012b: 32).

31% of the UK hospitality workforce is aged 16–24 (People1st, 2010).

UK housekeepers are comparatively older than the sector workforce as a whole with 7% aged 16–24 (compared with 33% in the sector as a whole) and 59% aged over 45 (compared with 29% of the sector as a whole) (Walker, 2011: 21).

Gender

57% of workers in the hospitality, leisure, travel and tourism sector are women and 95% of UK housekeepers are women (Walker, 2011: 21).

According to UK organization People1st (2014) women dominate in seven of 12 hospitality occupational categories: catering and bar managers, bar staff, kitchen and catering assistants, conference and exhibition managers and organizers, waiting staff, cooks, and housekeeping. They are only 20% of chefs and 48% of hotel and accommodation managers and proprietors.

'There are more women than men working in the sector (55% and 45% respectively). Almost 71% of employment contracts are full-time' (HOTREC, http://www.hotrec.eu/about-us/facts-figures.aspx, last accessed 07.04.13).

Education levels

Employees evidenced a lower educational level: twice as many workers in hotels and restaurants (11%) than the average for all sectors (5.3%) have completed primary education but the proportion of workers with third level education was 11.6%, significantly lower than the average 23.5% (Eurofound, 2009: 1).

14% of UK waiting staff are educated to degree level; 26% have A levels; 52% GCSEs; 7% no qualifications (Harris, 2012b: 32).

11% of the UK hospitality workforce hold no qualifications (People1st, 2010).

Ethnicity and nationality

14% of the hospitality workforce are from ethnic minorities and 21% of the sector's workers are from overseas (59% in London) (People1st, 2010).

26% of UK waiting staff were born overseas compared to 34% of restaurant and catering managers (Harris, 2012b: 32).

27% of UK housekeepers were born overseas (85% in London) compared to 21% for the sector as a whole (Walker, 2011: 21).

35% of ethnic minority workers worked in hotels, catering, distribution, transport and communications compared to 26% of white workers (Commission for Racial Equality, 2006: 5).

Two-thirds of Bangladeshis and nearly half of Chinese (47%) and Pakistanis (46%), and some 34% of Indians worked in hotels, catering, wholesale, retail, distribution, transport and communication (Commission for Racial Equality, 2006: 5). Bangladeshi men were overwhelmingly (81%) to be found working in hotels, catering, distribution, transport and communication industries where more than half of Pakistani and Chinese men also worked (Commission for Racial Equality, 2006: 5).

Part-time

'Within the EU, while the overall tendency leans toward more part-time employment in general, there is a broad variation between Portugal with 5 per cent part-time employment, the United Kingdom where 50 per cent are part time and the Netherlands where there are 68 per cent' (ILO, 2010: 14).

In the EU 27, the ILO (2010: 16) states that 7.7% of the workforce are male part-time and 44% male full-time; and 18% female part-time and 36.5% full-time.

Income

42.1% of workers are concentrated in the lowest income category compared to a cross-sector average of 25.1%, while a low proportion of workers fall into the highest income category (15.8% against an average of 24.3%) (Eurofound, 2009: 1).

The second usage of the term 'marginal worker' is one that would be more widely recognized by employment researchers. As Wood (1992: 179) puts it:

> To describe particular groups of workers as marginal is normally to identify them as having a weak labour market position. Marginal workers are disadvantaged in the sale of their labour to an employer because they have little bargaining power due to lack of skill and experience, or because the structure of labour markets allows them to sell their labour only in certain contexts on terms that usually favour the employer.

One inference that might be drawn from this quotation and an idea that recurs frequently in the research literature on hospitality employment is that many hospitality industry workers have limited choice in the kinds of jobs they can access. Thus, those with domestic and childcare responsibilities (usually women) seeking employment may only be available for part-time work (which in the UK hospitality industry is available in abundance). School leavers with few or no qualifications are restricted in the quality and variety of employment opportunities they can expect. Active discrimination against ethnic and national minorities may delimit opportunities for members of these groups. At the same time we can say that many advantaged – in particular young – people who defer their entry into the labour market (students and those enjoying a 'gap year' before becoming students) make the most of the easy availability of hospitality employment for short periods in order to finance their studies or some part of their lifestyle.

If the typical operative employee in hospitality is indeed 'marginal' in this sense then we would expect to see some or all of young people, females, less well-educated persons and people from ethnic and national minorities overrepresented in the workforce, occupying a disproportionately large number of part-time jobs and, concomitantly, fewer senior positions. Figure 3.1 shows a selection of statistics from European and UK sources. Even once all the usual caveats have been entered on the use of statistical data (see Chapter 2) the variety of information displayed is highly suggestive of the validity of the 'second' marginal worker thesis, and though far from conclusive, it suggests that the industry does indeed employ disproportionate numbers of young, female, ethnic minority, migrant and relatively poorly educated employees.

Marginal workers and labour instability

> Most organizations in the hospitality industry expect high turnover and employee dissatisfaction to occur … . The specific characteristics of the job that lead to high rates of dissatisfaction and consequently to employees' departure include seasonality of the operation, prevalence of small organizations, unpleasant physical working conditions, inconvenient working hours, lack of career opportunities for frontline jobs, and low pay. (DiPietro and Pizam, 2007: 22)

Labour mobility is a term that simply describes the movement of people in and out of employment with organizations. Labour turnover is a term sometimes used as a synonym for labour mobility but is more usually employed, whether accurately or not, to refer to the number of people who leave an organization in a given time period. In the hospitality industry, labour turnover rates are normally calculated at the unit (hotel, restaurant) level. The hospitality sector has a more or less global reputation for rates of labour turnover in excess of all other industries. The Eurofound (2009: 1) organization found that:

> Hotels and restaurants are less stable in employment terms with 52% of workers having been in post for one year or less and 10% only having served longer than sixteen years – as a corollary of this almost half (47%) of contracts in the

industry were found to be non-permanent compared to 23% across all sectors. (Eurofound, 2009: 1)

The International Labour Organization (ILO) (2010: 17) points out that: 'Labour turnover varies greatly from country to country, but in developed economies it tends to be significantly higher [in the hospitality sector] in relation to other sectors. In developing countries, workplace turnover is strikingly low and the industry is characterized by greater employment stability.' There is a lack of consistent evidence as to the latter, but in the case of the former the ILO is both historically and contemporaneously correct. In the UK People1st (2010) estimated a rate of labour turnover in hospitality, leisure, tourism and travel at 31%. Williamson et al. (2012: 675) write that: 'Labour turnover is a major issue in the New Zealand hotel industry, with almost twice the level of turnover against the national average.' In a study of 64 Australian four and five star hotels, Davidson et al. (2010) found that an average hotel spent A$109,909 (US$100,000) for replacing executive, managerial and supervisory staff each year excluding costs deriving from lost productivity and service quality. The average cost for replacing a member of operational staff was A$9951 (US$9000). In the 64 hotels studied, the total cost of labour turnover was A$49 million per annum. DiPietro and Pizam (2007: 23) quoted at the head of this discussion cite evidence to suggest that hourly employee turnover specifically in the quick service restaurant sector of the American food service industry costs in excess of US$3.4 billion a year. In another US study, Hinkin and Tracey (2000: 14) somewhat bleakly note:

In short, we know that turnover is high, and we have a good idea of why people leave. First, employees are poorly supervised, and they are often given little responsibility or authority in the work that they perform. Second, many jobs are mundane and repetitive, and working conditions are often unpleasant. Finally, compensation is low for work that can involve intensive interaction with guests. One conclusion of the research is that the hotel industry has been mired in many outdated human-resources (HR) practices for decades, while innovative management has resulted in major organizational and individual improvements in other industries.

One relatively recent 'innovation' in hotels that has the effect of rendering labour turnover less visible is the outsourcing of certain labour functions (see Chapter 4); employing temporary work agencies to supply personnel for specific short-, medium- or, increasingly, long-term assignments; and the use of zero-hours contracts. When employees are employed by another organization, as is the case with the first two of these arrangements, their departure does not register as part of the hospitality organization's turnover. Knox (2010: 463; see in addition the study by Soltani and Wilkinson, 2010, of temporary work agency employment in the Australian hotel sector) concluded:

> Overall … TWA [temporary work agency] employment has become a per-
> manent and embedded feature of the labour strategies deployed in this sector.
> Typically managers indicated that their reliance upon TWAs was driven by
> their desire to enhance numerical flexibility, eliminate recruitment/selec-
> tion and training/development costs, reduce costs associated with workers'
> compensation and overcome the variable nature of labour costs. In general
> then, managers' increased reliance on TWAs was associated with their need to
> enhance numerical flexibility while reducing costs.

A zero-hours contract is 'a colloquial term for an employment contract under
which the employee is not guaranteed work and is paid only for work carried out'
(Pyper and McGuinness, 2014: 3). A worker is expected to be available when their
employer needs them but are not legally obliged to accept work. In the UK – surprise,
surprise – the biggest user of zero-hours contracts in the pursuit of labour flexibility
is the hotels and restaurants sector, 19% doing so in 2011 as compared to 4% in 2004
(Pyper and McGuinness, 2014: 4). *The Independent* newspaper revealed in 2013 that
in the UK, 90% of McDonald's employees were employed on zero-hours contracts
(Hall, 2013). Employees on zero-hours contracts still count as employees and
therefore their departure from an organization counts as labour turnover. However,
as workers are only paid for work done, the cost of replacement is, arguably,
substantially reduced further empowering employers to ignore the effects of churn
on organizational performance and their bottom line.

Is It Like This Everywhere? International Comparisons

We saw in the earlier discussion of the social construction of skill thesis that an issue
with some researchers into human resources in hospitality is whether the 'low skill'
label attached to hospitality employment in the UK and other Anglosphere countries applies equally on a global scale. Baum (1993, 1995, 2006, 2008; Duncan et al.,
2013) has been a doughty proponent of this view and of the related assertion that
there are cultural and (inter)national differences in perceptions of, and rewards for,
hospitality work. In other words there are places where hospitality employment is
relatively highly regarded and the level of remuneration is, in local economic terms,
fairly positive. Other commentators, including this one (see Wood, 1997), have been
sceptical of this perspective.

The most persuasive evidence *contra* Baum's hypothesis comes from the periodic
reports of the ILO (e.g. ILO, 1965, 1974, 1980, 2001, 2010, 2014), which by and
large suggest that the 'Anglo-Saxon' experiences described in this chapter are widely – if
unevenly – generalized across the globe. Some 35 years ago, Mars et al. (1979: 153)
noted that: 'The I.L.O. reports describe the structural properties of the industry
in a number of different countries. Although there are some very obvious cultural
variations, particularly in terms of attitudes to the service role the industry performs,

many of the social and economic problems of the industry tend to have general applicability.' Wood (1997) reviewed certain of the then extant research evidence from other countries (the USA, Australia, Japan, France, Italy, Spain and Austria), which reported evidence of some or all of the characteristics of 'marginality' in the hospitality workforce. The old saying that if it walks like a duck and quacks like a duck then it *is* a duck seems to apply here but, once again, as is often the case with hospitality employment research, the evidence is highly suggestive but not conclusive and in this particular instance the possibility must be allowed that employer organization and employee experience of hospitality work is not entirely uniform.

Concluding Remarks

The issues discussed in this chapter represent only a part – albeit perhaps the most significant part – of a tapestry of reasons as to why hospitality employment is negatively viewed and experienced. Necessarily the focus of the discussion has been very narrow. We have not, for example, considered the absence of work–life balance in the industry (for recent observations on this phenomenon see Cleveland et al., 2007; Qu and O'Neill, 2010), which is increasingly cited as a reason either for not selecting, or for abandoning, a career in hospitality. However, we have covered a sufficient range of topics to obtain clear reasons for the poor image of hospitality employment: the image of the industry is poor because many aspects of employment practice are poor. If we are looking for someone or something to blame for the image of the industry then there is only one serious candidate – the industry's owners and managers.

Research into hospitality employment has long established that a core factor in the perpetuation of existing employment practices emanates from managers' acceptance of the 'inevitability' of low pay and high labour turnover, a reliance on 'traditional' industry practices and a corresponding lack of imagination and creativity in *how* to manage. There is an absence of extensive evidence on the effect of managers' interventions in these areas where they do occur, but see Choa et al. (2006), who found that the routine practice of basic human resource procedures can have significant effects on turnover rate of non-managerial employees. This said, two relatively recent global, if small-scale, surveys (Enz, 2001, 2009) have suggested that HRM issues are top of hotel managers' concerns. Enz's (2009: 581) most recent, 2009, investigation of global manager opinion (243 persons in 60+ countries comprising hotel general managers, corporate executives and middle managers) found that on a five-point scale (5 = very important concern), four specific issues scored on average in excess of 4.5 – namely attraction, retention, training and morale. Enz (2009: 581) notes regional variations as follows:

> Attraction is most important for managers in North America and the Middle East, while retention tops the list for European respondents, and training worries Asian respondents. Attraction, retention, and morale are tied for most important in Africa, while retention and training are tied for the top rating by respondents from South America.

Managers are thus not obviously oblivious to HRM problems in hospitality but appear unwilling, unable or incapable of enacting meaningful change for the better thus as likely as not offering the prospect of exacerbating future employee relations, not least among those young workers who are increasingly the mainstay of the industry. Young people (18–24) in Meudell and Rodham's (1998: 131) study of money as a motivator in the licensed house sector found that fringe benefits, money and bonuses were self-declared motivators to work harder, with older workers being more concerned with the threat of losing their job and with bonus payments. According to the website Travolution (2013) a study for the World Tourism Forum (WTF) by PricewaterhouseCoopers (PwC) of 1000 20- to 33-year-olds found that pay and promotion prospects rather than loyalty and company commitment were top priorities for younger-generation staff. Charles Donkor, PwC partner, human capital consulting, is reported as saying: 'The results show that companies in the tourism industry must modify their management of Generation Y if they wish to achieve success in the tourism industry, attract motivated young staff and keep them long-term.'

The best current explanation of human resource practice in hospitality is simple: it is essential to the enduring financial viability of hospitality businesses, and hospitality employers can get away with the behaviours we have described. As in any business, some financial surplus could theoretically be sacrificed at the expense of profit to modernizing working practices and paying better wages. However, the motivation to do so does not exist. Go and Pine (1995: 206–210) reported the results from a 1991 survey of the 200 largest hotel corporations which revealed that in terms of the importance of strategic policies in personnel management, paying 'relatively high wages' and providing both 'attractive benefit packages' and 'incentive programmes' ranked 5th, 7th and 8th on a scale of eight items. Sturman (2001: 76) points out, somewhat wearily, that one 'might argue that hotels and restaurants simply cannot afford to match other industries' pay rates for operations positions. Moreover, it is possible for organizations to operate successfully with a competitive human-resources strategy based on paying lower-than-market wages.' This is indeed a crucial point. So long as there are people willing to work, or resigned to working, in the industry for the wages on offer why should the industry change? We noted earlier the growth in use of zero-hours contracts in the UK. Amounting to little more than a form of legal slavery, thousands of employees have nevertheless signed up to them. It would be a mistake to assume that in all cases this was a matter of choice; more often than not it will be because there is little choice at all. In the end, we are thrown back once again on the argument introduced in the Preface to this book and revisited in Chapter 2: namely that parts of the hospitality industry at least are, in economic terms, rather marginal – i.e. a key element in their economic success is the ability to pay low wages. It is a situation unlikely to change in the near future.

Further Reading

Enz, C A (2009) 'Human resource management: a troubling issue for the global hotel industry', *Cornell Hospitality Quarterly*, 50, 4: 578–583.

International Labour Organization (ILO) (2014) *Employment in the Tourism Sector (Hotels and Restaurants as a Proxy)*, retrieved from http://www.ilo.org/wcmsp5/groups/public/–ed_dialogue/–sector/documents/publication/wcms_235636.pdf, last accessed 10.06.14.

Riley, M, Ladkin, A and Szivas, E (2002) *Tourism Employment: Analysis and Planning*, Bristol: Channel View Publications.

Wood, R C (1997) *Working in Hotels and Catering*, London: International Thomson Business Press, 2nd Ed.

4

IS YOUR ROOM ALRIGHT?
ACCOMMODATION MANAGEMENT IN
HOSPITALITY

After reading this chapter, you should:

(a) have acquired a broad range of knowledge pertaining to the management of accommodation in the hospitality industry, and in particular the hotel industry;

(b) understand issues pertaining to the role of design in hospitality; and

(c) be familiar with core concepts (e.g. the guest cycle, standard operating procedures, revenue management, outsourcing, sustainability) and key operational functions (e.g. front office, front desk, housekeeping, laundry, IT services, security and loss prevention) in the administration of hospitality organizations.

Introduction

You are checking into the hotel that you booked on the hotel company's own website. You resisted the website's offer to spend an extra €50 to upgrade to an executive room. You are on a business trip and will only be in your room for as much time as you are allowed to sleep and perform your ablutions. A more luxurious and expensive room is therefore not a requirement. At the front desk, the receptionist repeats the offer you have already declined. You decline again. The whole check-in process seems to be taking longer than it should. The receptionist is looking doubtfully at the monitor in front of her. You are then told that as it is before the hotel's advertised check-in time (2 p.m.) your room is not ready. The receptionist will gladly store your luggage for you until it is available. But you have just come off a three-hour flight and need to shower and change your clothes in order to go to a meeting. The receptionist sighs and picks up the telephone handset. She calls the housekeeping department. Naturally, you only hear her side of the conversation. She hangs up. A room might be available in about an hour. Would you like to have a drink in the bar while you wait? When, finally, you get to your room you run a finger across the furniture and ascertain that it has not been dusted properly. The bathroom appears clean until you look up to the ventilator grill above the bath and see it is furred up with months, possibly years, of detritus. In general, the room does not appear to have been redecorated or refurbished for a considerable time.

The foregoing vignette is a composite of some personal experiences as a traveller. These experiences are not unique, occurring daily all over the world. Other things happen too: being 'walked' – that is, transferred to another hotel because the room you pre-booked and pre-paid has been sold to someone else who has beaten you to checking in. Being told on the company website that the hotel has rooms for those who smoke, to find on arrival that it does not. To discover that the hotel is being refurbished and looks very much like the building site it effectively is. The basic message that hotel companies want us to believe is usually expressed in the form: 'You are our customer/guest, your comfort is very important to us'. The more you travel the more you suspect this is not the case: that hotel companies are often economical with the truth and engage quite shamelessly in what, to customers, appear as apparently dubious ethical business practices but which are, in reality, industry norms.

If this seems harsh then there is a more 'academic' way of analysing this type of behaviour which has its roots in the work of the sociologist Boas Shamir (1978) who observed that each hotel guest thinks of service as being rendered to them personally (a similar sentiment applies in restaurants) but, of course, the very rationale of a hotel is to provide service to large numbers of guests on a more-or-less collective basis. When tensions between the macro-objectives of the hotel clash with the micro-management of hospitality as delivered to individual guests, the kinds of experiences described in the vignette emerge. In this chapter, we review some of the key features of accommodation management in hospitality that present challenges to managers.

The Nature and Status of Accommodation Services in Hospitality Management

Accommodation and food and beverage management are the two features of hospitality that distinguish it from general management. In the majority of hotels around the world, accommodation is what makes 'the' money – i.e. sale of rooms to guests is the main driver of revenue (Hunter Powell and Watson (2006: 297) cite data from the British Hospitality Association suggesting that 55% of total hotel revenue in the UK is derived from rooms, 23% from food and 10% from beverages). Despite this, in the past, hotel management schools have devoted considerable time and money to food and beverage education. Food and beverage is 'sexy', it is not simply confined to hotels but embraces the whole of the restaurant sector and figures as an ancillary service in many other types of organization. For many years in hotels, and to some extent it is still so, attainment of, and success in managerial responsibility in the food and beverage department was seen as the dominant career route to a general manager position (see Chapters 5 and 7). With the possible exception of front office, accommodation management has not, and still does not, always share the same allure, and this is especially true of accommodation functions including housekeeping, maintenance and engineering, security and design. Nevertheless, as Frapin-Beaugé et al. (2008: 383) note:

> Thirty years ago in the UK and elsewhere, it was hardly possible to study for a qualification in hospitality management without touching on all these subjects. Changes in the industry, not least the increasing utilization of external experts (whether lawyers, architects, or interior designers); the increasing limitation of resources in many (especially state-funded) higher education institutes offering hospitality programmes; and a switch from technology based approaches to hospitality to managerially based approaches now make it much less likely that students will encounter these areas in much depth.

As examples, the authors refer to the fact that in the past many hotel schools taught the soft science underpinning housekeeping and maintenance, exploring technical subjects that included lighting, water and sanitary engineering, chemical treatment of various materials and fabrics, and the operation of ventilation and heating systems. One rationale for this approach was to equip students of hotel management with basic knowledge for dealing with specialists. While this approach can still be found in some educational programmes it is no longer the norm, and much of the scientific basis that underpinned – at least in the UK – hospitality higher education has been dropped in favour of a more purely managerial orientation of the curriculum. Indeed, as we shall see in Chapter 5, this retreat from science also applies to the theory and practice of food and beverage management.

Accommodation management is centrally concerned with the protection and management of the fixed assets of the organization and/or buildings' owner(s) with a view to generating profit (Schneider et al., 1999). In large corporate entities, it has, over the last quarter century, largely become an increasingly systemized and standardized process as a result of changes and development in construction technologies, design and business processes. Technological developments include advances in building-structural technologies (e.g. off-the-shelf modular construction packages – Robbins (2012) notes that hotel group citizenM prefabricates its rooms which are transported from a construction centre to the hotel where they are 'slotted' into the building frame – the technology is not new but continues to evolve). In addition to its functional role, design has acquired a greater centrality in hotel and restaurant design branding. Business process developments include those in internal management systems such as growing appreciation of the relationships between the evolution and application of the concept of the guest cycle; the increasing importance of standard operating procedures (SOPs); the theory and practice of revenue management; external opportunities furnished by the growth of specialist companies that facilitate the outsourcing of particular services (e.g. laundry) or whole functions (e.g. housekeeping); and the ever-present pressure to deal with questions of business and environmental sustainability. Together with comment on key operational areas in accommodation management (especially the 'Rooms Division' of hotels) it is these processes that frame the following discussion of the main aspects of accommodation management.

Design

We begin our discussion of accommodation management with the topic of design and another vignette drawn from personal experience.

An upscale hotel chain 'signatures' its design sensibilities via the postmodern irony of placing a rubber duck with sunglasses in its guest bathrooms. A Dubai hotel of the same chain has invested in a top-class German brand of kettle for the courtesy tray – with a two (round) pin plug in a country that uses the UK three ('square') pin plug system. There is no adaptor. A large international four star hotel chain has bathtubs (incorporating shower) that cannot easily be climbed into (except by those of athletic disposition). The reason – the sides are too high. With all the bathroom fittings being modular, the unusually shaped sink is not deep enough to allow for filling of the courtesy tray kettle provided. The executive rooms of the same chain have low free-form chairs with a seat that is approximately 15 centimetres off the ground making it impossible for the arthritic, the disabled or the elderly to rise from them without difficulty.

Other common design flaws found in hotels include: over-, under- or inadequate lighting; the absence of a bedside switch that turns all the lights in the room on and off; an insufficient number of power points; and power points in difficult-to-access positions that require rearrangement of the room's furniture in order to get to them. To this we can add the small open space with a hanging rail that substitutes for a wardrobe in many hotel guest rooms. Often, the hanging rail is fixed at a level easily accessible to a taller member of the Harlem Globetrotters but nobody else. Then there are the hangers affixed to the rail by a loop which is the hotel's way of unambiguously telling you that 'We charge you the earth but don't trust you not to steal the traditional type of hanger'. The openness of the space to the rest of the room allows the guest to enjoy the thought of the room cleaner daily kicking up clouds of dust that will envelop their clothes. A particular 'despoilment' of the design/brand concept, even more bizarre in the age of the netbook, tablet and smartphone, arises from the littering of guest rooms with different-sized bits of paper advertising, variously: the overpriced cable and internet–via–television daily package; the hotel's 'environmental' policy in respect of the changing of bed linen; a 'pillow menu' advising of the range of said articles available for your comfort; the similar notice in the bathroom extolling the virtues of reusing towels; and, in many upscale hotels, the small piece of paper placed on your pillow during turndown advising on tomorrow's weather (often accompanied by a gratuitous quotation or an 'on this day' factlet). There may be, additionally, an in-room dining menu from which you can order frequently unappetizing (and by the time it is delivered to your room, tepid) food. All of the above are usually additional to the provision of a hotel directory (usually – somewhat strangely – hidden in a drawer somewhere and often in loose leaf format allowing for the insertion of all that additional information contained on the various bits of paper strewn about).

From the publicity given to them, design and design decisions appear to have assumed greater importance in hospitality operations in recent years. Over the past three decades or so we have been inundated by innumerable picture books and magazines intended to showcase hotel design – and especially interior design. 'Designer restaurants' and 'restaurant chains' attract similar attention. Reporting on the Ping Pong dim sum restaurant chain, Lander (2006) compliments the Swiss architect and designer concerned, David Marquardt, on the 'stylish interior' (of the restaurant) and for, in opening a new branch, 'the manner in which – with only a simple, regenerating kitchen to install – they can turn round a site in no more than eight weeks, way below the restaurant norm' (see http://www.pingpongdimsum.com/, last accessed 07.04.13).

Academically, relatively little research has been conducted in the field of hospitality design (see Wood, 2011; Marée, 2013, for brief overviews). Design is cited as both a key differentiator of brand and a factor believed to encourage guest and customer satisfaction. Just as chefs have 'signature' dishes, for many operators, signature buildings and signature interiors are sought after to increase the marketing appeal of hotels and restaurants, sometimes seeking to employ design to create so-called 'destination' venues, i.e. hotels and restaurants that are primary attractions in their own right in much the same way as a museum, art gallery, theme park or particular natural environment is a principal motivation to visitors. Some hotels – called variously design, boutique or contemporary hotels (Strannegård and Strannegård, 2012) – are even operated and marketed on the back of their design appeal. Unfortunately, as the earlier vignette suggests, given the extent of interest in design it remains a mystery as to why most hotels and many other hospitality organizations still get so much wrong (and they do) in this respect. The answer may be quite simple – though not at present verifiable. It is that as the status of the so-called creative and cultural industries has grown (see Hartley et al., 2013), we have come to appreciate certain activities for their intrinsic rather than applied value. In his survey of the design field, John Heskett (2005) recounts the history of the idea that in design, form should follow function, reminding us that this idea became one of the most hotly contested among design professionals in the twentieth century. Common sense might suggest that a principle of design at all levels would be to factor in the needs and wants of a product's or service's end users in the spirit of ensuring the 'fitness to purpose' of those products and services. It appears, however, that this might be too optimistic a view.

The design devil is in the detail

From the perspective of a regular hotel user the two main issues with design are (a) the apparent disregard for basic human needs (the corollary of which is a tendency to elevate the designer's or operator's vision or needs over those of other stakeholders), and (b) the tendency to assume that design is an *absolute* process that once completed will be fixed in time for eternity – and this despite the fact that best design practice suggests that the process should – and will, as a result of the need for refurbishment – be otherwise (Heskett, 2005).

All this said, Robson and Pullman (2005; see additionally Goff, 2007) point out that in hotels at least, little has changed in the fundamentals of hotel design over the last 50 years despite the apparent growth in importance of design considerations. Guest rooms and associated spaces account for anything from 65% to 90% of total building area whereas back-of-the-house functions take up between 10% and 15% with the balance going over to lobbies, food and beverage outlets, recreational spaces and meeting facilities. The overall trend has been towards standardization and, in the case of newly built hotels, this extends to everything from room size and configuration and the placement of infrastructure services to the mode, quantity and quality of services available in guest and public areas. As long ago as 1984, Riley (Wood, 1994a, offers a partial development of his argument) noted that traditional modes of hotel service based on human delivery were giving way to forms of service centred on various forms of technology to which customers themselves added the human element (essentially self-service and to the provider, cost saving). In guest rooms, this included the provision of a minibar, complimentary tea- and coffee-making facilities and televisions (older generations can still remember hotel guest rooms *sans* televisions: some hotels had television lounges which could become battlegrounds over the choice of what to watch, a phenomenon captured in 'The Hotel Inspectors' episode of that paean to the UK hotel industry, the BBC's *Fawlty Towers*).

Riley's point about hotels is particularly useful because it captures a trend that at the time of his writing was instantly recognizable and remains so today, though these processes do not appear to have been uniform either in their application or focus. As an example we can take the case of minibars, which are rarely found in the guest rooms of budget hotels and are, indeed, absent from many luxury establishments (in the case of the latter permitting a more expensive 'room service' offering). Moreover, there has been much recent indication that the economics of the guest room minibar are no longer sustainable. Gaining ubiquity in hotel rooms across the world from 1974 when it was introduced by Hilton, Muston (2011) reported that many hotel chains were seeking to improve the quality of products offered in their hotel room minibars despite hotel chains complaining they are loss leaders primarily because of theft and the cost of employing personnel to maintain them. Some two years later, Mesure and Blagoeva (2013) noted that many hotel chains had decided to remove minibars from guest rooms because of the costs of maintenance and policing. They cited the growth of budget hotels providing vending machines instead of in-room minibars as another influence on this trend. Room service itself might be under threat. Muston (2013) again reports the New York Hilton, that city's largest hotel, as abandoning room service. Why? As with the minibar, room service is expensive to provide and not all that profitable, if it is profitable at all. This does not invalidate the arguments of Riley and others as to technological substitution of services or the role of guests/customers in contributing to product/service delivery. Rather it shows how trends can mutate, or be made to mutate, by operators in search of the elimination of 'unnecessary' costs and/or new and innovative products and the niches in which to market them.

In respect of the latter, the earlier mentioned Dutch group, citizenM, which opened its first hotel in 2008, has been lauded for its design imperatives. Walker and Mielisch (2010: 42) in an article in the UK Institute of Hospitality's magazine enthusiastically note that: 'Dutch hotel group citizenM has an innovative business model that keeps investment, labour and distribution costs low while providing "affordable luxury" to its guests. But it is citizenM's pioneering approach to technology that is making waves.' The article emphasizes the company's attention to detail in designing the guest experience. There is self-check-in; emphasis on 'a comfy bed and a good shower, where guests are unwilling to compromise'; free internet access; and an information technology system that allows guests to use their room's 'MoodPad' to control lights, window blinds and other functions and for preferred settings to be remembered. Robbins (2012) notes that the London hotel's guest rooms are very small (14 square metres) though the finish is to a high standard, and he name checks the use of Frette linen, a Hansgrohe shower and toiletries by Alessandro Gualtieri. However, the hotel's public areas are spacious and incorporate different zones – bar, restaurant (self-service) and office working space.

Without in any way distracting from the creative intentions behind the citizenM brand, it is essentially a budget hotel model that seeks to minimize costs while proposing a superior guest offer. The Chief Operating Officer, Michael Levie, is reported as claiming that the Glasgow hotel employs one employee for every five rooms against an alleged industry norm of one employee for every two rooms. The investment costs are noted as around £79,000 per bedroom against an industry average of £175,000 for a four star chain brand (Walker and Mielisch, 2010: 44). To what extent citizenM is superior in its offer to other budget chains is unclear precisely because its pitch is unashamedly to a niche market, defined by Levie as people 'interested in art and high culture but travel in jeans and T-shirts; they drink champagne but take the bus home' (quoted in Robbins, 2012: 7).

The limits of design standardization

Standardization of products and services is a force in all industries, including hospitality. There are, however, limits. Some limits arise from cultural differences. Thus, compared to Europe, in the Middle East and Asia both operators and guests have expectations of larger rooms and a full range of services. A number of international budget and midprice limited-service brands, when establishing themselves in these regions, are compelled to offer a full service product. Acquisition is a second factor mitigating standardization. Companies that acquire properties from other operators in order to expand and/or establish a presence in a particular geographical market often acquire properties that are by definition non-standard relative to the majority of their existing properties. This poses the danger of diluting a brand by presenting to guests different norms, standards and facilities within the same brand. In some cases, however, difference can be turned into a brand virtue as with Marriott's Renaissance Hotels, which are mostly non–standard acquisitions where potential guests are invited to:

> Choose from one of our historic icons, chic boutiques or luxurious resorts. Each offers its own personality, local flavour, distinctive style and charm. All will stimulate your appetite for discovery. (http://www.marriott.com/marriott-brands.mi, last accessed 18.08.13)

Another limit to design standardization is the need for periodic refurbishment. In their survey of the hotel industry for 2013, the consultancy company Ernst and Young (2013: 7) commented:

> The physical condition of a hotel property is one of the most important drivers of operating performance. A deteriorating property, whether on the exterior, in common areas, rooms, ancillary facilities or back-of-house, can be a significant challenge for investors and owners. In recent years, stagnant lodging fundamentals and capital constraints, exacerbated by slow economic growth in many parts of the world, have had a negative impact on the ability and/or willingness of hotel companies and owners to address portfolio capital expenditure needs. Today, in light of recovering industry fundamentals, hotel companies and owners are once again assessing the need for capital expenditure investments.

Refurbishment provides a considerable challenge to hotels. It is rarely the case that a whole hotel can be closed for refurbishment although with many prestige projects this does happen: London's Savoy Hotel was closed from 2007 to 2010 for a £250 million refit; the London Connaught for nine months in 2007 for a £70 million refurbishment (Harris, 2012b: 32–34). The scheduling of refurbishment in most hotels (normally) entails the phased closing of floors. Of course, this leads to revenue loss. The ideal balance in establishing the extent (in years) of a refurbishment cycle rests on the judgement as to when accommodation becomes so tired that it has a negative effect on occupancy. Information of this kind is more widely and easily disseminated by customers in a socially networked world. However, as any regular hotel user can report, there are many companies and establishments that apparently extend the life of their inventory to extremes. The reason for this is, of course, money, arising from the unwillingness of building owners to finance refurbishment on a systematic basis – leaving, in many instances, the operator/brand owner with only the threat of withdrawing from the unit (see Hassanien and Losekoot, 2002; JNA and HVS Design, 2013 offer a useful guide to the costs of renovation and refurbishment). Refurbishment/renovation cycles vary from company to company. According to White (2012: 41) guest room carpets are replaced around every five years with furniture expected to last 10–12 years. However, the same author cites numerous instances of poor quality including tired bed linen, outdated televisions and poor interiors in both guest rooms and public areas despite observing that hotels were expected to spend US$3.5 billion in 2011 on refurbishment/renovation (this figure appears to pertain only to the USA). Robson and Pullman (2005) indicate a number of fronts on which hotels and hotel companies are addressing specific customer needs, both in 'new builds' and through the process of adapting or refurbishing buildings; for example: providing rooms with longer beds and higher shower heads for taller guests; installing proper ergonomic furniture in work areas to reflect guests' increasing use of mobile computing; and placing soap dishes in elevated positions in the shower to improve safety. Refurbishment is also an opportunity to make existing buildings disabled friendly (in many countries this is, or has been driven by, legislation), both a necessary recognition of the needs of the disabled and a sound marketing decision – in the UK alone the disabled market is worth £2 billion year and accounts for 12% of all overnight stays in the UK, with disabled people staying on average longer (3.6 nights) than the able bodied (3 nights) as well as being more likely to travel with others (friends, relatives, carers) (Anon, 2013: 11).

In summary, the practical implications of design for hospitality organizations are rarely addressed in sufficient depth in the educational process. In the case of hotels, relatively few general or departmental managers will, in their career, have to contend with the opening of a brand new, freshly constructed hotel and even if they are, they are unlikely to be involved in the design standards which will almost certainly have been agreed at the building design stage. This robs the design process of necessary practical experience in conceptualizing the physical framework of a hotel building.

The Guest Cycle and Standard Operating Procedures (SOPs)

The guest cycle is a key concept underpinning the practice of hotel accommodation management. It is a four-part process model of the stages of a guest's stay at a hotel depicting the flow of business in terms of internal service and financial exchanges (see Kooi, 2013, for a brief but useful summary). The four stages are: pre-arrival (reservations); arrival (registration); occupancy (occupancy services); and departure (check-out). The *pre-arrival* stage links to other managerial functions – at executive/ corporate *and* unit level – including marketing, sales and revenue management, and is concerned with securing business for the hotel in the form of a room reservation. The key skills required are those that contribute to influencing potential guests in favour of 'this' hotel rather than 'that' hotel. The *arrival stage* entails effective registra- tion and check-in of the guest; procuring and verifying personal details (e.g. credit card validity); conforming to prevailing local legal requirements (e.g. securing a copy of a guest's passport for onward transmission to the public agency respon- sible for immigration); and attempts at selling additional or enhanced products and services (e.g. a better and more expensive room). The *occupancy stage* is everything between the arrival and departure stages and is committed to ensuring that guests have a comfortable and enjoyable stay in the hotel, as well as in many cases continuing to try to sell additional services. In the *departure stage*, the principal objective is to secure payment for the guest's stay, sell any onward services that the guest may require (e.g. limousine transfers to airports) and leave the guest with a positive final experience of the hotel.

Earlier in this chapter we noted Shamir's (1978) observation that individual hotel guests think of themselves as having service rendered to them personally whereas the rationale of a hotel is to provide service to large numbers of guests on a more-or-less collective basis. In the contemporary corporate hospitality industry this rationale is embodied in *standard operating procedures* (SOPs) – written guides to physical and process standards and the execution of tasks to meet these standards (see Frapin-Beaugé et al., 2008, for an extended discussion of this topic). Often called 'living' documents ('living' because ideally they should be modified as and when procedures, equipment or rooms change), SOPs often have significant monies invested in them by corporations; in addition to being reference points, they form the basis for training personnel. The guest cycle and standard operating procedures (the latter taken collectively) are *integrative concepts*. The guest cycle integrates customers into the payment and customer relationship management systems of the hotel. In many ways, SOPs perform the same function for an organization's personnel, as well as linking to guests in the sense of specifying the standards they are entitled to expect.

It is on the twin issues of guest expectations and entitlements that SOPs often falter. First, SOPs are not meant to be localized but mutually benchmarked throughout the organization to ensure integration of processes and procedures. For non-standard hotel buildings in a chain (often obtained through acquisitions), uniformity (and thus brand identity) can be undermined by necessary local variations in standards, processes and procedures. Secondly, SOPs are often grown and administered through departments, and integration within and between departments in hospitality organizations is often difficult to attain. A final reason for the frequent lack of success of SOPs is that the emphasis is on 'the standard'. A major objective of SOPs is a reduction in human variability in the delivery of products and services so as to achieve either an explicit or implied level of hospitality. This can constrain operatives' discretion to vary their actions according to guest needs and wants. Further, 'the standard' in SOPs is often constituted by quantitative rather than qualitative indicators in the form of performance criteria (e.g. what and how guest rooms should be cleaned) and productivity criteria (e.g. how many rooms should be cleaned by an attendant in a defined time period). These criteria often *become* the standard and are made manifest (for example in hotel housekeeping departments) in checklists. If all the boxes on the checklist are ticked then the standard has been achieved – irrespective of whether it meets guest expectations, needs or wants, or whether a room has a peculiar odour, or has tired decoration or some other failing that is not included on the checklist. One of the banes of frequent hotel users is the addition of supernumerary cushions to the bed, usually placed on top of the pillows. Remove them and the next day after the room has been serviced, they will be back. Hide the cushions – if you can – somewhere out of sight, and the room attendant will hunt them down and replace them on the bed: it is the standard operating procedure. There are occasions when a standard operating procedure is subverted by a hotel's management and the act of subversion itself becomes a standard. In higher-end establishments, what is known as 'turndown' service, whereby a guest room is prepared for sleeping (entailing drawing curtains, emptying waste baskets, turning down the corner of the bedding and, of course, leaving the ubiquitous chocolate on the guest's pillow) is costly to the hotel and it is increasingly normal to find management seeking to avoid having to meet this expectation. Consider the signs exhibited in Figure 4.1, found in the rooms of two hotels of the same chain in different countries. Standard operating procedures are, according to *The Economist* (2013d), at the heart of the 'industrial hotel' and they note with glee that:

> A veteran chef explains the grip that SOPs have. From Tokyo to São Paulo all omelettes must match a laminated picture (they should be cigar-shaped). A manager in Dubai says he follows 2,300 rules, including the phrases used to greet guests. ... A 2010 Hilton manual stipulates that staff must answer phones after three rings, that guests' pets may not weigh more than 75lbs (34kg) and that scuba-diving boats must provide free pieces of fruit. A 2004 SOP book for InterContinental allows staff to wait until the fourth ring, requires drinks to be refilled when two-thirds empty and specifies that rooms must offer at least four pornographic films.

Example (a): Five star international chain hotel, Cyprus

Evening Maid Service

Dear Guest

Our concern is to make your stay comfortable and enjoyable, by not disturbing you during the early evening hours.

Your bed has not been turned down. If you require this service, please contact our Housekeeping Department on ext. no. 18.

Hospitable [*sic*] yours

The Housekeeping Team

Example (b): Five star international chain hotel, Amsterdam

In order to guarantee your privacy, we offer evening turn down service only at your request. Should you wish to have your room made up for the night let us know before 9pm by using the Housekeeping button on your telephone.

The Housekeeping team

Figure 4.1   Getting out of the turndown

Revenue Management

Many factors influence hotel guests' purchase decisions but price is always of major importance to customers and hotels because: (a) if a hotel room is not sold for a night it is lost revenue to the hotel (assuming the revenue obtainable exceeds the maintenance and servicing costs of the room); and (b) many hotels operate in markets characterized by the close substitutability of products and services, and price can therefore be a determining factor in customer hotel selection. Hotel pricing is a complex process and one that was initially described in terms of 'yield management' but is now routinely termed 'revenue management' (a useful summary of the field is given by Josephi, 2013). Cross (1997: 3) defines revenue management as 'the application of disciplined tactics that predict customer behaviour at micro market level and optimize product availability and price to maximize revenue growth' and by Kimes (1989: 14-19) as 'allocating the right type of capacity to the right kind of customer at the right price so as to maximize revenue or yield'. Josephi (2013: 140) cites the popular definition of revenue management as selling 'the right *product*, for the right *price*, to the right *person*, in the right *period* and in the right *place*'.

Revenue management is becoming – in many places has already become – a specialist management role in hospitality, principally of course in hotels. The discipline of revenue management is based on a series of interlinked observations about consumer behaviour (especially the times at which bookings are made); about the timing of demand for hotel accommodation; and about the price sensitivity of different types of consumers. The word 'maximize' employed by Kimes in the remark cited above can be construed as a little misleading, as what is being practised in hotel revenue management is a form of optimization encompassing questions and decisions about what percentage of a hotel's total room inventory should be allocated at a particular time to specific market segments in order to 'maximize' revenue. These segments are, in practice, defined and redefined as a compromise between experiential marketing (including the kinds of guests a hotel knows it 'traditionally' attracts, knowledge and awareness of seasonal trends and so on) and guest characteristics (a typical 'business' hotel tends to attract expense-account business visitors with higher spending power during the week, and lower-spending leisure guests at the weekend – corporate or business rates are typically higher than weekend rates). A variety of other rates will be available for different market segments including group rates (where hotels have contracts with tour operators and travel agencies), rates for different numbers of occupants per room, rates according to the characteristics of the room (for example, more for 'a room with a view' or a suite) and conference rates.

The practices of revenue management have gained considerable importance in the hotel industry, possibly because of their veneer of quantitative, pseudo-scientific respectability linked to the prospect of generating greater revenues. However, it would serve us well to remember that as with many other ostensibly 'scientific' techniques, revenue management as a driver of the hotel business relies on a good deal of human judgement and not a little luck. Expertly performed by those with considerable experience, revenue management can indeed go a considerable way to optimizing income from hotel rooms but there is no magic – or even scientific – formula that can guarantee that outcome. The former British Prime Minister Harold Macmillan was alleged to have responded to a journalist's question as to the most difficult aspect of his job by replying, 'Events, dear boy, events'. The tourism and hospitality industries are particularly susceptible to the impact of events, whether natural disasters or economic and political ones. The tragedy of the loss of a Malaysia Airlines passenger jet in March 2014 (at the time of writing the plane has still not been located) carrying a majority of Chinese passengers saw a significant cancellation of existing airline and hotel bookings and a reduction in online enquiries for travel to Malaysia, not least from China. There is little that can be done in the short term by revenue managers or anyone else to ameliorate the effects of tragic events of this magnitude.

Outsourcing

Outsourcing is a growing phenomenon in many industry sectors. It entails the contracting out of certain of an organization's activities to another organization and is usually justified on the grounds that those activities not core to the host organization's business are best outsourced to specialist providers. What might be called the 'classic' model of outsourcing is where 'back office' functions of mainly western businesses are located in countries in the East with a suitably skilled but cheaper labour force. You telephone the customer care line because the television you bought in Birmingham has developed a fault and end up talking to a customer service agent sitting in Mumbai. In hotels, outsourcing is increasingly becoming a favoured approach to handling many hotel departments (Lamminmaki, 2011), including, notably (at least in the West): hotel car services; security (in many hotels, the person responsible for managing security will be a member of the permanent staff but the hotel will employ other personnel from external providers); laundry operations; and of course, housekeeping. It is, naturally, favoured where a hotel can reduce its costs by outsourcing particular activities, although some researchers, Bolat and Yılmaz (2009) among them, suggest that the actual cost effectiveness of hotel outsourcing is unclear. In part or in total, housekeeping is frequently the first choice of many hotels for outsourcing. As Ball et al. (2003: 151) state, 'The scope of the services contracted out can range from simply employing additional contract labour on a short-term basis through an agency or employing the services of a facilities management company that can take over the complete running of the housekeeping department.' That housekeeping activities tend not to be seen as a core activity, and that the marketing and selling of rooms is, says much about the modern hotel industry – what are hotels about if not the provision of good quality, well-maintained and clean rooms?

As Gunn (2003) notes, there is a tendency for outsourcing to be seen by hotels as a quick way out of providing a service, a form of risk deferral instead of a partnership where both companies stand together to provide a service. The prospect of reducing costs through outsourcing some or all housekeeping services has an obvious appeal

(Kappa et al., 1997). Housekeeping departments are often the numerically largest in the hotel in staffing terms and are no less affected by labour turnover and its concomitant costs than other hotel departments. In the hospitality sector, labour turnover rates are frequently higher than in other industries (Wood, 1997). Some outsourcing companies have grown to be global players. Integrated Service Solutions (ISS, http://www.issworld.com) can be found providing diverse services in hotels, airports and hospitals around the world. However, even if they have conglomerate ownership, many companies promote themselves as highly localized, providing support to organizations within a certain geographical area. This may improve symbiosis between a hotel and a service provider and alleviate some of the effects of the abandonment of direct control over services. Of course, a somewhat less sophisticated answer to the question as to why hotels outsource the housekeeping function is because they can get away with it. In an industry where the average stay of a guest is quite short, it seems plausible to assume that, providing a minimum set of standards is more or less maintained in housekeeping, most guests will not be in a position to experience significant causes for complaint (and of course, if they do, the company providing the outsourced service can always be blamed). To avoid a diminution in standards, organizations need to ensure that personnel negotiating outsourcing contracts are properly trained and that once established, specified standards are maintained. However, rarely do the skills of contract negotiation and maintenance/monitoring figure in the formal education of prospective hospitality managers.

Sustainability

The central (and noble) idea at the heart of the desire for sustainability is that physical and human resources should be directed to reducing the negative impacts of human activity on our biosphere and to actively encourage behaviours that have positive consequences for replenishing and/or improving the durability of resources. Occasional, radical, voices break through pointing out that probably the most sustainable forms of tourism and hospitality are no forms of tourism and hospitality whatsoever (or at least minimal tourism) but for the most part, tourism and hospitality scholars hedge their bets in this regard, their angst instead directed towards ways in which the 'negative impacts' of tourism can be ameliorated.

When raising the question of what they do to encourage sustainability with hospitality managers, not untypical responses include rolling of the eyes; a verbal expostulation that could not be repeated in front of a much-loved maiden aunt; and a rapid change of subject. In hotels, commitment to sustainability and environmental integrity is most evident in the rooms division and is/has been most often represented by the now clichéd sign often found in guest rooms illustrated here by Figure 4.2. Sustainability in hospitality has thus far attracted the attention of a limited – though growing – number of writers (see Sloan et al., 2011; Legrand et al., 2012; Nicholls and Kang, 2012). Melissen (2013a, 2013b) has skilfully reviewed some of the key issues, one of which (the central one arguably) is how a successful business case for sustainability can be made when managers regularly view sustain-ability measures as unaffordable and/or as not adding value to the products and services they offer, and/or as not a priority with customers and guests in the whole product/service mix.

The content of Figure 4.2 suggests it can be done if one appeals to naked (or enl-ightened) self-interest. The real meaning of messages of the kind shown in Figure 4.2 is that the guest can help the environment by simultaneously helping the hotel reduce costs even though the guest is not normally a practical beneficiary of the latter. However unthinking or unreasonable the tradition of a room rate including, *inter alia*, the daily change of linen (towels are of course another favourite), for the guest to forgo that convention without reimbursement adds to a hotel's revenue via a reduction in the costs of laundry. Hotel environmental notices, in common with much sustainability propaganda, rely to a large degree on inducing a sense of guilt in the mind of the guest. Many efforts to encourage interest in sustainability in the hospitality industry employ other rhetorical strategies, particularly the use of imperative language. Singh (2010, emphasis added) writes: 'Hotels, by their very nature, draw on huge environmental resources and depending on the positioning have high luxury standards. Hotels *have to* balance out the luxury coefficient of their operations with that of their impact on the environment and adapt accord-ingly.' 'Have to'? Hotels and other hospitality organizations do not have to do anything which Singh suggests (save where governments have legislated for certain sustainable behaviours). Where they do exist, environmental initiatives in hotels typically focus on energy saving procedures, waste recycling and use of environ-mentally friendly chemicals following what Schneider et al. (1999: 272) call 'the "reduce, reuse, recycle" credo of the environmental movement'. Frapin-Beaugé et al. (2008) note that sensors or heat detectors can be used to shut down power supply so as to avoid electricity wastage. Simple lock-out systems can be (and are) employed to switch off air conditioning when guest rooms are unoccupied. Other methods of addressing sustainability questions can be found in any of the references cited in this section.

Protect our environment

In an effort to protect the environment, we strive towards conserving water and energy, and minimizing the use of pollutants such as detergents. As our new guest, your bed linen is freshly laundered. Thereafter, bed sheets will be changed on:

- Every other day
- Every check out room
- Upon your request to contact Housekeeping on extension '6'

Thank you for helping us to protect our environment.

Figure 4.2   A typical hotel 'environmental' notice

Source: Four star local chain hotel, Hong Kong.

What, then, is a (potential) hospitality manager to make of demands for more sustainable products and services? Environmental and sustainability initiatives have appealed to some operators in terms of their marketing potential but the impact has not yet been widespread and can attract disapproval – Schneider et al. (1999: 272) arguing that concern for the environment 'is more than a marketing buzz word, it is a business-building decision'. Again, the sub-text here is that concern for the environment *should* be a business-building decision. One of the central difficulties with commentaries on sustainability in tourism and hospitality is that they often rely too heavily on moral insinuation without much evidence of understanding the wealth of philosophic insight on what it is to be 'moral'. This has allowed many operators to engage in the 'sins' of 'greenwashing', defined as 'the act of misleading consumers regarding the environmental practices of a company or the environmental benefits of a product or service' (http://sinsofgreenwashing.org/, last accessed 25.11.13).

On the other hand, as Melissen (2013a, 2013b) notes, there are many cases where companies in numerous industries have made a (relatively) cost-effective virtue of sustainability policies and practices and there are similarly a number of organizations engaged in the business of conferring independent accreditation for lodging businesses that meet specific standards (although principally confined thus far to the USA and Canada, the Green Key Eco-Rating Program is one scheme designed to encourage a more sustainable lodging industry; see http://www.greenkeyglobal.com/default. asp, last accessed 25.11.13). In most cases, progress has been made not because of moral appeals, but of appeals to common sense, in this case common economic sense. If it is indeed possible to make the hospitality industry 'more sustainable' then it seems likely that this will only be achieved by showing the benefits of a sustainability orientation to businesses' 'bottom lines'. Increasingly, advice to the industry based on this approach is generating a useful *practical* literature (see for example Goldstein, 2012; Goldstein and Primlani, 2012) as well as some small evidence that the economic benefits of sustainability are all of tangible, calculable and attainable (Assaf et al., 2012). One possible barrier to the wider adoption of sustainable practices is the domination of the hotel sector by small, independently owned businesses and indeed, Rahmana et al. (2012) in a study of the adoption of no-cost and low-cost sustainable/environmentally friendly practices in a sample of US hotels found that chains were stronger adopters of green practices than independent hotels (see also Yu-Chin, 2012). An earlier study by Chan (2011: 18) found that adoption of environmental management systems in small and medium sized hotels was hindered by nine barriers; in descending order:

(a) implementation and maintenance costs, (b) lack of knowledge and skills, (c) lack of a sense of urgency, (d) ambiguity of EMS standards, (e) lack of qualified verifiers/consultants, (f) lack of motivation and professional advice, (g) conflicting guidance, (h) outcome uncertainty, and (i) inconsistent support.

The demand for sustainable initiatives in industry in general and hospitality specifically is unlikely to diminish in the years ahead – whether or not industry is willing or able to rise to this challenge remains to be seen.

Operational Management of Hotel Accommodation

Hotel accommodation management is, in larger and chain hotels at least, increasingly organized in terms of the 'rooms division' with a single senior manager responsible for all of a hotel's accommodation functions. Depending, as ever, on the size of the hotel and any particular corporate traditions, the rooms division manager/director of rooms will typically have line responsibility for any or all of the key accommodation sub-departments including front office (normally headed by a front office manager or assistant manager depending on the hotel's size, and covering – again any or all of – concierge, switchboard, guest relations and reservations); housekeeping (normally headed by a head or executive head housekeeper); information technology services; security and loss prevention; and engineering and maintenance.

Front office and front desk

The front office is the communication and dissemination centre of the hotel, providing numerous services to guests (including, often, concierge services) and information to the other hotel departments on guests' requirements. It embraces a 'back office' which may be predominantly concerned with reservations and night audit. The 'front office' is not the same as the 'front desk': the front desk is merely the visible focal point of the front office department and normally the first (and often last) contact point a guest has with the establishment (premium service guests staying on executive floors usually have their own check-in facilities and in many deluxe hotels, the front desk has all but disappeared to be replaced by guest service team members who will accompany guests to their room and register them there). Guests' perceptions of the overall level and quality of service provided by the hotel can be extensively influenced by their experience of interactions with the front desk.

In the mythologies that have grown up around the hotel industry, the front office (and certainly the front desk) is often depicted as the 'glamour' end of the rooms division department. Not for front office and front desk workers the low-status 'dirty work' associations of the housekeeping department. Dirty work need not, of course, always involve physical contamination: it can arise from dealing with frequent customer disgruntlement. This disgruntlement can emanate from both reasonable and unreasonable guest dispositions but a major source for front office is overbooking, that is, deliberately accepting more bookings than a hotel's capacity permits (a 'policy' that has penetrated the soul of hotel accommodation management, textbooks directed to students increasingly depicting overbooking as a necessarily integral element of revenue management approaches to guest procurement; see for example Baker et al., 2000: 277). Revenue management approaches to hotel accommodation sales encourage overbooking because opportunities for revenue optimization always contain an element of uncertainty: e.g. guests who do not have guaranteed reservations, or those who have guaranteed reservations but do not materialize (so-called 'no shows' who can account for 10% of capacity in some hotels and who are increasingly punished by being charged either part or all of their 'guaranteed' booking). To compensate for variability, hotels overbook slightly – all very sensible but a source of considerable frustration to those customers who arrive to find no room at the inn and have, in the parlance of the industry, to be 'walked' to other hotels, similar frustrations are faced by guests who arrive at a hotel to find that their room is not ready (it is a matter of some shame to the hotel industry that hotels in destinations that rely on international guests for the bulk of their business still enforce an afternoon check-in).

Housekeeping and laundry

Frequent surveys show that cleanliness comes top of travellers' lists of must-have hotel attributes (e.g. F.L.C., 2000). Housekeeping work is physically demanding, conducted largely away from the public eye (at least while cleaning guest bedrooms) and goes largely unnoticed in another sense, namely, as Rawstron (1999: 115-117) notes, housekeeping staff are the 'unsung heroes within the hotel', rarely tipped by guests and viewed as relatively low-skilled. Walker (2011: 18) notes that housekeeping has a 'Cinderella' status within the hospitality industry (or at least within the UK hospitality industry), with fewer than 1% of hospitality students choosing to take the housekeeping route into management (useful studies on the occupational image of housekeeping and housekeepers are provided by Hunter Powell and Watson, 2006; Harris et al., 2011).

The main responsibilities of the housekeeping department lie in the need to 'provide clean and serviced bedrooms on a daily basis to the agreed standards' (Rawstron, 1999: 114). These responsibilities extend to the cleaning of the whole property and are obviously 'critical to the smooth daily operation of any hotel' (Kappa et al., 1997:3). The condition and cleanliness of guest rooms are generally asserted as being the most important factors in determining customer satisfaction ratings (Walker, 2011: 20), a point supported by the research of Falbo (1999, cited in Ball et al., 2003). Challenges involved in the delivery of housekeeping services are numerous. The value of the physical assets involved is significant and their care and protection complex. It is not simply a case of a guest room's established assets – the bed, the furniture – but includes movables (e.g. towels and linen). Simpson and Rossiter (2012: 18) suggest that large hotels can hold £30,000 worth of linen at any one time, with around £30 per room, much or all of it rented from specialist commercial laundries. The pursuit of cleanliness can be complicated by infestations. In recent years there has been growing concern over the spread of bedbugs. Henson (2011) reports a USA National Pest Management Association survey of institutions that found that 99% of respondents encountered bedbug infestations in the year prior to the survey with the biggest increase being in hotels and motels, 80% reporting infestation (the delightfully named Bedbug Registry, which sadly only covers the USA and Canada, offers regular updates on the alleged presence of bedbugs in hotels and other forms of accommodation (http://bedbugregistry.com/)). Perhaps most importantly, it is difficult to improve the performance of housekeeping tasks beyond the direct labour of the room attendant. As Ball et al. (2003: 141) note, 'the nature of the work involved and the variety of tasks to be completed in each room mean that introducing technology any more complex than a vacuum cleaner is very difficult.'

Guest information technology services

Travellers now expect as routine the provision of Wi-Fi in hotels and other hospitality establishments. Some larger single hotel establishments will have a small IT department in terms of personnel but in most cases the provision and maintenance of information technology systems is outsourced. Regular hotel guests are well aware of the long history of hotels charging what the website Independent Traveler.com calls 'unreasonable fees' (see http://www.independenttraveler.com/travel-tips/hotel-and-b-and-b/hidden-hotel-fees, last accessed 12.01.14; and flyertalk.com, one of many sites offering travellers' insights into the good, the bad and the ugly in transport, hotels and restaurants). Wi-Fi is the latest battleground and increasingly hotels are following many restaurants in providing 'free' Wi-Fi for their clients. In reality, of course, internet access charges are incorporated into general product and service pricing and are not free at all.

Nevertheless, one has to admire the resistance that some hoteliers have put up to the idea of 'free' services in this area. Walker (2010: 40) reports a symposium in Britain between hotels and an IT company to discuss the question of IT provision in hotels noting that 'The IT managers present felt more should be done to prioritise IT needs during the construction or refurbishment of a hotel given IT's increasing importance to the guest experience.' This is fair comment. For hotel new builds those conducting business feasibility studies have a possible interest in keeping cost projections as low as possible, particularly if, in an asset light environment (see Chapter 2), external investors are sought. Reflecting the observations made earlier in Chapter 2 about the economic 'marginality' of the hotel business, one participant in the symposium commented: 'In the hotel business at the moment, it's all about the extra charges as we have become so competitive and price-sensitive. … We need those extra charges' (Walker, 2010: 41). Smith (2012) for the UK *Daily Telegraph* newspaper surveyed 70 hotel groups. A number of individual properties, some 24, did not impose Wi-Fi charges. Smith found that luxury hotels in London were the most expensive, several charging £20 per day for Wi-Fi access while noting that Holiday Inn in the UK charges up to £15 per day and €24 in the Eurozone. The highest hourly rate identified was €10 per hour in certain Marriott hotels. Smith writes that 'TalkTalk, the internet service provider, estimated that the cost to a business, such as a hotel, of providing broadband, would range from £10 a month for a small property to £300 a month for a 100-room property, or £700 a month for a larger, 300-room property.' He further notes the remarks of Paul Charles, Chief Executive of Perowne Charles Communications, a PR company specializing in travel, that the firm will not work with hotels that still charge for Wi-Fi access. 'Free Wi-Fi should come as standard in a hotel these days', said Mr Charles, 'Hotels that continue to defy the odds will be losers in the long term because customers will go elsewhere.'

Security and loss prevention

Although there has been a growth in public discussion about security in hotels in recent years (see Banerjee, 2013, for a useful short review and Ellis and Stipanuk, 1999; Feickert et al., 2006; and Chan and Lam, 2013, for more wide-ranging commentaries), the very nature of the subject means that there is a certain reticence in circulating too much information for wider scrutiny, or even sharing it within the hospitality community. In many hotels and some other hospitality organizations in certain parts of the world access and egress security is very obvious in the form of barriers, car searches and bag inspections. Sometimes internal security can be very obvious in the form of surveillance cameras or the physical presence of security guards even on guest floors in hotels. Security not only relates to physical and other defences against terrorism but also to routine activities that include theft and fire prevention and, increasingly, prevention of IT fraud.

Much recent activity in the development of hotel and hospitality security is motivated by the increasing tendency of terrorist groups to bomb hotels (18 attacks against hotels since 2002 according to *The Economist*, 2013d; see Table 4.1 for a small selection of more notable examples; for a very useful review of employing anti-terrorist strategies in hotels see Paraskevas, 2013), but security measures are, of course, necessary to discourage and detect more mundane crimes, particularly theft. Many organizations issue advice on security to their personnel. The Department of Safety and Security of the United Nations (2006) has issued 'Special Guidelines for Women', although why these suggestions should be seen as being specific to women is something of a mystery as they might be regarded as having general application (see http://www.eisf.eu/resources/item/?d=1599, last accessed 10.04.13).

Increasingly, security is becoming an important element of the hospitality product and service offer. Conference and convention organizers and meeting planners in their routine booking of hotel and restaurant services will consider the level of security prevailing in potential venues as part of the process of due diligence. A key issue facing hotel managers is that hotel owners (as opposed to operating companies) are sometimes reluctant to make the necessary investment in appropriate security. A report by the (British) Institute of Hospitality (2010: 12) pointed out that reduced insurance premiums are a good incentive to invest in security. However, in 2012, Walker (2012a: 22) in the Institute's news magazine reported Dr Alexandros Paraskevas of Oxford Brookes University as stating: 'After the 2008 economic crisis, when I looked at the budget cuts made by hotel companies worldwide, laundry was first and security was second.' Further difficulty can arise in ensuring that strategic risk management is taken seriously as a training objective. Paul Moxness, Vice President, Corporate Safety and Security for Rezidor, is cited in the UK Institute of Hospitality's magazine as saying education is not serving industry needs: '40% of an area manager's or GM's induction is related to risk management … . Today GMs take on huge legal responsibilities and they aren't prepared for them. There is a huge gap in education' (Institute of Hospitality, 2011: 11).

Table 4.1 Some significant hotel bombings

Date	Location	Hotels	Other information
12 October 1984	Brighton, England	Grand Hotel	An attempt by the Irish Republican Army (IRA) to assassinate the British Prime Minister and other government members during their annual party conference. Used a long delay time bomb installed in September 1984 under a guest room bath.
20 September 2008	Islamabad, Pakistan	Marriott Hotel	A dump truck filled with explosives was detonated in front of the hotel killing at least 54 people.
26–28 November 2008	Mumbai, India	Taj Mahal Palace Hotel and Oberoi Trident Hotel	Part of a wider attack on public buildings in Mumbai, over 60 people died in the two hotels shot by terrorists.
17 July 2009	Jakarta, Indonesia	JW Marriott Hotel and Ritz-Carlton Hotel	Seven people died and more than 50 were injured in a suicide bomber attack, the suicide bombers having checked into the hotels previously as paying guests.

Sources: various; see also The *Guardian* (2009) 'Timeline: hotel bomb attacks: bombings and sieges of hotels around the world in recent years', http://www.guardian.co.uk/world/2009/jul/17/indonesia, last accessed 10.04.13.

Engineering and maintenance

Given its centrality to the success of a hotel business, there is remarkably little research into either hotel engineering or the role of the engineering manager in the industry. Two recent studies confirm the paucity of literature (Lai and Yik, 2012; Lai, 2013) beyond a handful of textbooks and textbook contributions (e.g. Adamo, 1999) despite the existence of a number of national and international representative bodies for hospitality engineering (e.g. in the USA the National Association of Hotel and Lodging Engineers, http://nahle.org). One possible explanation for this neglect is that the hotel engineering function is sometimes outsourced but a more plausible reason is that a hotel engineer is usually, first, an engineer, and the principles of engineering are well established requiring only adaptation to specific contexts (Corrigan, 2002). Though some hotel schools still offer options in hotel engineering, they do not qualify one to become an engineer. Anecdotal evidence suggests that there are some hotels where the chief engineer is paid substantially more than the general manager, as one might expect of a technical specialist. In the manner of the philosopher Wittgenstein, 'whereof one cannot speak, thereof one must be silent' – but readers interested in learning more about the hotel engineering function could do worse than consult the articles cited in this section.

Concluding Remarks

Accommodation management covers a wide range of functions and activities that are simultaneously core to the success of the hotel business and complex in their coordination. The hotel sector is increasingly experimenting with outsourcing to defer certain kinds of risk but relatively little is known from research about the circumstances that can contribute to an increase/decrease in the complexity of coordination as a result of the pursuit of outsourcing strategies. The accommodation function in lodging has often been treated as subordinate, even on occasions inferior, to the provision of foods and beverages (see Chapter 5) but in recent years a balance of sorts has begun to reassert itself. No longer is the accommodation function seen simply and disparagingly as 'bricks, beds and bathrooms' but, in an era of increased competition, and when integrated with sales and other functions (see Chapter 6), it is (re-)establishing itself as the essence of the lodging sector.

Further Reading

Frapin-Beaugé, A J M, Verginis, C and Wood, R C (2008) 'Accommodation and facilities management', in B Brotherton and R C Wood (Eds) *The Sage Handbook of Hospitality Management*, London: Sage, 383–399.

Melissen, F (2013) 'Sustainable hospitality: a meaningful notion?', *Journal of Sustainable Tourism*, 21, 6: 810–824.

Verginis, C S and Wood, R C (1999) (Eds) *Accommodation Management: Perspectives for the International Hotel Industry*, London: International Thomson Business Press.

Wood, R C (Ed) (2013) *Key Concepts in Hospitality Management*, London: Sage.

5

ARE YOU ENJOYING YOUR MEAL? FOOD AND BEVERAGE MANAGEMENT IN HOSPITALITY

After reading this chapter, you should:

(a) understand the role of food and beverage administration within hospitality management and the extent to which its significance is on occasion exaggerated;

(b) appreciate that evidence which shows both the relative constancy over time of public taste in food and beverage and the relatively slow pace of change in such taste; and

(c) comprehend key aspects of the operational management of food and beverage – for example the core challenges facing restaurants (including consumer choice and food preference); the nature of food production and service systems; the value of menu analysis techniques; and the nature of the meal experience.

Introduction

As noted in Chapter 4, accommodation and food and beverage management are the two features of the hospitality industry that distinguish it from other forms of industry and management. Attainment of, and success in food and beverage management have long been seen as the dominant career route to a general manager position in hotels, although this may be changing. As recently as 20 years ago, Nebel et al. (1994: 3) found that in the US, food and beverage directors received the highest pay of all hotel departmental heads and that more hotel general managers in the USA follow career paths in food and beverage than any other department. Indeed, in their sample of 78 food and beverage directors of hotels, Nebel et al. (1994: 6) noted that

57% of respondents reported no hotel management experience other than in food and beverage management.

The importance given to food and beverage management by the industry has traditionally been reflected in hospitality education, with hotel schools devoting a good deal of their curriculum to education in food and beverage management even down to prospective managers learning how to cook as 'chefs' and how to serve food as 'waiters' (see Chapters 7 and 8). The educational model of food production and service model has usually embraced to some degree the world of 'classical' French food and 'silver' service, which in the twenty-first century applies at best to a minority of hotel and fine dining restaurants (though it does have the virtue of being the 'apex' model of food service, incorporating most of the major skills that a food service operative would require in any form of food service employment). In some countries, for example the United Kingdom, the relevance of this aspect of hospitality education has been frequently questioned and the model has come under pressure, largely because of its resource intensive-ness and the perceived inappropriateness of 'training' to university level study (for a competent elaboration of the issues see Alexander, 2007, 2008; Alexander et al., 2009). Furthermore, in the 'real' world of apex restaurants, emphasis has shifted in the last 30 years or so from emphasis on the rituals of service to emphasis on the (admittedly largely whimsical) artistry of the chef, with the result that there has been a trend towards plated service.

If we examine the handful or two of food and beverage management textbooks that are marketed to hospitality students then it is immediately evident that the majority exhibit a bias towards operational management of food and beverage amplified by an emphasis on (not usually very profound) technical knowledge and skill sets. These works are supported by a plethora of general and specialist litera-ture in the form of cookbooks/recipe books and manuals of service and etiquette. However, for an area that is of critical importance and centrality to the hospitality industry, research into the food and beverage function has at best been piecemeal and, at worst, marginalized in hospitality education. We should not be surprised by this. Beyond nutritional science, the study of food and eating has been neglected in other academic disciplines. Curtin (1992: 3), from a philosopher's standpoint, comments: 'Philosophers in the dominant western tradition have been uninterested in those aspects of life that "give colour to existence" … . Our relations to aspects of life that can only be understood as concrete and embodied (primary among them our relations to food) have been marginalized. They have been pushed to the periphery of what is regarded as important.' Lupton (1996: 2–3), from a sociologi-cal/social anthropological stance, observes:

> The practice of cooking has similarly received little serious scholarly atten-tion because of its transitory nature and link with physical labour and the servicing of bodies rather than with 'science', 'art' or 'theory'. Cooking is identified as a practical activity, enmeshed in the physical temporal world. It is therefore regarded as base and inferior compared with intellectual or spiritual

activities … . To pay attention to such everyday banalities as food practices is to highlight the animality always lurking within the 'civilized' veneer of the human subject.

With some exceptions, it is certainly the case that food and beverage management research has failed to link study of public food and beverage provision, trends and developments to wider societal contexts, or indeed the growing philosophical and sociological understanding of food consumption (Wood, 1995b; Baggini, 2014). Indeed, the main locus of food and beverage management activity – the restaurant, whether chain or independent – has itself been subject to only intermittent research attention. As Rahman (2010: 330) notes, 'Restaurants have seldom been the subject of theory-driven empirical research. Moreover, extant literature has generally focused on food and service quality issues.' Even with regard to food and service quality issues, Johns and Pine (2002: 130) note that:

A significant problem is that attributes of restaurant experience vary between different outlets and dining occasions. Some researchers have therefore conceptualised restaurant outcomes as service quality, for which a generalizable set of attributes exists. However this is unsatisfactory because service quality attributes alone do not describe the restaurant experience as fully as attribute sets derived empirically from consumer data.

One implication of this important short quotation is – correctly – that any study of the food and beverage consumer should *begin* with the consumer rather than abstruse and poorly developed concepts that render the consumer almost invisible. Unfortunately, just as food and beverage management research has largely failed to link the study of provision to wider elements in business and society, then so it is equally lacking consistency in placing the customer at the heart of analysis. In general, two principal categories of food and beverage management research can be identified (see Wood, 2007) which for convenience here are labelled:

- production-oriented research, including food technology and food science; the construction and operation of food production and service systems; and the quantitative analysis of food and beverage performance employing various forms of what has become termed 'menu engineering'; and

- consumption-oriented research, including consumer food and restaurant choice, the menu as a driver of food and beverage management and the meal experience.

Later in this chapter, we shall examine some of the key themes embraced by both approaches in an effort to draw out their relevance and implications for managers. Before proceeding to this task, however, it is first necessary to examine the context in which these themes have emerged and are sustained. This context has two dimensions – the tendency of the hospitality industry to 'mythologize' elements of food and beverage management theory and practice, and, secondly, the often contrasting realities of the food and beverage management function in practice.

The Mythologization of Food and Beverage Management

The basic processes of food and beverage management do not, at first sight, seem either exciting or complicated, at heart they involve managing the preparation, cooking and serving of food – or 'catering' as it used to be called before the lowly sentiments attached to that word made it unfashionable (Riley, 2005). It is important to keep this thought in mind precisely because it is difficult to get to the theoretical and practical essence of food and beverage management without first understanding that no area of hospitality management has been as mythologized, or as touched by pretension. That, as we have noted twice before, it has been seen as the necessary and natural route to hotel general management when (at least in most western cultures) the sale of accommodation is, for most hotels, the principal source of revenue, hints suggestively at a distortion of both perspectives that upon closer inspection can be found to infuse the culture of the hospitality industry. In a stimulating commentary on food and beverage management in the hospitality industry, Riley (2005: 88-89) in two passages (and somewhat unintentionally it must be said) exposes the extent to which this process of myth-making is embedded in the hospitality industry when he asserts that recent change in food and beverage management has:

> emphasized the business aspects of profitability and marketing over the more, for want of a better word, romantic issues of food as a cultural entity and hospitality as a human propensity. In a very real sense, change has brought technological innovation and conceptual creativity.

Riley (2005: 92) later remarks:

> Managing food and beverage is more complex than managing rooms and it demands a greater range of knowledge and a degree of creativity, which room management does not. ... Designers and chefs have come together with entrepreneurs to innovate in the industry, adding a level of creativity to the 'catering process' that lies beneath.

We can certainly agree that recent change in the food and beverage field has emphasized profitability and marketing. Whether it is 'change' that has led to technological innovation and conceptual creativity (rather than innovation and creativity that has led to change) and whether a business orientation has largely been at the expense of the 'romantic' issues of food as a cultural entity (and, we can add, hospitality as a human propensity – see Chapter 1) are more contentious issues. 'Romantic' notions are not absent from the processes of myth-making that characterize food and beverage management theory and practice. The exaggerated importance attached to the creative powers of chefs, marketers and food and beverage managers to which Riley alludes would make any spin doctor proud. Certainly it might be possible to settle upon examples of these powers in elite fine dining markets (Stierand and Lynch, 2008; Lane, 2010; Tresidder, 2011) and even to track their wider adoption in reduced and ersatz forms as a result of 'trickle down' to other consumer segments (Mennell, 1985). Yet within the hospitality industry the 'celebrity chef' phenomenon embraces a minority of chefs and (once again, the point can never be made enough) fine dining represents a small percentage of the eating-out market – most dining-out experiences are probably more affected by products developed in the laboratories of the large international restaurant chains. Widening this argument somewhat, Riley advances no evidence to support the propositions that food and beverage is more complex, more knowledge intensive or more creative than accommodation management and yet it is a fairly safe bet that most of those involved in the industry (revenue management and sales management executives of large hotels being possible exceptions) would recognize his remarks as essentially accurate. However, as we sought to demonstrate in Chapter 4, the management of accommodation is highly complex with a considerable and increasing amount of managerial energy being expended on this function. It is also uncertain as to what extent food and beverage management is more complex than other managerial functions except that a single element (and an arguably diminishing one at that) requires the expertise of skilled cooks. What we appear to have here is an instance of the exceptionalism we noted in the Preface to this book, only in this instance the claims for exceptionalism are being made for an element of hospitality management rather than hospitality management itself.

Every industry, every organization, develops its own mythologies. In the case of food and beverage management the wellspring of myth-making is the elevation of aspects of food (procurement, cooking and service) and food work (its supposedly creative nature and its certain potential to be physically taxing) to the status of a fetish – that is, something regarded with irrational irreverence. This fetishistic quality has in recent years been buttressed in wider culture. Culinary television channels, programmes, websites, applications and more traditional media including cookery magazines and books attract people in their hordes, including many whose interest in food and cooking is at best superficial. The 'irrational reverence' with which the activities of celebrity chefs are often imbued (Wood, 2000b) is the most egregious manifestation of this fetishism in a world where the United Nations Food and Agricultural Organization estimates that about 12% of the global population regularly go hungry (http://www.fao.org/hunger/en/, last accessed 25.03.13). Of course, the levels of interest generated by the antics of celebrity chefs have been generally good news for operators in the hospitality industry, stimulating demand for food and beverage products and services, although bringing with this demand the dangers attendant on the growth of amateur or semi-professional 'knowledgeable diners' or wine 'buffs' who can put up a good show of knowing as much as or more than the providers of these products and services in the commercial hospitality sector.

Food and Beverage Management in Practice

The theory and practice of commercial food and beverage management, then, have been profoundly affected by models of food production and service and their associated values that originally evolved in the course of satisfying the demands of social elites, principally in hotels. They are models and values that still exert a far from vestigial influence on the field lending the food and beverage function in hospitality an importance that is, in any objective sense, difficult to justify. If, for the moment, we set aside elite dining – whether in a hotel or those relatively few independent restaurants where it is practised – and exercise due scepticism about the mythologies considered in the previous section, what are we left with in terms of the practice of food and beverage management?

A moment's *intuitive* consideration of food and beverage provision – that is without resort to examining the evidence – suggests that while change certainly occurs over time, it is usually very gradual, giving a continuing appearance of constancy and the absence of wide-ranging variation or, for that matter, exceptional creativity (Mennell, 1985; Wood, 1995b). There are good reasons for this. Public taste for food and beverage in general changes very slowly and most restaurant diners, *contra* common beliefs, do not wish to be excessively challenged when eating out – i.e. they wish to eat foods with which they have an actual or imaginable familiarity. Good restaurateurs know this and by and large give their customers what they want. A successful restaurant operator offers what s/he knows they can sell, although there will be occasions when poorly performing menu items are retained in the hope that their sales will improve, or for some other non-business reasons. Once a restaurant menu has been determined, changes to it are gradual unless the viability of the business model demands more radical action. As Auty (1989, reported in Auty, 1992: 325) comments in regard to how restaurateurs determine their menus:

> restaurateurs suited their own inclinations in running their restaurants rather than taking note of the competition in the area. If their style did not suit a regular set of diners, they went out of business rather than making dramatic changes. Changes tended to be in small increments, like adding garlic bread to the menu. Proprietors on the whole denied being competitive, though they admitted keeping an eye on what similar restaurants were doing. None could remember changing their way of doing business in response to a competitor's action, but at the same time they were quite sure that any innovative action of theirs would be copied.

Putting intuition aside, a wide variety of evidence testifies to the slow speed of change in food consumption patterns (e.g. Driver, 1983; Mennell, 1985) and the consistency of industry 'offers' in terms of the range available (Wood, 1995b). A 1994 report of Sutcliffe Catering Group's review of favourite lunches in their staff restaurants, comparing 1994 to 1968 (reported in *Caterer and Hotelkeeper*, 27 October 1994: 18) gives some insight into change over a 25-year period (see Table 5.1). Although two of the top three items on the 1994 list are curry and lasagne, the menu is still dominated by 'traditional' British dishes. While 'foreign' foods have undoubtedly become staples of the British diet, they have done so as part of a very slow process of assimilation. More generally, a report by the specialist food marketing intelligence company Horizons (2012b) identified the dishes that appear most frequently on menus (not the same as the most popular purchases, but a reasonable surrogate); these are shown in Table 5.2. Again, in a world in which we are periodically told that the UK's most popular dish is chicken tikka masala, or 'Chinese' stir fry or some other exotic concoction, reality steps somewhat starkly in, and Table 5.2 is further suggestive of the slow assimilation of non-indigenous foods into the national menu. It is the case that the market for dining out and the places where people eat are,

Table 5.1 Favourite lunches in workplace restaurants serviced by Sutcliffe Catering Group, 1968 and 1994

	Rank, 1968	Rank, 1994
Battered fish and chips	2	4
Braised steak	4	–
Brown stew and dumplings	5	–
Chilli con carne	–	10
Cottage pie	7	8
Curry	9	1
Homemade faggots and peas	8	–
Homemade meat pies	–	5
Lasagne	–	3
Mixed grill	6	–
Pasta dishes (not lasagne)	–	9
Roast beef	–	6
Roast meats	1	2
Salads	10	–
Steak and kidney pie/pudding	3	7

Table 5.2 Dishes appearing most frequently on restaurant menus, 2012

Rank	Dish
1	Beefburger
2	Pizza
3	Fish and chips
4	Chicken burger
5	Rump steak
6	Chicken curry
7	Grilled chicken
8	Roast chicken
9 =	Beef lasagne/Sausage and mash

Source: Retrieved from http://www.hrzns.com/mint/pepper/tillkruess/downloads/tracker.php? url=http://www.hrzns.com/files/Consumer_eating_out_trends_10_things_you_need_to_know.pdf&force&inline, last accessed 05.06.14.

respectively, less dynamic and more conservative than the food service industry would have us believe, as the following points illustrate:

- Warde and Martens (1998: 147) note that in 1991, the Family Expenditure Survey showed that the proportion of food expenditure devoted to food eaten away from home rose from 10% in 1960 to 21% 1993. For 1991, some 3.6% of total household expenditure was spent on meals out.

- A UK Cabinet Office report of 2008 suggested that consumers spent roughly the same proportion of their income on eating out as they did in 1968 (http:/www.cabinetoffice.gov.uk/media/cabinetoffice/strategy/assets/food/food_analysis.pdf., last accessed 03.05.14).

- By 2012, the UK government's Department for Environment, Food and Rural Affairs (DEFRA) noted that the amount of food eaten outside the home had been in decline since 2001, and in the three years to 2012 household spending on eating out fell by 5.6% with food eaten away from home constituting around 3.1% of total household expenditure (https://www.gov.uk/government/uploads/system/uploads/attachment_data/file/265245/familyfood-2012statsnotice-12dec13.pdf, last accessed 03.05.14).

In terms of publicly available research on the choice of venue for eating out, the UK Cabinet Office (2008) report cited a 2005 Mintel (http://www.mintel.com) survey which showed that 22% of dining-out sales value was accounted for by public houses; 15% by hotel catering and 14% by restaurants. The last category excluded the following, named, kinds of outlet:

- burger restaurants (8%)
- cafés, coffee shops (7%)
- ethnic restaurants (7%)
- in-store catering (5%)
- pizza and pasta restaurants (5%)
- ethnic takeaways (6%)
- fish and chip shops (4%)
- fried chicken restaurants (4%)
- roadside catering (2%)
- other fast food (1%).

The Horizons (2011) marketing intelligence company suggests that the top two growth sectors in food service by sales in 2011 were pub restaurants and managed branded pubs, and in a related report (Horizons, 2012a) notes that whereas in the USA, fast food restaurants account for 28% of all consumer spend in the food service sector, it is half of that figure in the UK. Nicholls (2013) notes that in 2012 pub restaurants accounted for 20% of all meals eaten out. Horizons (2014) currently estimate the

2013 market structure of restaurant provision at 258,000 units, distributed as shown in Table 5.3, indicating that hotel eating places and pubs are almost on a par in terms of numbers.

Table 5.3 Market supply of eating places, 2013

Hotels	45,256	17.50%
Pubs	44,377	17.16%
Education	34,308	13.27%
Fast food/quick service restaurants	32,353	12.51%
Health care	32,116	12.42%
Restaurants (excluding fast food/quick service restaurants)	29,090	11.25%
Leisure	19,968	7.72%
Staff catering	17,960	6.94%
Services	3,071	1.18%

Source: Horizons, 2014.

The general message to be taken from the discussion so far is, first, that in recent times, the proportion of income spent on dining out has remained remarkably constant and secondly, where it is spent – mainly in public houses – has shown a remarkable conservatism. What could be more traditional, more conservative and more gently assimilating than eating lunch or dinner in one's 'local' pub? Thirdly, the very (slow) speed of social change, notably with regard to eating habits, gives a little more prompting to our critical faculties in further considering whether hospitality industry provision of food and beverage can really be so complex. In situations of production and service complexity we might reasonably expect the problems associated with food and beverage provision to be numerous. In practice, the principal ongoing challenges of food and beverage provision are limited in number and well-established in the culture of the hospitality industry.

Restaurant and hotel restaurant challenges

When they reviewed the food service industry some years ago Johns and Pine (2002: 120) asserted that:

> food service is an important industry in its own right, not least in terms of financial turnover, and although it contributes in part to both hotels and tourism, it has its own separate characteristics. Restaurants (including those in chains and those that are part of hotels), take-aways, and even contract catering, are more volatile, changeable and fashion-prone than hotels or tourist attractions.

Whether food service outlets are indeed more changeable and fashion prone than hotels or tourist attractions is, in the light of the evidence so far considered, a point that might be legitimately argued in the context of the mythologizing of the hospitality industry discussed earlier. In contrast, and in practice, the volatility of the industry is well illustrated by the fact that away from the rarefied atmosphere of food and restaurant provision in hotels, and in the independent restaurant sector at least, business failure is very high. Parsa et al. (2005: 309) calculated US restaurant failure for one-, two- and three-year periods from 1996 through 1999. The highest failure rate was during the first year (26%): in the second and third year the failure rates were 19% and 14% respectively. A report from UHY Hacker Young in 2007 found that 'Restaurants and bars are three times more likely to go bust than other UK businesses … . 15.5% of businesses in the UK hospitality and catering sector (restaurants, pubs and hotels) fail every year, compared to just 5.2% for the economy as a whole (http://www.uhy-uk.com/resources/news/restaurants-three-times-more-likely-to-go-bust-than-other-businesses555/, last accessed 29.03.14). Citing the UK Office for National Statistics, Yahoo! Finance report that in 2012 the business 'death rate' was 13.3% for the accommodation and food sector (https://uk.finance.yahoo.com/news/the-industries-most-likely-to-fail-114700979.html, last accessed 29.03.14). In contrast to the independent sector, branded restaurants offer a different proposition being inherently more stable, although brands come and brands go – not all are successful. However, we can remind ourselves that many western brands that have been 'exhausted' are often found, resurrected and thriving, in new and emerging markets. Moreover, in recent years, an increasing solidity has characterized the list of leading global brands (see Table 5.4).

The volatility of the stand-alone restaurant sector can be contrasted with the situation of many hotels where the performance of restaurants can be, as a matter of practice, highly problematic. As Rushmore (2003: 30) observes for the USA:

Table 5.4 Leading global restaurant brands, 2013

Rank	Global top 10 (all US)	Top 10 non-US brands
1	McDonald's	7-Eleven (Japan)
2	KFC (Yum! Brands)	FamilyMart (Japan)
3	Subway	Lawson (Japan)
4	Pizza Hut	Sukiya (Japan)
5	Starbucks	J D Wetherspoon (UK)
6	Burger King	Hotto Motto (Japan)
7	Domino's Pizza	Mister Donut (Japan)
8	Dunkin' Donuts	Yoshinoya (Japan)
9	Dairy Queen	Dicos (Taiwan)
10	Papa John's	Paris Baguette (South Korea)

Sources: http://www.forbes.com/pictures/feji45hfkh/top-10-global-fast-food-brands-2, and http://nrn.com/international-top-25/2013-international-top-25-chains-sales-growth, both items last accessed 03.05.14.

> Most hotel food and beverage departments are big money losers when all expenses are properly accounted for. Hoteliers tend to regard foodservice as an amenity – a necessary evil that must be available to guests to be competitive. Very few hotel operators have been able to … run the foodservice businesses like a real restaurateur.

(Riley, 2000, makes a similar case in respect of UK hotels; see also Mansbach, 2010, for the USA.). Rushmore's point is that it is normal for certain expenses *not* to be allocated to the food and beverage department of a hotel – for example, for administration, sales, heat, light, power and so on. When these costs are included, he avers, most hotels cannot fail but to make a loss on their food and beverage operations. Riley (2000) examines the factors that contribute to a lack of demand in hotel restaurants and makes two important points. First, hotel guests do not want to eat all their meals in the place where they are staying. Secondly (and this remark has very clear applications in Anglophone cultures but is less certain elsewhere), non-resident customers are put off dining in hotels because of, potentially, lack of awareness as to the offerings available and the 'threshold' effect of having to enter a restaurant via the main hotel which can make at least some people uncomfortable (see Riley, 1984). Given that restaurant space is deemed necessary because of breakfast provision, the responses to the problem of demand for the services of hotel restaurants have been, Riley (2000) argues, twofold. The first is to outsource provision either by buying in an established concept or by contracting out management of the restaurant facility. The second response is what Riley calls the 'coffee shop' solution and what is now more commonly termed 'all-day dining' where at least one hotel restaurant will be open more or less all day for the service of all meals, employing a buffet concept. This is a particularly prevalent model in Asia but is to some degree found in most countries around the world in branded hotels.

For independent restaurants therefore the real world problem appears to be staying in business; for hotel restaurants – or at least some of them – it is sourcing the business. To the list of factors potentially reducing demand in the latter one might add pricing – often dining in a hotel restaurant carries a price premium compared to dining in an independent restaurant. As Riley (2000) suggests, however, culture needs to be considered as an important demand factor. Buffets are highly popular in many Middle Eastern and Asian countries and to dine in a hotel restaurant is a mark of status, or at least an opportunity to demonstrate one's wealth by engaging in conspicuous consumption. The buffet is, however, in economic terms a double-edged sword for any food and beverage establishment. It can lead to both high food wastage rates, on the one hand, and 'abuse' by customers, on the other. We conclude this section by noting the events in Brighton's 'Gobi' restaurant when, in 2012, the owner of this independent restaurant offering an 'Eat as much as you can for £12' deal based on a buffet banned two customers for alleged overindulgence. One of the customers concerned told the BBC: 'As we were eating the last bowl, the owner came up and said never to come back again, we're disgusting, and we're eating him out of business, so we're nothing but filthy pigs' (http://www.bbc.com/news/uk-england-sussex-19817457, last accessed 04.05.14).

Production-Oriented Research in Food and Beverage

Having examined in some detail both the 'mythological characteristics' associated with food and beverage management and some key aspects of the practice of that function, we now examine what food and beverage management research teaches us about the field. In the case of both production- and consumption-based research an underlying theme is the degree of control that food and beverage operators can exert over provision. In this section we shall briefly consider food and beverage research focusing on the construction and operation of food production and service systems, and the quantitative analysis of food and beverage performance employing various forms of what has become termed 'menu engineering'.

Before we do this, a brief comment on food technology and food science is appropriate. As with the study of accommodation management (see Chapter 4), the early curricula of higher hospitality management courses often underpinned food and beverage education with scientific components – food technology and food science being especially popular. The orientation towards a more managerial focus has reduced or eliminated the role and significance of scientific subjects (although the literature on food production and service systems often refers to the *employment* of technology in a management context). Research into food science and technology continues, but largely separate from the sphere of hospitality management. Periodically this state of affairs has attracted insightful if somewhat acid criticism, as with Rodgers (2009: 74; see also Rodgers, 2005a, 2005b, 2007), who writes:

> Currently, hospitality research is represented by two dominant themes, management and social science. These are mostly descriptive replication studies based on surveys, case studies and multivariate techniques, which 'do not lead to formulation of new theories' … . At the same time, the hospitality science model with well-established theories and research tools in natural and physical science is overlooked.

Rodgers is undoubtedly correct that within the specific context of hospitality management education and research, and food and beverage management in particular, the role for scientific knowledge has been delimited. This is due in no small part to the advance of catering technologies where knowledge that might have been required of individuals is embedded in machinery and mechanized processes. Pre-prepared and in some way preserved and/or partly-cooked food that can be 'finished' employing a particular form of technology (for example, *sous-vide*) requires a person only to follow the instructions for preparing that food for consumption by the consumer.

Food production and service systems

A food production and service system is a planned and integrated set of resources, processes and procedures designed to deliver one or more product and service offerings (Pickworth, 1988; Waller, 1996; Rodgers, 2005a). One commentator – Peter Jones – has dominated contributions to this field of study (see especially Jones, 1993, 1994; Huelin and Jones, 1990; Johns and Jones, 1999a, 1999b, 2000; Kirk, 2000). Much of Jones's work (e.g. Jones, 1993) has been directed towards evolving a utilitarian classification of food production and service systems. Noting that, traditionally, most food production and service systems have been conceived and implemented as unified forms with production and consumption taking place spatially and temporally more or less together, Jones elaborates the ways in which changes in technology have broken, or produced the potential for breaking, the direct link between production and consumption. For Jones (1993: 4–7) this is best illustrated by adopting a 'materials flow' approach to food production and service systems. Beginning with the traditional catering service delivery system that has its origins in nineteenth-century hotels and identifying the flow of materials through the system, Jones generates eight essential stages, namely: storage, preparation, production (cooking), holding, service, dining, clearing, and dishwash.

The development of food technologies, and particularly regenerative techniques based on food preservation (notably cook-freeze, cook-chill and *sous-vide*), allows the decoupling of production and service by lengthening the time that food can be held between its production and service – the so-called 'holding' stage. Technology thus permits food production and consumption to be separated both temporally and spatially leading Jones to add two stages to his eight-stage model – being 'transportation' and 'regeneration' thus: storage; preparation; production (cooking); holding; transportation; regeneration; service; dining; clearing; and dishwash. According to Jones, some or all of these 10 elements can be combined in different ways, to produce various permutations that are representative of real food production and service contexts. For example the combination/permutation storage–preparation–cooking–service–dining–clearing–dishwash is operationalized as an *à la carte* restaurant where fresh commodities are employed and dishes cooked to order. Further, specific combinations and permutations arising from the generic can be classified according to a tripartite typology:

- integrated food service systems where production, service and consumption take place in the same location – in other words the 'traditional' concept of the restaurant;

- food manufacturing systems where decoupling occurs between the production and service of meals and the role of transportation is emphasized; and

- food delivery systems where operations have little or no on-the-ground food production activities but rather centre on the assembly and/or regeneration and service of meals.

As indicated previously, food and beverage management research does little to link key themes to wider societal trends in food and eating. Research on food production and service systems exemplifies this. Wood (2008) argues that Jones's modelling exercise is a useful descriptive tool providing a framework for the possible arrangement of technologies and the variables influencing these arrangements – but little more. Wood (2008, 2013b) suggests that much of the food production and service systems literature ignores the role of human agency in influencing how systems operate, change and develop. The development of any system results from intentional human acts but intention, design and 'rational' planning do not lead automatically to *what* is intended and designed *actually* working, in a rational or any other way. Indeed, deviations in performance that derive from human interaction *with* a system tend to be treated as dysfunctional, as something to be corrected by improving the system in order that 'rogue' human influence is minimized. To this, Wood adds the observation that Jones's model is underpinned by an uncritical belief in the rationality of systems, so that solutions to catering 'problems' are sought within the boundaries of the system(s) employed rather than by reference to the functioning of the system(s) in wider social, economic and technological contexts. And yet, however Jones's 10 (or fewer) categories are arranged they only represent a snapshot of part of the wider food system. As an example, we can consider the role of food supply chains as essential to instances of both production and service in terms of food availability, the susceptibility of different foods to different types of processing and preservation and restaurateurs' marketing choices (in the case of the last, increasing interest in locally sourced 'authentic' foodstuffs – whether or not as part of concerns for sustainability – can have implications for the choice of configuration of a restaurant system, as may a myriad of other factors in the wider food system).

Menu engineering and menu analysis

Menu engineering is *one* technique of menu analysis and management, but the term menu engineering (apparently coined by Kasavana and Smith, 1982) is often used to refer to all similar techniques. In essence, menu analysis comprises a set of ostensibly quantitative approaches to identifying the economic and financial (cost, revenue and sales) performance of dishes on a menu, thus facilitating management decisions as to which items on a menu should be retained, which removed and which modified and (hopefully) encouraged to better performance. The earliest and now most well-known models of menu analysis are:

- the Miller Matrix (Miller, 1980)

- menu engineering (Kasavana and Smith, 1982)

- cost/margin analysis (Pavesic, 1983, 1985) and

- the profit and loss approach (Hayes and Huffman, 1985).

The first three of these rely on matrix analyses similar to the so-called 'Boston Matrix' (Boston Consulting Group, 1970) whereby the performance of dishes is judged in terms of their placement within one of four quadrants on the basis of computation of the intersection of (usually) two principal variables (see Figure 5.1). Thus, the Miller Matrix proceeds from the view that the 'best' menu items have the lowest food cost percentage and highest level of consumer popularity (sales volume). In the menu engineering of Kasavana and Smith (1982), the two principal variables are an individual menu item's contribution margin (the difference between the selling price and direct cost of a menu item) and its popularity with consumers. In menu engineering the best menu is one that maximizes contribution margins.

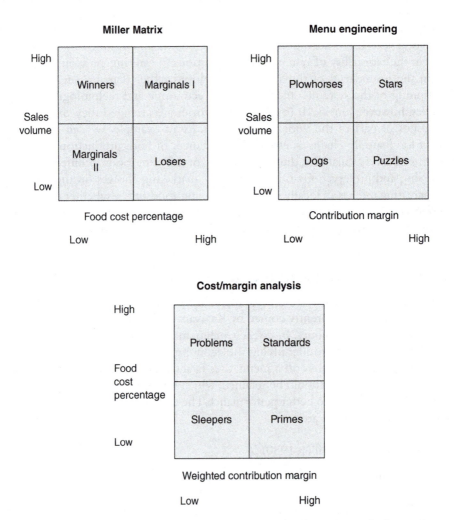

Figure 5.1   Miller Matrix, menu engineering and cost/margin analysis quadrants

Pavesic (1983, 1985) developed his cost/margin analysis in response to what he perceived as weaknesses in the Miller Matrix and menu engineering approaches. With regard to the former, he argues that the design of a menu geared to the lowest overall food cost will run the risk of sacrificing total sales revenues because low food cost items are usually priced lower than high food cost items. In respect of menu engineering, Pavesic suggests that an emphasis on contribution margin courts the danger of restaurants focusing on costly items (thereby reducing margins and damaging profit) because items returning a higher amount of gross profit are most typically those with the highest food cost and menu prices. Thus, menu engineering may work in restaurants where one or more of total revenues are high or increasing (as in fine dining) and/or where the market is relatively price-inelastic (Pavesic, 1983: 127–128; 1985: 72). Pavesic's (1983: 129) cost/margin analysis therefore *combines* the relationship of food cost percentage and contribution margin with an appraisal of volume on the basis that: 'the optimum sales mix is the one that simultaneously optimizes (not maximizes) dollar contribution margin relative to achieving the lowest overall food cost percentage, while optimizing total sales revenue.' The Pavesic Matrix has axes representing food cost percentage and the weighted contribution margin and the four quadrants are produced by calculating the average weighted contribution margin (a straightforward division of the sum of total weighted contribution margins by the number of menu items) and potential food cost (weighted food cost divided by weighted sales). In all the matrices shown in Figure 5.1, the performance of individual dishes on the specified criteria can be mapped, leading to classification in one of the four quadrants. In the Miller Matrix, a dish that appeared in the 'Winners' quadrant would have a low food cost and a high sales volume; in the cost/margin analysis model a 'Prime' would be a dish with a high weighted contribution margin and low food cost.

As early as 1985, these matrix models of menu analysis were attracting doubt, not least because they failed to take into account any of the additional costs involved in food production. As an alternative to matrix analysis, Hayes and Huffman (1985) suggested developing individual 'profit and loss' statements for each dish, with each statement taking into account the percentage of fixed and variable costs borne by the item. For computational purposes they assumed that each menu item bore an equal proportion of the total daily fixed cost simultaneously acknowledging that this is an essentially arbitrary and thus contentious procedure. In a recent and authoritative review of the field, Taylor et al. (2009: 214) note in passing that menu engineering 'remains more art than science'. This is undoubtedly the case: the veneer of quantitative respectability which characterizes the techniques discussed cannot disguise the qualitative, judgemental elements required to make them work. As with revenue management (see Chapter 4) menu engineering is a pseudo-scientific technique that allows the appearance of control and controlling but which at best offers indicative information that has to be set against experience and other sources of information to be of genuine use.

Consumption-Oriented Research in Food and Beverage

As with production-oriented research into food and beverage management, consumption-oriented studies are to a greater or lesser degree concerned with control, and in particular the directing of consumers towards particular structures and conventions that in general 'favour' operators in terms of the provision of food and beverage products. Thus in this section we are concerned with the nuances of restaurant and food selection and the meal experience.

The problem of restaurant and food choice

The concept of choice is central to individual and social identity in western liberal democracies. However, as Warde and Martens (1998: 130) note, there is good reason for thinking that there has been a tendency for 'exaggeration of the scope of the freedom implied by the concept of consumer choice'. These authors identify four shades of meaning associated with the word: (1) to select; (2) to pick in preference; (3) to consider fit or suitable; and (4) to will or determine. They suggest that in the area of food consumption there has been a tendency to conflate the first two meanings with the fourth. In practice this means that consumers rarely encounter 'pure' states of choice (characterized by their absolute freedom to select and pick in preference something of their choice); this choice is instead always to some degree pre-determined and pre-structured by those providing the 'choice'. In food and beverage management, the principal device within an organization for pre-structuring choice is the menu. Mooney (1994: 46) notes that: 'In reality, more often than not, the menu also serves as a limit on what a foodservice operation is willing and able to prepare and serve.' Wood (2000a) goes further, arguing that though invariably presented as a vehicle of customer choice, the menu is an illusory device whose real purpose is antithetical to choice. The menu's real purpose is to state at its simplest what the vendor is willing to offer, it is a limiting device, with dishes 'chosen' by the vendor providing a list from which the consumer selects items that the vendor is willing to provide (this view of the menu has been picked up and extended to social life more generally in a fascinating piece of conjecture by Korczynski and Ott (2006)). Of course, restrictions on choice are not only found *within* a food service organization. We can add the observation that we do not all approach food consumption choices equally. Limits of income, geography, transport and home facilities (e.g. in the case of domestic food consumption, the possession of a 'deep freeze') can all influence the markets to which people have access or from which they are excluded. In terms of dining out in the public sphere, for some people a visit to a fast food restaurant is equivalent to other customers' visit to a three star Michelin establishment.

Research on consumer restaurant selection has tended to focus on eliciting the role of key variables in the choice of restaurant and/or meal selection given a number of alternative scenarios (e.g. anniversaries, family get-togethers) and then ranking the resulting factors. In general, these studies suggest that concrete factors – and especially perceived quality of food, quality of service, price of food – are most important in consumers' choice of restaurant. Furthermore, friends and peer group influence, rather than formal marketing influences, are usually more important in selecting a *particular* restaurant. In the USA, Jolson and Bushman (1978: 69) found that in deciding whether to dine at a restaurant for the first time, consumers depend primarily on personal recommendations and remarks by critics in contrast to restaurant advertising. Similarly, Barrows et al. (1989: 90) found that recommendations from friends were the most valued factor in determining whether to go to a restaurant for the first time. A Mintel survey for the *Caterer and Hotelkeeper* trade magazine (Anon, 1992: 14) pertaining to the UK found that 90% of people listed recommendation by a friend as most important in choosing a new place to eat with 25% saying they took note of reviews in newspapers or magazines. A later NOP poll for the same publication found that the most influential factor in selecting where to eat out was prior experience: 84% of the sample had bought a meal from a place where they had dined before (Anon, 1998: 60–62).

The meal experience

An intervening factor in our understanding of the reasons why people choose particular restaurants (and indeed, particular foods) is the idea of the meal experience. This concept was developed in terms of its applications to the commercial hospitality industry by Campbell-Smith (1967, 1970) and thus pre-dates the concerns of those 'experience economy' perspectives on service industries that we briefly examined in Chapter 1. Indeed, the concept of the meal experience is one of the few genuinely original concepts generated by hospitality research. Campbell-Smith (1967) argued that when dining out, customers assess their overall meal experience by reference to (a) the quality of food and drink and (b) other less tangible elements, including quality of service, atmosphere, ambience of the restaurant and so on. This seems a commonplace idea in the twenty-first century but at the time it was something of a revolutionary notion and it has become part of the received wisdom of the hospitality industry, the concept suggesting, as it does, that providers of public hospitality can compensate for a less than outstanding quality of food and drink by manipulating other elements within the meal experience – in other words it offers food providers the prospect of exerting (further) control over customers' food and beverage experiences.

As we noted in the previous section, the general consensus of research undertaken in the area of food and beverage consumer choice is that the quality and price of food and drink are of primary importance to restaurant/food selection. This does not obviously mean, however, that other, less tangible, elements of the meal experience are *unimportant*. After all, the recurring success of experience-oriented thematic restaurant brands suggests that the restaurant industry believes theming to be of value (Weiss et al., 2004). A fair amount of research energy has been expended on exploring the significance of the less tangible aspects of the meal experience but with no firm conclusions. At one extreme, the nature of human variability and the complexity of studying this particular type of behaviour lead some writers to be sceptical that we will ever be able to fully establish the nature of the meal experience. Johns et al. (1996: 23) suggest that it is 'impossible to identify clearly the factors which make up the meal experience' although suggestive associations in their data indicated that 'food was the most important element of the majority of meal experiences'. At the other extreme and despite this gloomy prognosis, a number of hospitality researchers have established a loose programme of research centred on the five aspects (5A) model of the meal experience which is dedicated to nothing less than providing 'a tool for understanding and handling the different aspects involved in producing commercial meals and offering guests the best possible meal experience' (Gustafsson et al., 2006: 90). The kindest thing that can be said about this research is that it is yet to produce any meaningful insights that advance our knowledge of the meal experience (see Stierand and Wood, 2012, for a thorough review of the 5A model). As a model it, like Campbell-Smith's original, begins with the *a priori* assumption that meals are experiences which restaurant customers seek. More importantly, the word 'experience' is loaded here – it means, in practice, the creation of a 'positive' experience. As we saw in Chapter 1, however, there are good reasons for doubting the fundamental validity of 'experience' approaches, not least their tendency to reductionism and oversimplification.

Beyond this, researchers who would seek to persuade of the importance or primacy of intangible factors in the meal experience have yet to adequately address two issues. The first is to explain why consumers normally cite as a matter of priority *material* reasons for choosing restaurants and/or particular types of food. The Horizons (2012b) food marketing intelligence company referenced earlier confirms the fairly consistent trend over time that food quality (79%), price (70%), cleanliness (64%) and standard of service (55%) – all subjective but nevertheless tangible, material elements – rank most highly in consumers' choices when dining out. 'Ambience' comes in fifth out of 13 factors cited as important by only 51%. The second issue to be addressed – and which is notably absent from the 5A model of the meal experience literature – is what will be termed here 'the Finkelstein Question'. In 1989, Joanne Finkelstein published a study that offers a somewhat different view of the nature of dining out. Finkelstein notes that restaurants are, culturally, depicted as places of, variously, excitement, pleasure, wealth and luxury, these values and emotions being articulated in their ambience, décor, furnishings, lighting and tableware. To this extent she is in accord with the Campbell-Smith concept of the meal experience but she goes on to make two critical points. *First*, individuals mistakenly believe themselves to be acting from choice when they dine out and they have expectations that restaurants will help them realize both 'objective' desires – for good food and service – and deeper emotional desires for status and belongingness. In fact, according to Finkelstein, dining out is not a wholly individual act but one instance of 'uncivilised sociality', whereby restaurants encourage styles of interaction that make dining out an example of mannered behaviour. The interactions in question are imitative of the behaviour of others, of prevailing images and fashions; they are actions of habit, without the need on the part of the consumer for self-scrutiny or reflection. In other words, when dining out, Finkelstein (1989: 12) argues, people act 'from habit or in response to the anonymous edicts of conventions' that is, within a framework of interaction already laid down for them, where they have little need to engage meaningfully with others (Finkelstein, 1989: 5). *Secondly*, and following from this, Finkelstein at least implies that public meal experiences can rarely be anything other than desultory, empty affairs, a view quite contrary to that of promoters of the meal experience concept and 'experience economy' notions more generally.

Finkelstein's views have been largely ignored by 'meal experience' researchers and no wonder – her assertions undermine the very basis of their claims and assertions. A significant critique of her position has come (in a different context and research tradition) from Warde and Martens (1999: 128-130; Warde and Martens, 2000). In their survey they found that some 47% of respondents 'agreed strongly' with the proposition that 'I always enjoy myself when I eat out' with a further 35% 'agreeing slightly' and 82% had 'liked a lot' their last experience of eating out. Warde and Martens found that aspects of sociability – those very aspects of the meal experience that Finkelstein suggests are at best artificial and at worst acted out without any 'real' enthusiasm – were experienced as most pleasing, nearly 97% of their respondents saying they enjoyed the company and the conversation (compared to 94% saying they enjoyed the food and 87% the service and value for money: Warde and Martens explain these levels of satisfaction by arguing that people guard against poor experiences by revisiting those restaurants that have previously yielded positive experiences, with some 62% of their respondents having eaten out before at the venue of their most recent dining-out experience). The difficulty with Warde and Martens's position is that their results are exactly what you would expect to find if Finkelstein was correct – her main argument being, remember, that people *expect* to have positive experiences in restaurant dining. It would thus be unusual if members of Warde and Martens's survey responded negatively to the kind of questioning posed. Indeed, it is widely recognized that in all direct questioning methodologies there is a danger that respondents will tell questioners what they think the latter want to hear. 'The Finkelstein Question' simply put is: is Finkelstein correct in her assertions about the mannered 'uncivilised sociality' of dining out? Integral to any answer to this question would be determining what kind, level and significance of evidence could, or would, be accepted. It is an important issue because if Finkelstein is correct then our understanding of 'meal' and many other 'experiences' may have to be significantly reoriented. That Finkelstein herself fails to sufficiently evidence her own assertions does not diminish the importance of the issue.

Concluding Remarks

Food and beverage management is the most mythologized aspect of both the hospitality industry and hospitality management education. Its role as a vehicle for senior management ambition (see Chapter 7) is out of all proportion to its significance in the revenue mix of many (though by no means all) hotels. It is an area projected as complex in nature and in its administration, despite the skills of cooking being the only immediately obvious area of complexity. Given the nature of public taste, the industry's interpretation of that taste, and the general reluctance to innovate, even cookery more frequently evidences predictability and routine than novelty and innovation, the latter being generally confined to the small 'fine dining' section of the market. Branded quick service/fast food restaurants do not have to pretend to be operating in the gourmet market and the majority of small and medium sized restaurant enterprises operate in well-established markets whether for indigenous or foreign cuisines. In the UK, it is significant that the leading locations for consumption of food outside the home are public houses – pubs.

The mythological qualities appended to the food and beverage function in the hospitality industry appear to arise primarily from the insularity of the industry both at the operations level and at the level of academic research. The 'conventional views' of food and beverage management promulgated by the latter could easily be avoided, and/or placed in perspective, if research in the field was not itself quite so insular. As noted earlier in the chapter, and as expressed most elegantly by Beardsworth and Keil (1997), hospitality-related food research tends to investigate localized food systems, including the meal experience, in isolation from other parts of the food system or the wider social fabric of which dining is part. This leads to a tendency to underrate the importance of factors *external* to commercial food service that influence both the nature of supply (including the state of food technology and the number and quality of supply chains) and the nature of consumer motivation. With regard to the latter, different externally generated motives for dining out may give rise to different expectations and hence different parameters for judging meal experiences. Consider the work of Frisbee and Madeira (1986: 173), who hypothesized that, in the case of the two-earner middle-class households they studied, 'as time becomes more valuable to household members, the total cost of home-prepared meals (food costs plus time costs) increases relative to the total cost of restaurant meals (which are generally less time-intensive)'. Pavesic (1989: 45, italics in original) is more emphatic in asserting that: 'Customers will evaluate a restaurant as a place to *eat-out* or as a place to *dine-out*. If a restaurant is considered an *eat-out* operation during the week (a substitute for cooking at home), customers will be more price conscious. If a restaurant is considered a *dine-out* operation, the visit is regarded more as a social occasion or entertainment and price is not as much of a factor.' These two examples hint at the range of 'external' factors that can bear upon commercial dining and which, in much of the literature reviewed here, tend to be reduced to a cipher if they are considered at all.

In much hospitality research into food and beverage management there is a tendency to treat the customer base as homogeneous. Thus, fundamental differences in social class, gender, racial and ethnic characteristics, and cultural heritage are rarely marked in hospitality research. Yet in one area where we do have some fairly substantial information – gender – we know that for many women, participation in the hospitality industry can be an uncomfortable experience. Research as recent as the 1970s and 1980s showed that women customers tend to be stereotyped by hospitality organizations' employees as fussy, demanding, low spenders and poor tippers (Bowey, 1976; Mars and Nicod, 1984) without very much regard for the fact that many women are economically disadvantaged relative to men. Mazurkiewicz (1983), in what remains a landmark commentary, reflects upon the observation that as consumers in restaurants and other public places, women have traditionally been carefully controlled, or policed, and the stereotypes of female restaurant customers that abound in the hospitality industry are as much an aspect of the rhetoric of this control as they are a marketing judgement.

Food and beverage management is an important component of hospitality management but its significance and managerial complexity should not be exaggerated. Outside certain multi-service organizations (e.g. hotels and hospitals), the scale of operation or the proffering of simple products easily produced using various technologies, when combined with the predictability of consumer tastes (and an understanding of how slowly these change) means that relatively unskilled operatives can execute food and beverage functions with limited training. In recent years the general societal elevation of food and cooking to the status of a fetish has combined with the hospitality industry's own mythologies to reinforce an almost sexual image of the food and beverage function. A more grounded approach is required, one that links the study of provision to wider eating behaviours and begins with the reality of provision in the hospitality industry.

Further Reading

Finkelstein, J (1989) *Dining Out: A Sociology of Modern Manners*, Cambridge: Polity Press.

Riley, M (2005) 'Food and beverage management: a review of change', *International Journal of Contemporary Hospitality Management*, 17, 1: 88–93.

Stierand, M and Wood, R C (2012) 'Reconceptualising the commercial meal experience in the hospitality industry', *Journal of Hospitality and Tourism Management*, 19, 1: 143–148.

Wood, R C (2008) 'Food production and service systems theory', in B Brotherton and R C Wood (Eds) *The Sage Handbook of Hospitality Management*, London: Sage, 443–459.

6

WOULD YOU LIKE TO JOIN OUR CUSTOMER LOYALTY PROGRAMME? MARKETING AND CONSUMPTION IN HOSPITALITY

After reading this chapter, you should:

(a) understand that at the operational level at least, marketing plays a limited role in hospitality (and particularly hotel) management whereas the sales function is of critical importance;

(b) appreciate those marketing concepts - segmentation and branding - that do have immediate implications for hospitality operations, including developing an awareness of the fickle nature of customer and brand loyalty and comprehending the importance of direct examination of the expression of customer needs in providing products and services; and

(c) be able to place in context the importance and basic limitations of the use of social media in marketing and sales in hospitality.

Introduction

As we saw in Chapter 2, the hospitality industry has much formal and informal structural assistance in marketing and promotion from national governments' ministries of tourism, from international, national and regional tourism organizations and, increasingly, from web-based travel retailers. In respect of hotels, the old aphorism that the most important thing determining the desirability of a property is 'location, location, location' points to the importance of a traveller's destination in hotel marketing. Many global destinations have established themselves over many years as locations for business, or for one form or another of tourism. Some have deliberately set out to make themselves a destination for particular activities, the most notable success in recent years in this regard being the United Arab Emirates city of Dubai, which has positioned itself as a leading finance, business, shopping and leisure destination in a remarkably short period of time. Some destinations have retained and continue to retain a near permanency in their popularity – for example, in the field of business and finance, New York, London, Shanghai, Singapore, Hong Kong and Frankfurt. Other destinations, notably those devoted to various forms of leisure-based tourism, wax and wane in their popularity. The hotel industry in many ways gets a free ride off the back of destinations' marketing efforts when these are successful – and of course suffers when such efforts are unsuccessful. Similarly, when negative economic circumstances prevail as in recent years, then much travel, as a (relatively) discretionary item of expenditure, is curtailed, with all that this entails for hospitality businesses. Of course, sometimes particular – usually expensive and high end – hotels or restaurants can ride out economic troughs because they have become destinations in their own right and their products and services are sought out by those of sufficient financial independence to be unaffected by poor economic circumstances.

Marketing plays a role in the curricula of almost all management, including hospitality management, courses. As with strategy and strategic management (see Chapter 2) this is a little surprising for very few hospitality management graduates will ever be extensively involved in marketing (those involved in new hotel and restaurant openings may have some involvement in devising initial marketing plans). Because most graduates are directed towards operational careers they will be mainly restricted, even as senior managers at unit level, to implementing and monitoring marketing strategies and policies determined by 'head office'. In one of the genuinely useful practitioner volumes on hotel management, Venison (2005: 83) writes: 'In a perfect world … a well-run hotel should not need the manager (or anyone else) to do any marketing … . marketing … is one area of focus that is primarily conducted outside the walls of the hotel.' If, broadly defined, marketing is likely to be an activity not much encountered in the working lives of hospitality managers then sales is another matter. The last few years have seen growing general concern over the priority given to marketing over sales. One of the current gurus of sales, Philip Delves Broughton (2012a) has fought to bring this issue to a wider attention (see also *The Economist*, 2011a, 2012; Fitzhugh and Piercy, 2010; Piercy, 2012). In an article for the *Financial Times*, Delves Broughton (2012b) noted not only that sales is absent from the curricula of most MBA programmes and other business school curricula but that this absence is attributable to (a) a combination of the quantitative, scientific pretentions of management as a discipline and (b) academic snobbery, both of which we touched upon in Chapter 1. He writes: 'The effects of this omission from academe are grave. Many supposedly well-educated people in business are clueless about one of its most vital functions: the means by which you actually generate revenue.' Delves Broughton observes that in the USA, more people are employed in sales jobs than there are in manufacturing, let alone, he notes, 'marketing, strategy, finance or any of the other parasitic business functions'. The snobbery to which Delves Broughton alludes is arguably particularly acute in the UK where 'commercial travellers' (salesmen – and they were usually men) have traditionally been viewed in a somewhat jaundiced light. In the USA the situation is slightly different, at least in hospitality, where the sales function is often emphasized over marketing (the principal global specialist organization, the Hospitality Sales and Marketing Association International, is based in the USA, http://www.hsmai.org/).

In many parts of the world and especially in larger hotel properties, general and other senior managers will have at their disposal a significantly sized sales team and will often be required to engage in sales activities themselves, not least in securing leads for their teams and clinching particularly important deals at their final stages. There thus seems little merit in an abbreviated summary of what is readily available in the numerous introductory marketing texts available (including those specialized in 'services marketing' and 'hospitality marketing' – for one of the best short reviews available see Bowen, 2008; for one of the most comprehensive textbook treatments refer to Kotler et al., 2009); indeed, given the predictably limited role of marketing in most hospitality managers' careers there seems little point in discussing the subject at all. No doubt many marketing specialists will find comments of this nature controversial, even gratuitously contrarian. However, doubts about the integrity of marketing's disciplinary claims and aspirations to practical business utility have been long current in the discipline. From the point of view of the hospitality industry they are well stated and critically reviewed in Williams's masterly text on the hospitality consumer (Williams, 2002, especially ch. 7). Further, if we revisit the top 10 hotel companies mentioned in Chapter 2, and add the top 10 international restaurant chains, then with the benefit of further research we can note in passing that of those hotel company senior executives responsible for marketing on whom information is available, only two have a formal qualification in hospitality management; for restaurants the figure is zero (see Tables 6.1 and 6.2: it may be of some comfort to know that very few of those listed appear to have marketing qualifications either).

The knowledge taught in basic marketing modules within hospitality courses may well be intrinsically useful and useful to those few graduates who eventually assume senior executive roles in marketing. This chapter will give a brief overview of those concepts and issues in marketing which are most likely to be encountered by managers at an operational level. These are *first*, segmentation, which is important at both macro-level (how a unit or group of units is positioned within the international, national and local markets) and at micro-level, that is, the level of the unit. The latter is more important to hotel than restaurant managers because within their total guest count there will usually be different segments for accommodation purchases, food and beverage purchases and so on. *Secondly*, we shall briefly examine the related concepts of branding and loyalty. Again there is a macro- and micro-dimension to consider here. A brand is the proposition a company makes to one or more segments of the market and it is thus embedded in the physical and social structures of the hotel. At the micro-level this is reflected in the implementation of brand standards which may replace, be incorporated in or sit side-by-side with standard operating procedures (SOPs, see Chapter 4). Marketing generates its own myths and from time to time in any field of production or service one is left wondering whether the end users of those products and services were ever consulted as to what they wanted. We shall thus briefly consider, *thirdly*, the implications of what we know about what customers want for hospitality provision. *Fourthly*, no contemporary discussion of marketing and consumption in hospitality would be complete without a brief consideration of the implications of the rise of social media for the sector. Up until this point the discussion will focus primarily on hotels so, *finally*, we shall briefly turn attention to some of the issues in restaurant segmentation, loyalty and branding.

Table 6.1 Senior marketing executives: formal hospitality educational qualifications (top 10 hotel companies, 2013)

Company	Executive and title: formal educational qualifications in hospitality management
IHG	Gavin Flynn, Senior Vice President Strategic and Portfolio Marketing – no apparent hospitality qualification
Hilton	Mark D Wang, Executive Vice President of Global Sales and President of Hilton Grand Vacations Company – no information located
Marriott	Stephanie C Linnartz, Executive Vice President and Chief Marketing and Commercial Officer – no apparent hospitality qualification
Wyndham	No marketing executive apparently *in situ*
Choice	Alexandra Jaritz, Senior Vice President Brand Strategy and Marketing – hospitality qualification
Accor	Vivek Badrinath, Deputy Chief Executive Officer with responsibility for Marketing, Digital Solutions, Distribution and Information Services – no apparent hospitality qualification
Starwood	Phil McAveety, Executive Vice President and Chief Brand Officer – no apparent hospitality qualification
Best Western	Dorothy Dowling, Senior Vice President Marketing and Sales – no apparent hospitality qualification
Home Inns	No marketing executive apparently *in situ*
Carlson Rezidor	Eric De Neef, Senior Vice President, Marketing, Customer Relationship Management and Global Branding – hospitality qualification

Sources: (all items last accessed 28.04.14):

http://www.hospitalitynet.org/news/4060119.html
http://www.ihgplc.com/index.asp?pageid=789
http://www.hiltonworldwide.com/about/leadership/mark-wang/
http://www.linkedin.com/in/stephanielinnartz
http://investing.businessweek.com/research/stocks/people/people.asp?ticker=CHH
http://investing.businessweek.com/research/stocks/people/person.asp?personId=3330552
    8&ticker=ORA:FP&previousCapId=367964&previousTitle=ORANGE
http://www.starwoodhotels.com/corporate/about/leadership/McAveety.html
http://www.bestwestern.com/about-us/press-media/executives-detail.asp?ExecID=25
http://www.rezidor.com/phoenix.zhtml?c=205430&p=irolexecutive#sthash.1VVjFFa0.dpuf
http://www.rezidor.com/phoenix.zhtml?c=205430&p=irol-executive
http://investing.businessweek.com/research/stocks/people/people.asp?ticker=WYN

Table 6.2 Senior marketing executives: formal hospitality educational qualifications (top 10 branded restaurant companies, 2013)

Company	Executive and title/possesses formal educational qualification in hospitality management
McDonald's	Steve Easterbrook, Executive Vice President and Chief Brand Officer – no apparent hospitality qualification
KFC (Yum! Brands)	Nobody listed either on the board of directors or list of senior officers
Subway	Christopher Carroll, Senior Vice President of Marketing – no apparent hospitality qualification
Pizza Hut (Yum! Brands)	Nobody listed either on the board of directors or list of senior officers
Starbucks	Sharon Rothstein, Global Chief Marketing Officer – no apparent hospitality qualification
Burger King	Axel Schwan, Executive VP, Global Chief Marketing Officer, experienced restaurateur: *Bloomberg Businessweek* states that no details on Mr Schwan's educational qualifications are available
Domino's Pizza	Russell J Weiner, Executive Vice President, Build the Brand – no apparent hospitality qualification
Dunkin' Donuts	John Costello, President, Global Marketing and Innovation – no apparent hospitality qualification
Dairy Queen	No board member/senior executive responsible for marketing could be identified
Papa John's	Robert C Kraut, Senior Vice President and Chief Marketing Officer – no apparent hospitality qualification

Sources: (all items last accessed 28.04.14)

http://www.forbes.com/pictures/feji45hfkh/top-10-global-fast-food-brands-2/
http://www.aboutmcdonalds.com/mcd/our_company/leadership/steve_easterbrook.html
http://www.theguardian.com/business/2008/may/16/fooddrinks.mcdonalds
http://www.yum.com/company/srofficers.asp
http://news.starbucks.com/leadership/sharon-rothstein
http://investor.bk.com/burgerking/web/conteudo_en.asp?idioma=1&conta=44&tipo=43568
http://investing.businessweek.com/research/stocks/people/person.asp?personId=24
    8480712&ticker=BKW&previousCapId=821389&previousTitle=Burger%20King%20
    Worldwide%2C%20Inc.
http://phx.corporate-ir.net/phoenix.zhtml?c=135383&p=irol-govBio&ID=183449
http://investing.businessweek.com/research/stocks/people/person.asp?personId=49120901
    &ticker=DPZ
http://news.dunkinbrands.com/Leadership/John-Costello-91.aspx
http://investing.businessweek.com/research/stocks/people/person.asp?personId=1551077
    &ticker=DNKN
http://www.linkedin.com/pub/bob-kraut/7/994/535
http://investing.businessweek.com/research/stocks/private/person.
    asp?personId=21974945
http://investing.businessweek.com/research/stocks/private/people.asp?privcapId=
    280746

Segmentation

Segmentation is a central and familiar concept in marketing referring to the process whereby possible target markets of consumers are sub-divided according to one or more sets of their commonly held characteristics. A seller of products and services then directs the resources of their organization to position themselves so that they may satisfy, profitably, the needs of one or more of these segments. In economic terms, many hospitality products and services are close substitutes for one another because all hotels and restaurants provide accommodation and/or food. To use the jargon of strategic management, their threshold capabilities (capabilities required in order to function in a market) are simultaneously their necessary and essential capabilities – the provision of accommodation and/or food. Of course, in practice, not all hotels and restaurants may be actual substitutes for one other. Companies seek to meet the needs of particular consumer segments which are differentiated according to income, taste, lifestyle disposition and other needs. A kind of 'standard' way of expressing this would be to say that a Ritz-Carlton hotel is not a substitute for a Travelodge even though both offer accommodation. The companies' offers differ in degree in terms of the nature, range, extent and quality of products and services on offer which, together with price, are the main signals of difference, usually packaged, in the case of chains in the hospitality industry, into one or more identifiable brands. However, the concepts of both 'segmentation' and 'close substitute' are quite fluid. If you travel to a destination that has no Ritz-Carlton and the only other branded hotel product in town is a Travelodge then the latter may indeed become a close substitute, engendered by a willingness to trust in the Travelodge brand in preference to staying in an independently owned facility about which you know nothing.

A hotel company can seek both to comprehensively segment the market and then to satisfy the needs of multiple segments with differentiated product and service offers. One of the world's largest hotel companies, Accor, has, in effect, pursued this strategy (see http://www.accor.com/en/brands/brand-portfolio.html, last accessed 13.04.14) via careful branding. According to their own classification, Accor offers the following brands to the markets shown:

- economy hotels – Ibis, Ibis Styles, Ibis Budget

- midscale hotels – Novotel, Novotel Suites, Mercure

- upscale hotels – Pullman, MGallery, Grand Mercure and The Sebel (these last two in Asia-Pacific)

- luxury hotels – Sofitel.

Accor have been among those branded hotel chains pursuing a strategy of developing multi-branded hotels which essentially combines two or more hotels with different brand identities in one location, often under the same roof and with a single general or city/area manager. According to Wright (2013), the 'two hotels share construction and operational expenses as well as facilities, resulting in attractive cost savings for developers'. An arrangement of this kind often works to the benefit of both operator and consumer, optimizing the attractiveness of the proposition to multiple segments of the market. Other segments increasingly commonly provided for by the branded hotel sector are, as we saw in Chapter 2, long-stay products offering a more 'homely' type of accommodation based on the apartment concept and offering a variety of service levels. Marriott, who offer 16 brands addressing various market segments, have hotels, suite hotels and apartments for long-stay guests (http://www.marriott. com/marriott-brands.mi, last accessed 13.04.14).

Segmentation by some socio-economic classification or by type/motivation of guest is by and large the norm in the hotel industry; other forms of segmentation are called into being according to what might turn out to be temporary fashions or until the segment is diluted so as to effectively lose distinctive meaning. Boutique hotels could be seen as falling into this category. Developing from the 1980s onwards, the original boutique hotels usually offered no more than 100 rooms, were design oriented and associated with sentiments like 'hip' and 'trendy' (Balekjian and Sarheim, 2011). Initially, most were independently owned, and many, perhaps most, still are (many hotels have simply adopted the term because of what it signals rather than actually implementing the ethos). As Balekjian and Sarheim (2011) note, the success of the boutique hotel concept has led to hotel chains getting in on the act, brands including W (by Starwood), EDITION (Marriott) and Hotel Indigo (InterContinental Hotels Group). These authors see the next stage of the segment as being characterized by the growth of budget boutique hotels. Developments of this kind arguably dilute the boutique hotel concept, rendering it meaningless.

A similar phenomenon can be seen in the budget hotel segment. Walker (2012b: 20) reports a round-table discussion with industry representatives in which the growth of budget hotels was identified as a major innovation in the hospitality industry in recent years. It is indeed the case that the last 20 years or so have seen significant growth in this segment. Originally intended to address the concerns of price-sensitive travellers and, in particular, motorists, early entrants to the market were often located at or near motorway service stations or motorway/main road junctions and/ or business parks (a large number still are). Many hotels provided no catering facilities but were located adjacent, or very proximate to, a public house, tavern or restaurant that provided meals. Now, the budget hotel sector is much more diverse. Campos Blanco et al. (2010: 4) identify 27 budget brands operating in Europe and divide the segment into four: ultra-budget (including easyHotel); core-budget (including Travelodge and Premier Inn); upper-budget (including Holiday Inn Express); and design-budget (including citizenM). This is suggestive of highly calibrated differential positioning by brand owners and, as with the question of dilution of the boutique hotel market, differential positioning raises the question of whether the term 'budget hotel' has real meaning anymore. Part of Premier Inn's promotion and positioning is (a) the lauding of the beds they install in their rooms, a top-end brand enjoying a Royal Warrant, and (b) the availability of traditional 'British' meals. The group citizenM (see Chapter 4) markets itself to the design conscious who want 'budget' luxury.

Segmentation is thus an increasingly complex and not always obviously rational process – you can have budget hotels offering virtually no food and beverage, or budget hotels with reasonably substantial catering operations; budget hotels that offer beds of a quality that would shame many deluxe upscale hotels; and budget hotels that offer the simplest furnishing and fittings, or those that make design statements. Some forms of segmentation are, potentially, easier to comprehend. A possible future area of interest will be the growth of Sharia-compliant hotels outside countries that follow a strict Islamic code. Rosenberg and Choufany (2009) outline the operational requirements for Sharia-compliant hotels, which include: no alcohol; only halal food; Muslim staff in the majority; female staff only for single-female floors and male staff for single-male floors; a conservative television service; and Koran and prayer mats available in each room. In design and interiors, these authors argue, larger function rooms will be required to cater for males and females separately; markers will need to be placed in rooms indicating the direction of Mecca; hotel art will not depict the human form; there will be separate wellness facilities for males and females; and separate floors for single males, single females and families. In financial terms Sharia-compliant hotels will need to be financed through Islamic financial arrangements.

Brand and Loyalty

In its simplest form, a brand is a single element or combination of elements that differentiates one product or service from another. According to *Forbes* magazine, the world's top 10 most valuable brands in descending order are: Apple, Microsoft, Coca-Cola, IBM, Google, McDonald's, General Electric, Intel, Samsung and Louis Vuitton (http://www.forbes.com/powerful-brands/, last accessed 27.04.14). Differentiation is only one aspect of branding however. In addition to creating 'separateness' from other products and services one objective of branding is to conjure in the minds of consumers certain physical and psychological/emotional qualities associated with particular brands. These qualities may be obvious, or they may be more subtle, or a combination of the two. For example, the name 'Rolls-Royce' or the badge used on Rolls-Royce cars with the two interlinked 'Rs' are verbal and visual signals that 'stand' for particular qualities. A less obvious element of Rolls-Royce branding is the winged statuette that adorns each car's bonnet (hood). Surprisingly few people know that this is called the 'Spirit of Ecstasy', but what an association for the product when they do know! Brand value is measured in various ways – in raw terms (e.g. sales in the market(s) for which the brand is intended); in more abstract ways like the degree of loyalty to the brand (and particularly the extent to which people are able and/or willing to switch to or from the brand); and in terms of the extent to which a brand is 'top of mind', that is a brand is recalled when asked to name a particular generic product or service (when asked to name an instant coffee brand, Nestlé would be delighted if Nescafé appeared top of everyone's list, less so if it was Maxwell House).

Loyalty

Brands come and brands go. In their review of hospitality marketing research as it has appeared in the published papers of the US journal *Cornell Hospitality Quarterly*, Dev et al. (2010: 465) identify over 200 hotel brands created from the 1800s onwards. *The Economist* (2013d) reports that branded chains currently operate around 7.5 million rooms. Hotel branding has become a key feature of the sector in the last 30 years or so. It provides, in the words of O'Neill and Mattilla (2010: 27), 'a "shorthand" method of establishing a particular property's quality by giving the customer important information about its product and service, sight unseen'. The main purpose of branding, however, is to create long-term loyalty which in turn is meant to add value to the guest experience and to the hotel company.

Mixed messages are to be found in the research data with respect to the nature of customer loyalty. Somewhat interestingly, since so much weight is put on the role of branding in developing customer loyalty, in hospitality there are very few *direct* studies of the relationship between the two. Bell et al. (2002: 79) argue that:

> programs to cultivate relationships with high-value customers are central to marketing management. The head of Hilton Hotels Corporation's guest rewards program calls them 'the industry's most important marketing tool'. Despite the fact that each member belongs to an average of 3.5 hotel loyalty programs, management is optimistic that they can be used to cultivate loyalty. Membership constitutes permission for the chain brand to build a customer profile for each member, to assess the potential value of each member, and to measure marketing's efforts to realize the potential value.

They go on to argue that only 9% of guests who stay in a Hilton hotel in any one year belong to its frequent guest programme. Further, only 3% are in the elite silver, gold and diamond status yet these groups contribute disproportionately to the chain's profitability. In fact around 3% of guests contribute 11% of revenue and 46% of net profit (Bell et al., 2002: 79-80). According to *The Economist* (2013d) the five biggest hotel loyalty schemes claim 198 million members. But are guest loyalty schemes really all that effective? *The Economist's* travel columnist (2013) reported a Deloitte survey of 4000 US frequent travellers which found (http://www.economist.com/blogs/gulliver/2013/01/business-traveller-trends):

- only 8% of frequent travellers routinely stay at the same hotel brand;

- only 14% of frequent travellers routinely fly on the same airline;

- 44% of travellers had two or more loyalty cards – the schemes lacked significance for many travellers with the consequence that rather than ensuring loyalty they encouraged the 'switching' behaviour between brands they were intended to discourage; and

- the main factors in choosing a hotel or airline was value for money with loyalty schemes ranking 20th out of 26 variables for hotels and 19th out of 26 items for airlines.

What are we to make of this? In essence, consumers are a lot more alert to the wiles of marketers than they once were, and further, they are not always, or usually, very loyal. In 2011, *Business Insider* (Bhasin, 2011) reported results of a US survey of the 10 industries with the most loyal customers (see Table 6.3). A notable aspect of these data is that none of the 'top 10' sectors scores more than 50%. In its classic definitions, marketing as a set of disciplinary practices is supposed to enable organizations to meet the needs, wants and desires of customers and service users. As the subject has matured however, so has the suspicion grown that more often than not, the consumers and purchasers of goods and services lack centrality in the marketing planning process, often being reduced to ciphers rather than being seen as active drivers of demand. Put another way, there is less a concern with what consumers want and more a concern with what marketers think they should want – in addition to price competition, this may go some way to explaining the lack of willingness of at least some people to give their undying loyalty to an industry, sector or particular supplier.

Table 6.3   The 10 industries with the most loyal customers (US)

Rank	Industry/Sector	Loyalty index score %
1	Groceries and supermarkets	49
2	Online shopping	47
3	Department, wholesale and speciality stores	46
4	Online search and information	43
5	Car insurance	35
6	Brokerage and investments	35
7	Computer hardware	32
8	Consumer software	31
9	Household insurance	27
10	Mobile phone	19

Source: After Bhasin, 2011.

What Every Guest Wants (or Does Not Want)

Following from the last statement in the previous section, we can observe that one element at the heart of modern management 'philosophy' is the rhetorical emphasis on customer service which in hospitality at least has sometimes become a means of diverting attention from badly conceived and maintained products and services. It is as if the industry says to us 'Yes, our rooms are badly designed, they are cold, a draught blows through the window frames and the shower is not powerful enough – but our service is magnificent' (in fact a not unreasonable description, even today, of many 'grand' European hotels!). Conventional management (and, rather slavishly, most academic) wisdom centres on the suggestion that successful organizations are those that put their customers or clients at the heart of their strategy and thus their marketing approach. Most recently this has taken form in a focus on customer relationship management which avers a somewhat more realistic approach to customer management (Dev et al., 2010; Hermans, 2013). While nobody would suggest that the consumer is perceived as *unimportant* in marketing there are myriad examples from many industries of 'service failure'. As we observed in Chapter 4, if hospitality organizations, and particularly hotels, really listened to their customers all of the time, hotels would not be so badly designed. One of the main topics of research in hospitality marketing/consumer behaviour research is measuring and improving service quality, which has generated a huge literature of doubtfully coherent conclusions as very few of these studies actually address the importance of product and service *design* to quality.

There is never any shortage of advice to operators in the hospitality industry as to what guests want. In addition to the almost innumerable websites allowing direct communication of guests' feelings to hoteliers, airlines and other kinds of service provider, frequent advice is regularly proffered on what guests 'want' in both traditional and electronic media by professional commentators on travel and lifestyle. In addition, from time to time, someone bothers to ask the customers/potential customers about their needs and wants and survey results spring up in various media. Professional commentators, usually journalists of one type or another, generally produce rather more refined lists of wants and do-not-wants. Tyler Brûlé (2010: 35-36) in the male lifestyle magazine *Monocle* lists at least 23 features of 'good' hotels including provision of:

1. their own laundry;
2. guest rooms furnished with solid wood furniture and heated wooden floors;
3. combined lavatory/bidets that allow for the washing of private parts;
4. low and welcoming lighting that changes according to the time of day;
5. a valet locker with a lockable door outside and inside the guest room so that items can be left without interrupting the guest who can access them at their leisure;
6. room service delivered on trays rather than trolleys;
7. a welcome for dogs;
8. a level of service that ensures that guests are always greeted the moment they arrive and never have to use the front desk to check in, being taken directly to their room; and
9. a level of service whereby cleaning staff stop vacuuming as guests walk by and staff do not have casual conversations with each other in front of guests.

If it were not for the humourless earnestness with which these features are proffered one might suspect that the list was intended as some kind of postmodernist joke.

Polizzi (2012) in UK newspaper *The Daily Telegraph* online appears slightly more grounded, listing 10 'pet hates' regarding hotels as follows:

1. tatty hotel frontages;

2. inadequate lighting provision in guest rooms;

3. tipping – Polizzi argues that personnel are paid to perform their tasks and tipping should only be entertained where service has been truly exceptional;

4. generally intrusive service which breaks up guests' conversations, such as being interrupted while eating to be asked by a server if 'everything is all right';

5. the poor quality of hotel coffee;

6. towel art;

7. inadequate hygiene protection in guest rooms;

8. the availability of a bath butler – Polizzi writes: 'a hotel that needs to enhance its guest experience by offering this service cannot be sufficiently honed in the skills … considered the hallmarks of a good or even great hotel: prompt and efficient service, comfortable, clean and well-designed rooms, wonderful food and every attention offered to ensure your stay is just as you had hoped it would be';

9. sheet and pillow menus (provision of which Polizzi sees as pointless gimmicks);

10. children's menus consisting of fried food, pizza and pasta.

Many of the items in Polizzi's list recall much of the discussion on hotel accommodation in Chapter 4. More than this, they suggest that if many of those elements supposedly designed to enhance guest experience are the product of marketing 'intelligence' then, as we noted earlier, there must be some doubt as to the real centrality of customers' 'needs' in this process. At the very least, some of the affectations and weaknesses identified by Polizzi give pause to consider whether hotel owners and operators are really in tune with their guests.

Somewhat unsurprisingly, surveys of hotel guest needs rather less obviously fussy than Polizzi's tend to produce simpler and indeed starker lists. Egencia, the corporate travel arm of the Expedia group of companies, provided familiar data in its 2012 *Business Travel by Business Travellers* report focusing on business travellers within the European Union. The typical traveller was male, aged 31–50, travelling once or twice a month in economy class and working in senior management, sales or technology. When asked what they wished hotels would provide as a standard, 59% wanted mobile/MP3/computer chargers; 50% toothpaste; 44% voltage converters; and 32% slippers. Hotel 'luxuries' in which travellers indulged included the use of hotel swimming pools (40%), use of in-room tea and coffee making facilities (39%) and use of hotel spa and fitness centres (32% and 31% respectively). A later (2014) US survey of business travellers commissioned by Choice Hotels International and reported on ehotelier.com (http://ehotelier.com/hospitality-news/item.php?id=27506_0_11_0_C, last accessed 02.05.14) indicated that 73% of business travellers valued location, 61% room value and

55% free Wi-Fi when selecting a hotel. Some 76% of travellers had made hotel reservations online and just over half had used their in-room fridge and microwave, while 61% used their in-room coffee maker.

Other important aspects of consumer needs and wants relate to gender differences. Gender is a key issue differentiating guest needs in hotels and other hospitality organizations. Mazurkiewicz's (1983) study (noted in the previous chapter) showed how, historically, women have been treated differently by the hotel industry, a treatment reflected in the variety of initiatives from the 1970s onwards introduced to secure female custom, including female executive rooms provided with cosmetic products. Despite the efforts of the hospitality industry to render itself more welcoming to women unaccompanied by men, doubts remain as to how successful these efforts have been. A survey in London reported by Golding (1998: 18) found that lone businesswomen claimed frequently to 'experience leering waiters and patronising managers with more than 70% feeling that service was "secondary" purely because of their gender'. When dining with a male companion 74% of Golding's respondents said waiters assumed the man to be settling the bill and selecting wine. Some 41% claimed to feel uncomfortable dining alone and 62% chose to eat in their rooms, thus avoiding public areas. Eating out is a far from sociable activity for many people. Underhill (2011) suggests that women hotel guests, particularly those travelling alone, expect discretion from hotel employees notably in respect of not having attention drawn to them in public places. Further, he argues, women are more discriminating in their evaluation of the cleanliness and amenities of hotel guest rooms. Numerous other industry surveys available via a simple Google search elaborate these themes and issues (e.g. Harlow, 2014; Williams-Knight, 2014).

Social Media

Before the advent of social media potential hotel customers could obtain some idea of the market position of a hotel by its 'star' rating or some similar classification scheme (in some countries, parallel schemes ran for grading other forms of accommodation, e.g. guest houses and self-catering facilities). Many of these schemes were (and often still are) run by national tourist organizations and membership organizations (e.g. the Automobile Association, AA). In most cases grading schemes were (are) constructed on the basis of the range of facilities offered by an establishment rather than its perceived quality. The biggest challenge to businesses in recent years has been the rise of social networking and similar websites containing customer feedback. In the hotel context the most significant has been TripAdvisor, which offers reviews and ratings of hotels and other accommodation written by users. According to *The Economist* (2013d) TripAdvisor is now worth more than all but two of the big hotel groups and sees guests 'scroll through TripAdvisor's candid camera shots and algorithmic scores as cold-bloodedly as hoteliers design SOPs'.

Some hotel companies have taken heed of these developments and responded to them positively by having general or other senior unit managers reply to both positive and negative reviews. Indeed, several hotel chains include evaluation of TripAdvisor reports and managers' responses to them in the annual human resource appraisal process. There are increasingly numerous sources of advice on how to treat online reviews. Rivera (2013) outlines a number of 'rules' for dealing with social media including:

- do not outsource the response function but employ literate senior personnel within the hotel to do so;

- ensure reviews are discussed widely both within the unit's excom (executive committee) and/or senior management team and with front line staff;

- respond regularly and quickly, especially to negative comments, which should be precisely addressed, with apology;

- to avoid appearing contrived, do not reply to all comments;

- train gatekeeper personnel (front desk; seating station) to solicit positive reviews from satisfied customers as they leave and/or follow up with guests by sending an email and suggesting that they could post comments on preferred websites (the latter is now standard practice with many hotel and restaurant chains and independent hospitality businesses); and

- do not offer compensation for negative reviews.

Just as many hoteliers have adapted quickly and well to social media, many have adapted badly, sometimes crying 'foul play' in suggesting that some negative reviews are placed deliberately by rival competitors. Hickman (2010: 1) reported that around 400 UK establishments were considering a group defamation action against TripAdvisor. The business travel blog of *The Economist* (2010a) newspaper reported that some hotels were using information in TripAdvisor reviews in an effort to seek to identify reviewers and reward – and more sinisterly – perhaps punish them, in the latter case by putting a black mark against their name in the guest database. A later business travel blog in *The Economist* (2011b) reported that hotel company Starwood was encouraging guests to post reviews of its hotels on the company's own website, suggesting efforts to circumvent the impact of TripAdvisor and similar independent sites (see also Lanz et al., 2010). Other hotel and restaurant chains have followed Starwood's lead. More recently, Starwood has begun to feature Instagram on its property websites (see http:// www.marketwatch.com/story/starwood-hotels-resorts-among-the-first-to-feature-instagram-on-all-property-websites-showcasing-the-40000-images-guests-capture-and-share-every-month-2013-12-11, last accessed 19.04.14). Their Aloft brand has featured in the Second Life simulated world website (http://secondlife.com/).

Numerous examples can be easily found reported across multiple sites of cases where hoteliers and restaurateurs have responded robustly to customer reviews, some of which have been picked up by the national press, thus generating thousands of pounds of free publicity (see for example http://www.thebraiser.com/chef-epic-tripadvisor-smackdown/, last accessed 30.04.14, and http://www.tnooz.com/article/georgian-house-hotel-tripadvisor/, last accessed 01.05.14). A more interesting question is whether social media and particularly advisory sites actually matter in the travel, tourism and hospitality fields, in terms of influence. As yet, there is an insufficient quantity of evidence to make a categorical judgement on this issue. The Deloitte survey of 4000 US frequent travellers referred to in the earlier discussion on loyalty found that:

> 63% of respondents did not want to interact with a travel brand via social media and 44% never visited social media and review sites for travel. Additionally, 80% of respondents never downloaded a hotel or airline app to their smartphones. The majority of consumers were still using tried-and-trusted methods to book travel reservations – 61% using hotel and 59% using airline websites most frequently. Most important to consumers was a secure and easy purchase process, email discounts and the latest news. (retrieved from http://www.economist.com/blogs/gulliver/2013/01/business-traveller-trends, last accessed 22.11.14 and http://www.prnewswire.com/news-releases/new-deloitte-survey-uncovers-the-erosion-of-travel-loyalty-187878311.html, last accessed 28.01.15)

The situation described in this quotation reinforces the earlier articulated view that despite the beliefs and practices of marketers, it is the case, as Williams (2002) argues, that those to whom marketing ploys are directed are much more skilled at resisting these blandishments than is often allowed.

Restaurant Segmentation and Branding

In terms of segmentation, restaurants follow a similar pattern to hotels. Once again, a Michelin-starred gastronomic restaurant is not a close substitute for a Burger King, although both serve food and drink. As is often the case with the larger hotel chains, however, within segments the close substitution effect can assert itself so that in quick service/fast food restaurants centred on burger products, Burger King is a close substitute for McDonald's, which is a close substitute for Wendy's. It is even possible that fast food restaurants offering different core food products become close substitutes – thus a burger joint is a close substitute for any of the fast food restaurants that offer chicken products. The key here is what is important to the customer – fast or food?

An incredible success story, branded restaurants – and especially the fast food sector – have become part of the urban landscape. They are, however, relatively little studied. As we noted briefly in Chapter 1 many chain restaurant businesses rely at least to some extent on the principles involved in running a retail rather than hospitality business, albeit an extreme form of retail business. Thus, characteristically, product lines are short; cooking or regeneration techniques are precisely defined and capable of being executed by those other than highly qualified chefs; and wastage rates and wages and salaries are kept low. In this sense chain restaurant businesses differ again from most independently owned and managed restaurants where motivations to engage in the sector may exhibit greater variance. The most successful branded and franchised food and beverage service organizations (think McDonald's and Starbucks) not only exhibit considerable adaptability around their core products but also meet (or are perceived as meeting) quotidian needs. Brand loyalties have developed as a result of highly focused marketing, frequent merchandising and the creation of broadly understood, if not always obviously rational, value systems. Thus, McDonald's is associated with family dining (for which read children) and frequently links up with film companies to produce child-oriented merchandising. At the same time, its reputation, and that of similar companies, for providing 'fast' food at economic prices appeals to many other kinds of custom. Adaptation occurs at a variety of national and regional levels, the Netherlands has the 'McKroket' and in India, where for Hindus the cow is sacred, there is the 'Chicken Maharaja-Mac' (see http://money.howstuffworks.com/10-items-from-mcdonalds-international-menu.htm, last accessed 14.06.14). In respect of coffee shops, Starbucks undoubtedly leads the way but differentiation and dissent tend to centre on professed preferences to particular brews of coffee: some people prefer Starbucks's coffee, others prefer Costa or some other brand. The philosophy of the coffee shop revolution differs slightly to fast food – lingering is often encouraged and in contrast to hotels, few branded coffee chains are without free Wi-Fi for customers.

As we saw in Chapters 1 and 3, branded fast food restaurants have attracted the attention of theorists (McDonaldization) and employment researchers concerned with quality-of-work issues. They have inspired many health campaigners across the world to argue that the culinary offerings purveyed by many chain restaurants are nutritionally deficient and damaging. Despite this, the sector remains a mainstay of the hospitality industry with largely undiminished popularity.

Concluding Remarks

If, as American entrepreneur Edwin Land is alleged to have said, 'Marketing is what you do when your product is no good', then the scope of marketing in some areas of production must almost be limitless. There are tangible measures that can be employed to measure the success or otherwise of marketing campaigns and it is generally agreed that marketing is an indispensable business function. Yet as critics including those from within the marketing discipline have noted for some time, the underlying assumptions of the scientific efficacy of marketing as a set of practices do not bear much close scrutiny in a world in which consumers are both better informed and more sceptical of marketing claims, and in which marketers are required to anticipate and control for the multiple complexities of human behaviour. Some products and services are almost certainly easier to market than others. This said it cannot be automatically assumed that restaurant meals and hotel stays as discretionary goods are more complex to market because the competition is 'stiffer'. Indeed, as we have seen in the case of the hospitality industry at various points in this book, the principle of close substitution when combined with increasing standardization of products and services and the lack of loyalty to brands demonstrated by customers suggest that the complexities of hospitality marketing arise from a different set of factors altogether, a set of factors which may allow effective segmentation at some levels, but not at others; and a set of factors which need to pay attention to consumer scepticism and a lack of willingness to 'fall in' with the more obvious strategies employed by marketers.

Further Reading

Bowen, J (2008) 'Marketing and consumer behaviour in hospitality', in B Brotherton and R C Wood (Eds) *The Sage Handbook of Hospitality Management*, London: Sage, 302–315.

Dev, C, Buschman, J D and Bowen, J T (2010) 'Hospitality marketing: a retrospective analysis (1960–2010) and predictions (2010–2020)', *Cornell Hospitality Quarterly*, 51, 4: 459–469.

Fitzhugh, K and Piercy, N (2010) 'Improving the relationship between sales and marketing', *European Business Review*, 22, 3: 287–305.

Lanz, L, Fischhof, B and Lee, R (2010) *How are Hotels Embracing Social Media in 2010?*, Mineola, NY: HVS, retrieved from http://www.hvs.com/staticcontent/library/nyu2010/Journal/articles/SocialMediaIn2010.pdf, last accessed 19.04.14.

7

CAN I SPEAK TO WHOEVER'S IN CHARGE? THE ROLE OF MANAGEMENT IN HOSPITALITY

After reading this chapter, you should:

(a) understand the kind of research that has been conducted into the nature and functions of management in the hospitality industry;

(b) comprehend the significance of the particular content of managerial roles in hospitality including reasons for general variations in the career trajectories of male and female managers; and

(c) have gained insight into the nature of managerial rewards in the sector.

Introduction

> Myths abound in management, for example that senior managers sit on 'top' (of what?), that leaders are more important than managers (try leading without managing), and that people are human resources (I am a human being). (Mintzberg, 2012: 4)

Despite over a century of research generating many useful insights (and a lot of flannel) we are no closer to obtaining definitive answers as to what is 'good' management. One might argue, following that luminary of management theory Henry Mintzberg (2004), that the proper subject of 'management' is what managers do, what they think, how they operate. In this chapter we will review what is known from research studies about management (touching briefly also on leadership) in the hospitality industry. The chapter concludes with a brief consideration of managerial salaries, employing the UK as a case, and a short reflection on the status of hospitality managers.

Becoming and Being a Manager in Hospitality

Most research on managerial work in the hospitality industry focuses on *hotel management* roles (Wood, 1994b). People come to hotel management careers via three principal routes (Baum, 1989): formal hotel school training; training for management within the industry after starting either in craft positions or being given a traineeship; and via an early career in another industry followed by late entry into the hotel industry. Those who commit themselves to a hotel and catering career early on rarely leave the industry. Baum (1989) found that two-thirds of his sample of Irish hotel managers had no working experience outside the hotel industry, a trend confirmed by Guerrier (1987) in the context of British hotel managers. Ladkin (2002: 386) found a high degree of managerial mobility within the Australian hotel industry, but little mobility out of and back into the industry: 75.6% of respondents had never worked in a different industry, against 24.4% who had.

Most senior hotel managers obtain their appointments at a relatively early age (Commission on Industrial Relations, 1971). Formal qualifications do not seem to affect either position on entry or promotion prospects and career patterns (Guerrier, 1987; Baum, 1989). In their study of UK managers, Riley and Turam (1988) argue that vocational education and time spent working in the industry gaining experience are alternative uses of time that make little difference to long-term prospects. Harper et al. (2005: 55–56) in a study of Scottish hotels of over 50 rooms found that:

> Managers without a formal qualification, on average reached their first position as hotel general manager at the age of 28 years and one month, marginally sooner than their qualified counterparts, who were 29 years and four months. Excluding time spent at college/university the qualified manager took a mean nine years and two months to reach a general management position, with the actual times ranging from five to 18 years. The unqualified manager by comparison took an average 11 years and ten months to reach the same position with the actual times taken ranging from seven to 21 years.

These authors further found that one-third of their sample disagreed or strongly disagreed with the view that formal qualifications were integral to a manager's career development in hospitality with only 57% of older managers (over 35 years old) agreeing with this statement compared to 72% of younger managers. In her sample of Australian general managers, Ladkin (2002: 383) found that some 52% of respondents were without a vocational education, a factor she attributes to the relative youth of vocational hospitality education in Australia when compared to Europe.

Positional and unit mobility is a crucial factor in the development of a junior manager and can be similarly important once the position of general manager has been achieved. The first part of a manager's career is likely to find him or her in a very junior position. In the UK, Guerrier (1987) found that assistant managers gained seniority usually by acquiring functional responsibility for a department, often in what would be called today the rooms division, and in food and beverage. As we have previously noted, experience in both (but especially the latter) has traditionally been seen as necessary to advancement. In her Australian study, Ladkin (2002: 385; see also Ladkin and Juwaheer, 2000) found that 40.9% of her general manager sample had prior experience in food and beverage and some 22% in front office; a very low number had prior experience in housekeeping, accounting, human resource management and marketing. Managers' experience is gained through multiple positions, often in numerous units. More specifically, junior managers move frequently between hotels, 'collecting' experience of both specific functions and different types of hotel. Both Guerrier (1987) and Riley and Turam (1988) found mobility a crucial feature of management career development and this appears to be true of the USA as well (Nebel et al., 1994). In Riley and Turam's (1988) study, some 43% of career moves examined involved a change of company, with the change to hotel (general) manager involving a change of company in 41% of cases.

The attainment of the general manager (GM) position in a hotel rarely means an end to mobility. Guerrier (1987) found that the average age of attaining a general manager position was 30, but this was often to a smaller hotel within the company – the pattern to promotions seems to be appointment to a small unit and subsequently – to use Guerrier's naval metaphor – to larger and more prestigious ships in the line. Harper et al. (2005) identified 29 as the average age at which Scottish general managers assumed their first role and Peacock (2012) reports that in the Malmaison and Hotel du Vin group of hotels, 75% of managers are under 35. In many countries, however, more conservative standards seem to operate in respect of the suitable age for promotion to general manager. Birdir (2002) in a study of Turkish hotels found the average age of general managers to be 42, with 33 as the average age of their first managerial role.

It is therefore unsurprising that many managers change company to gain a unit manager's post since mobility offers opportunities to 'short circuit' traditional patterns of promotion. Stalcup and Pearson (2001: 17) note that during the 1980s and 1990s lodging industry managerial turnover was estimated in the US to be as high as 46%. In their own study, these authors found that the greatest stimulus to turnover was career and financial advancement (Stalcup and Pearson, 2001: 23). Veller (2007) with a sample size of 60 global hotel general managers found that from a first entry level position to general manager took on average 14.75 years in North America, 15.8 years in Europe, and 16.5 years in Asia. Persons entering as management trainees took 14.8 years on average to become a GM, with the figures of 15.3 and 16.5 applying to rooms division and food and beverage respectively. The majority of GMs had entry level positions in food and beverage (40%) but this was more pronounced among Europeans whereas in America the rooms division route was a more sure way to a general manager post. Ladkin and Riley (1996) found the average number of years taken to attain a GM role in the UK was 12.2 and in a later study Ladkin (2002: 383) found that the figure for Australian hotel general managers was 12.6 years.

What do hospitality managers do?

It has long been recognized that hospitality managers have substantial freedom in the running of their units. Nailon (1968) found that British hotel managers engaged in a much larger number of activities than counterparts in other industries, spending considerable time in direct supervision of staff, contact with customers and continuous monitoring of their unit through brief contacts with personnel and regular movement about the establishment. Fifteen years later, the UK Education and Training Advisory Council (1983) found that over half the managers in their sample were frequently or sometimes involved in these activities as well as, at times, food preparation, cooking and service. The discretion granted to managers in the control of their units may be moderated by a number of factors. Pickworth and Fletcher (1980) found that restaurant food service managers in medium sized companies had more discretion than managers of smaller and larger companies but this latitude for control was heavily operational in nature. Managers enjoyed most discretion in the area of determining staffing requirements and had considerable autonomy to allow complimentary meals and the establishment of inventory levels.

There is a strong tradition in hospitality – hotels in particular – of senior managers being action oriented in their management practice that is, physically mobile within their unit and, to marshal two clichés, 'hands on' and 'walking the talk'. The roots of this approach lie in the Germanic or Swiss-Germanic notion of 'mein host' in which the proprietor or manager of a hotel or restaurant is always visibly in evidence and engaged in greeting and meeting guests. Guerrier and Lockwood (1989: 84) note that:

> The traditions of hotel management emphasise the hotel manager as the person who is always around to greet guests as they arrive. The Victorian hotelier was almost like a host welcoming a guest into his own home ... the 'greeting' and 'being there' aspects of the role remain important.

Such traditions still persist. Cullen and McLaughlin (2006: 514) found that hotel managers are highly conscious that they are perceived as the public face of the hotel and that they offer 'brand value' in being continually present. Guerrier and Lockwood (1989: 85) found that managers expressed a preference for active management and disliked the 'sitting behind a desk' aspects of their job and doing paperwork. They write that managers:

> saw their jobs very clearly in terms of being out and about in the hotel. This very often involved working long hours - an average of 12-14 hours a day was not seen as unusual and with very few and irregular days off, if any. Rather than seeing this as a potential source of dissatisfaction, they saw it more as perfectly normal for the industry.

Similarly, Worsfold (1989: 150) quotes a respondent to the effect that:

> It's pointless the general manager sitting behind his desk all day, he needs to be out and about encouraging his staff. … If he's going to be stuck in an office all day then he's going to be away from that team and not know what's going on in his hotel.

More recently, Waryszak and King (2001) found that managers least enjoyed desk work so the peripatetic 'being there' (now normally labelled as 'presenteeism') culture of managers in hotels is fortuitously self-serving. Despite, as Baum (1989) notes, there being little evidence to show that 'being there' styles of management are costed relative to the benefits which may accrue from them, getting involved in basic operative work – even if this involves encouraging managers to be 'downwardly mobile' in their activities – tends to invite the respect rather than disapprobation of peers and other employees (Guerrier, 1987; Guerrier and Lockwood, 1989). Guerrier and Lockwood (1989: 86) further note that:

> Having sorted out the immediate problem … the manager does not pause to analyse the problem but passes on to the next operational crisis. The hotel culture sees this activity based behaviour as the 'right way' and will reward it with praise and career progression, so passing the approach higher up the organization.

'Being there' styles of management encourage the use of informal communication between management and operatives and a paternalistic and authoritarian (or at least directive) approach to staff. In Guerrier and Lockwood's (1989) study managers saw the development and care of their staff as a central part of their role whereas staff saw management as being rather critical, autocratic and controlling. Cullen and McLaughlin (2006: 514) found that hotel managers believed they had a clear duty to provide emotional support for their staff with some of their respondents estimating that they spent up to 40% of their time 'counselling' staff members, despite not being trained to do this. Interestingly, the 'being there' culture that prevails in hotels and other hospitality organizations is not necessarily what corporate level management *believes* is going on in a company's units. Hales and Nightingale (1986: 9) found that:

> Senior/head office staff expectations of unit managers seem to be predominantly focused on tasks, rather than activities, upon what the unit manager should achieve rather than what he should actually do … and reflect a concern for broad organisational objectives in the areas of standards, customers, staffing and finance.

Further, Umbreit (1986: 56) observes:

> Traditionally, the hotel industry has had a strong operational orientation with concern primarily focused on short-term results. Hotel managers have been

evaluated on profitability measures and control of expenses. Additional criteria, if any, have included a list of key traits not necessarily related to job performance.

In a subsequent study, Umbreit and Eder (1987) developed a list of 14 performance measures which managers themselves felt they ought to be assessed against (see Figure 7.1). Magnini and Honeycutt (2003: 268) writing some 15 years later on the topic of expatriate managers observe that:

> Numerous indicators of a manager's technical competence exist in the hotel industry. A proven track record of maximizing revenue per available room (REVPAR), exceeding budgeted P&L goals, and achieving favourable guest satisfaction scores are recognized measures of technical competence.

- Guest comments on product experience cards
- Market share attained – the percentage of room nights achieved by a hotel relative to the total available in the market
- Room nights sold in a given period
- Reduction of labour turnover in a given period compared to a previous period
- Budget control – the extent to which budgets are achieved and income and expenditure reconciled
- Food and beverage profit attainment
- Rooms profit attainment
- Employee complaints and grievances – the extent to which these are reduced in a given period relative to a previous period
- Training attainments of employees – the number of employees achieving completion of training courses in a given period
- Collection of receivables
- Number of leadership positions held in the wider community by the manager
- Hotel ratings – by independent organizations
- Health and safety record, i.e. reduction of accidents in a period relative to earlier periods
- Adherence to productivity standards by employees

Figure 7.1 Performance measures against which hotel managers believe they should be measured

Source: Umbreit and Eder, 1987.

Many studies of what hospitality managers do have been conducted using the 10 managerial role categories identified by Mintzberg: figurehead, leader, liaison, monitor, disseminator, spokesperson, entrepreneur, disturbance handler, resource allocator and negotiator (for readers unfamiliar with Mintzberg's work, see Chareanpunsirikul and Wood (2002) for a brief summary in the context of hospitality management). Their findings again point to the reactive nature of managers in hospitality services. Ferguson and Berger (1984: 30) observed nine restaurant managers using a modified version of Mintzberg's schema and found that they spent an enormous amount of time on a variety of contacts – telephone calls (13%), unscheduled (35%) and scheduled (29%) meetings, and 'tour' meetings (those initiated as a result of touring the unit) (6%). For each hour of a normal working day, there were, on average, 10 of these contacts. Desk sessions accounted for 17% of the restaurant managers' time. We can conclude this discussion by citing Ferguson and Berger's (1984: 30) comment that pithily captures the nature of much hospitality managerial work:

> Mintzberg described executives' activities as brief, fragmented, and reactive. The restaurant operators' activities in this study seem even further from the textbook description of a planner, organizer, coordinator, and controller than did those in the Mintzberg sample. Planning seems to have been eclipsed by reacting; organizing might be better described as simply carrying on; coordinating appears more like juggling; and controlling seems reduced to full-time watching.

In concluding this section of the discussion we can note how the factors considered reflect the operational imperatives of managerial roles in hospitality, indeed how the very nature of hotel management work is confined within an operational framework to the apparent extent of precluding measures of managerial performance based on creative general contribution and future potential.

A note on leadership

The quest to find the 'secrets' of leadership is a defining feature of a century-plus of management research. Put crudely management plus 'x' equals leadership. The problem is that there are, as one would expect given human variability, many different forms of 'x' most largely dependent on context. It is not even clear why leadership is important – or indeed if it is important. Robbins (1992: 151-152) makes the point that:

> Leadership may not always be important. Data from numerous studies collectively demonstrate that, in many situations, whatever behaviours leaders exhibit are irrelevant. Certain individual, job, and organizational variables can act as substitutes for leadership, negating the formal leader's ability to exert either positive or negative influence over subordinate attitudes and effectiveness.

Common in contemporary approaches to the study of leadership is the desire to have one's cake and eat it. Thus leadership often appears as both a process and a property (Moorhead and Griffin, 1989: 322). As a process, leadership involves the use of non-coercive influence to direct and coordinate people. As a property, it is a quality attributed to those who appear able to exert this influence successfully. The key phrase here is 'non-coercive' for most popular definitions of leadership emphasize that leaders are able to inspire others to 'follow' them without resorting to the formal structures of authority attendant on the role of manager. From this are derived the familiarly aphoristic views that a manager is not always a leader, and that leaders are defined to some extent by the presence of followers.

Those interested in the current status of leadership research in the hospitality industry could do worse than consult Boyne's (2010) masterly review but they should expect to be disappointed. Leadership research in hospitality is neither extensive nor systematic and the findings of studies frequently differ. We can illustrate these differences in the context of two studies utilizing Mintzberg's managerial roles. In a small-scale study of seven American managers of a single company, Ley (1980) observed the work of management personnel and classified their activities according to Mintzberg's schema. Following from this, the ratings of managers' effectiveness as perceived by corporate superiors were obtained. Two managers were graded highly effective, three effective and two less effective. The grades were then compared to the role ratings. Ley argues that the highly effective managers allocated *less* time to the leadership role than the two less effective managers, and more time on entrepreneurial activities than managers with lower effectiveness ratings. In a much larger study of American general managers, Arnaldo (1981) secured 194 responses involving self-classification of activities according to Mintzberg's model and a note of the time spent on each plus a rating of the importance of individual roles. No corporate ratings of effectiveness were available here but it is worth noting that in terms of time allocated, the most important roles were leader, disseminator and monitor while in terms of importance they were leader, entrepreneur and monitor.

In contrasting the findings of the two studies, we can observe, first, that in Ley's study there is the hint of a suggestion that an 'objective' or at least external, assessment of the roles performed by managers leads to an outcome suggestive of superiors attaching value to roles other than leadership. Secondly, where managers self-classified the various managerial roles as in Arnaldo's research, then leadership was viewed as the most important role and was the role managers most spent time on. This possibly suggests that managers believe they are, or should be seen (by superiors and others) to be operating in the leadership role. A third point here is that Mintzberg's model of managerial roles depicts leadership as one component of a broad skill-practice set. This is perhaps ill-suited to modern times where an almost obsessive preoccupation with the 'need' for leadership detracts from other desirable qualities. Arnaldo's managers seem in keeping with this *zeitgeist* – so possibly were Ley's, we shall never know, but the researcher's intervention in employing his own judgement as to the roles performed and comparing them to third party performance ratings challenges reliance upon subjective managerial assessments as to the nature of their work.

In these two simple studies we can observe some of the difficulties involved in assessing the nature and quality of leadership. If there is something we can call 'leadership', is it a skill or some other kind of quality? How do we judge when leadership is 'present', as opposed to effective management – and more importantly, who makes these judgements? Contemporary obsessing over the need for leadership has, as Eric McNulty (2013: 17), Director of Research of the US National Preparedness Leadership Initiative, observes, led to 'a proliferation of leader labels and a gutting of the understanding of what it actually means to be a leader'. An instance of this phenomenon might be the term 'thought leader', a concept suggestive of monumental immodesty, often self-evidently inaccurate and normally applied to 'motivational' speakers of one kind or another. McNulty (2013: 18) is firmly in the Mintzberg camp seeing management and leadership as complementary skills, leadership being differentiated from management by the clear presence of followers. To this we can add that while we remain uncertain of the value of leadership, we should not exaggerate its importance among the wider repertoire of management skills.

Women Managers

Women managers in hospitality have attracted research attention not least because higher education courses in hospitality have attracted a greater proportion of women than men yet few women make it to senior management positions in the industry. As long ago as the 1990s Brownell (1994: 112) noted that although just as many women graduate from hospitality management programmes as men, they leave the industry at up to three times the rate of their male counterparts. Walmsley (2011: 36) reports that some 67.5% of UK hospitality students are female compared to 57% in the total UK student population. Yet, the number of female general managers (or women holding more senior corporate roles) in hospitality remains much smaller than would be suggested by the number of women graduating from college each year and entering the industry. Walker (2011) states that only 12% of UK company directorships are held by women, dropping to 6% in the hospitality sector. Research into the role of women hotel managers suggests that the relative absence of females from general manager positions is a global phenomenon (see, for example, Li and Wang Leung, 2001; Ng and Pine, 2003; Kattara, 2005).

It has long been established that gender differences in rearing and education orient girls to careers which involve an extension of male-defined roles for women – usually entailing caring and nurturing. Similarly, general reasons that explain the lack of progress of women in business apply to the hospitality sector (see Brownell, 2013, for a recent short summary). These are:

1. the 'channelling' of women away from roles, positions and career paths that would facilitate progress to senior positions;

2. explicit and implicit discrimination against women, both from male co-workers and as institutionalized within the organization in the form of, *inter alia*, inhospitable corporate culture; social exclusion from informal power and communication networks; lack of mentoring; and lack of appropriately planned career development; and

3. women's own attitudes, aspirations, career decisions and experiences relative to traditional career paths to general management in hospitality.

Before briefly examining each of the above in turn, we consider the role of women managers in hospitality.

What do women managers manage?

Research into what women managers do in hospitality is very clear in its implications. In the commercial sector, women managers tend not to be found in operations departments from which the route to general manager and other senior positions is most easily accessed. The exception to this is housekeeping, which despite its operational nature is, in western countries at least, more defined by the fact that it is viewed as a 'women's department' (see Guerrier, 1986). Otherwise women tend to be found in lower status 'support' departments, e.g. sales and marketing (Hackett, 1981; Hotel and Catering Industry Training Board, 1984; Guerrier, 1986). Purcell (1993: 131-136) reported research showing women comprised 94% of house-keepers; Walker (2011) found 95% of UK housekeepers were women, 61% were personnel and training managers, 18% general managers and 5% food and beverage managers. This last statistic is significant for as we have noted on multiple occasions, mobility and experience of food and beverage and accommodation/front of house management are necessary in order to achieve general manager positions.

Channelling

A range of factors contribute to the occupational and hierarchical segmentation of women managers in the hospitality industry. 'Channelling' is a difficult phenomenon to define not least because the forces behind it are often hazy and informal and part of a wider network of socially discriminating values and practices. A UK Hotel and Catering Industry Training Board (HCITB) (1984) report found that the majority of women on hotel and catering management courses expressed considerable interest in a career in operational management but were relatively rarely offered opportunities for this kind of training by their employer. Indeed, some women managers received no training at all and those that did, had done so in sales, marketing and personnel. This is suggestive of direct interventions by organizations to focus women into support roles. We should not be surprised by this – disgusted, but not surprised. Even in the twenty-first century it is still common to hear male educators and male hospitality managers rehearsing the hoary old platitude that there is little point in putting women into operational roles because eventually they will leave, get married and have children. The same HCITB report noted that both male and female students had similar aspirations concerning the post they would hold five years after leaving college, but women had lower expectations of their employment prospects upon graduation – which for the most part appear to have been realized. Formal channelling may also be present before women select their university course of study. Guerrier (1986) noted that many women chose to study hospitality management because it represented a resolution of pressures in the form of interest in management with interest in the traditionally female field of domestic science and cookery. Guerrier argues that women are misled in their career choices and not told of the extent of either the general or industry-specific discrimination they will face. When the extent of discrimination and lack of opportunity *is* discovered, many withdraw from hospitality employment altogether or limit their aspirations, resigning themselves to lower levels of achievement.

A related 'channelling' phenomenon concerns the conventional role of hotel manager which, as Guerrier (1986) observes, is carried out in a semi-social setting, often leading to promotion decisions being affected by what she calls 'extrafunctional variables', primarily, sex, race and education. For women, jobs where contact with the public is involved may be particularly problematic as: (a) male managers and clients expect women to be attractive, servile and compliant with the demands of men and (b) it is often antithetical to the strategy adopted by token women in organizations which is to become socially invisible. In the case of the first, women thus have to contend with the twin difficulties of sexism and maintaining their authority. In the case of the second, the consequences can be more severe in that women managers will forgo a more high profile career accepting low profile jobs and promotions in order to maintain their invisibility. Guerrier (1986: 235) captures this when she writes: 'Hotel companies may prefer men to women in certain management jobs because of their greater acceptability to (predominantly male) clients, as they might prefer an older man to a younger man. And a woman who is appointed to the job of hotel manager may find it harder than a man to acquire the status and credibility she needs with clients.'

Discriminating forces

The sources of direct and indirect discrimination against women in the workplace are, generally, and in the case of hospitality, numerous. Brownell (1993) surveyed 374 US women middle managers and found that they ranked 'old boy networks' as the most serious obstacle to their professional development followed by a lack of women mentors and role models, and then by quality-of-working-life issues. These often informal networks are major sources of discriminatory behaviour. Guerrier (1986) notes that career moves within the industry tend to be handled informally and managers higher in the organization may sponsor individual mobility. Since the majority of managers are men they tend to sponsor men in preference to women, with the result that women do not acquire the mobility deemed necessary for the attainment of senior positions.

For those women who wish to raise children, the relative absence of affordable and otherwise satisfactory childcare facilities is an important source of discrimination. In the commercial hospitality industry where mobility can be important in reaching senior management positions, removing oneself, however temporarily, from the workforce can be a source of missed opportunities. Necessary consideration of the needs of partners and children can be career inhibiting. Regular uprooting and relocation is not always possible, let alone conducive to a satisfactory personal life. Many surveys over the years have found that women senior managers in hospitality are, in the majority, single and/or childless. Brownell (1994: 112) noted from her own research of a sample of hospitality organizations that one-third of women general managers were single compared to only 7% of men (see additionally HCITB, 1984).

Attitudes and aspirations of women

However cautiously one approaches discussions of the role of women's attitudes and aspirations in and beyond the workplace it is necessary to guard against the phenomenon of victim blaming as this diverts attention from sexist and other discriminatory behaviour of the kind described above. Nevertheless, it is reasonably clear that in response to the behaviours they encounter, many women managers in hospitality modify their attitudes and aspirations, lower their career advancement expectations and settle for roles more favourable to work–life balance. Underlying such adaptations, however, is evidence of the damage that discriminatory behaviour – whether experienced prior to or while working in the hospitality industry – can cause. The HCITB (1984) study cited earlier administered attitudinal tests to its women respondents and found that many shared male stereotypical views as to the nature of women as lacking in confidence to push themselves, insufficiently ambitious, more influenced by their emotions (which affected their behaviour as managers), less worthy as employees because of their physiological capacity for child-bearing and not aggressive or competitive enough.

A study by Boone et al. (2013: 12) examined senior male and female global hospitality executives and (somewhat peculiarly) argued that 'a shift has occurred in that the barriers to women's advancement are more *self-imposed* and largely involve choices they make about family and household.' This is peculiar because, as we have tried to show, this is a long-established phenomenon. Indeed, the authors' own data largely resonate with other evidence considered here. Only 7.3% of men had never been married compared to 17.8% of women (12% in the total sample). Some 76.4% of male respondents had never been divorced compared to 42.2% (61% in the whole sample). More importantly, Boone et al. (2013: 6) note that in regard to childcare arrangements: 'male executives rely more heavily on their spouses, while the female executives rely more heavily upon school or day care and extended family.' The Boone et al. (2013) study makes many positive suggestions about how organizations can be better structured to facilitate female careers while, however, not exploring very much the reasons behind women's 'self-imposition' of limitations to career advancement.

A Note on Managerial Salaries

We saw in Chapter 3 that, allowing for cultural variations, pay and other rewards in the hospitality industry usually compare unfavourably to those in other industries. Superficially at least, the same is true of managerial salaries, at least in the UK. In 1994, independent evidence suggested that an average management salary for those in the hospitality industry was £15,103 but around 58% of all managers earned less than this (NTC/Bacon and Woodrow, 1995). McBride (2012: 19) reports his company's 2011 general-industries salary and benefits data and comments that 'the perception of the hospitality industry as being low-waged as a whole has some substance'. He notes that median rates for corporate and management roles in the general labour market compared to the hospitality sector reveal that median rates in hospitality were lower than national rates in 57% of roles and higher in only 30%.

More recently Peacock (2012) cites a spokesperson for the Malmaison and Hotel du Vin group of hotels as quoting GM salaries of between £70,000 and £100,000 but the Berkeley Scott (2013) *Hospitality and Leisure Salary Survey 2013* (http://www.berkeley-scott.co.uk/2013-hospitality-and-leisure-salary-survey, last accessed 03.04.13) suggests that these are possibly exceptional. The survey found that:

- For 19 out of 21 roles examined in England, salaries in London were higher than elsewhere.

- Hotel general managers averaged £85,000 in London, £60,000 in the southwest and southeast and £58,000 in the Midlands and north.

- Hotel food and beverage managers averaged £38,000 in London, £27,000 in the southeast, £24,000 in the southwest and £24,000 in the Midlands and north.

- Hotel head housekeepers averaged £35,000 in London, £25,000 in the southeast and £23,000 in the southwest, Midlands and north.

- Hotel executive chefs averaged £50,000 in London, £39,500 in the southeast and Midlands, £35,000 in the southwest and £35,500 in the north.

Table 7.1 Speculative comparison of hospitality managerial job categories analysed by Berkeley Scott compared to median gross annual earnings as determined by the Office for National Statistics

| | Number/percentage of Berkeley Scott job categories in England with average annual salary falling below the national average of £26,500 | | | |
| | Hotels (no. of job categories = 21) | | Restaurants (no. of job categories = 13) | |
Region	Number	Percentage	Number	Percentage
London	7	33	7	54
Southeast	16	76	8	62
Southwest	17	81	8	62
Midlands	16	76	8	62
North	16	76	8	62

Berkeley Scott note that in the restaurant sector, branded restaurants tended to offer salaries towards the lower end of the ranges observed.

According to the Office for National Statistics (2012): 'For the year ending 5 April 2012 median gross annual earnings for full-time employees (who had been in the same job for at least 12 months, including those whose pay was affected by absence) were £26,500, an increase of 1.4% from the previous year.' Although not directly comparable (the Berkeley Scott data pertain to the first quarter of 2013) of the 21 job categories reviewed for the five areas examined the number in each which fall below the national average salary is as shown in Table 7.1.

Concluding Remarks

Given the expectations of hotel managers in terms of the time spent *in situ* on the job and other pressures which they routinely face, the reward situation does not appear that favourable. However, the good news (that appears to hold true inter-nationally) is that upon reaching the rank of unit general manager the rewards often exceed those of managers in many other industries. That in many countries GM positions can be attained at a relatively youthful age means that those who can survive several years of the kind of work described earlier can look forward to generous rewards – and generous responsibilities! Far less positive is the observation noted earlier by Riley and Turam (1988) and others that vocational education and time spent working in the industry gaining experience are alternative uses of time that make little difference to long-term career prospects. This raises the question of why anyone would want to study hospitality management at college. While much more categorical information is required as to the (financial) benefits of formal qualifications in the field, there is more than a suggestion in some research that the possession of qualifications makes little difference to earnings. For example, Bañuls and Ramón Rodríguez (2005: 128-129) write: 'Returns on education in the tour-ism sector are lower than in other service sectors in Spain. This lower valuation of the workers' level of education in the tourism sector contrasts with the results obtained from other studies of all Spanish workers, which demonstrate that the elas-ticity of the general education–earnings ratio is double that of the Spanish tourism sector.' (Thrane, 2010, offers a somewhat contrary view.) Also pertaining to Spain, Marchante et al. (2007) found no evidence that 'overeducated' workers gained better jobs from their initial entry position and inferred that many were therefore 'trapped' leading *inter alia* to moves to other sectors. A recent report for the UK Council for Hospitality Management Education (CHME) by Walmsley (2011: 36) showed that six months after graduating, hospitality students were as likely to be in graduate as non-graduate level employment although for those in small or medium sized enter-prises there was a greater probability of them being in graduate level employment. In some senses this is unsurprising but it does raise questions about why expensively trained graduates in the *corporate* sector are not immediately engaged in graduate level employment (see Chapter 8).

Managerial work in the hospitality industry is demanding, requires multiple skills and abilities and at the most senior levels is usually well rewarded. As with many graduates of business and management studies courses, hospitality graduates will (if they are reasonably lucky) find themselves initially in a series of specialized or semi-specialized roles but upon attaining a general manager position will be called upon to practise a very wide range of skills whereas the majority of their business management graduate counterparts will continue in relatively narrow and specialized areas. In this respect, relatively high levels of reward are justified, as the business and moral responsibilities of hospitality unit managers are extensive. That the number of available general manager positions is relatively small goes some way to explaining the 'survival of the fittest' atmosphere that permeates, in particular, the hotel sector and inevitably contributes to driving good managers out of the industry at early stages in their career thus reducing the size and quality of the talent pool available from which to draw these senior appointments. As with so much in the sector, imminent change in the near future seems a distant prospect.

Further Reading

Brownell, J (2013) 'Women, gender and hospitality employment', in R C Wood (Ed) *Key Concepts in Hospitality Management*, London: Sage, 157–162.

Guerrier, Y (1986) 'Hotel manager: an unsuitable job for a woman?', *The Service Industries Journal*, 6, 2: 227–240.

Ladkin, A (2002) 'Career analysis: a case study of hotel general managers in Australia', *Tourism Management*, 23, 4: 379–388.

Pizam, A and Shani, A (2009) 'The nature of the hospitality industry: present and future managers' perspectives', *Anatolia – An International Journal of Tourism and Hospitality Research*, 20, 1: 134–150.

8

SO YOU GIVE DEGREES TO WAITERS? HOSPITALITY MANAGEMENT EDUCATION

After reading this chapter, you should:

(a) understand in outline the history of higher hospitality education and the relevance of such understanding to other themes in this book;

(b) have gained insight into the nature of the relationships that continue to exist between higher hospitality education and the hospitality industry; and

(c) comprehend at a basic level the nature of, and potential for, variation between countries in the provision of higher hospitality education and in relationships with the hospitality industry.

Introduction

'Tell the truth' was a common response from colleagues in the hospitality industry when they learned this book was in preparation. The 'truth' in question was that a hospitality business is just that – a business – and its main function – and by extension the main function of managers – is to make money. While this assertion may be 'true' it is not necessarily the whole truth: as we have previously noted, there are many instances of hospitality services being provided at cost, or not-for-profit, as in certain hospitals and schools. Indeed, saying that the purpose of a business is to make money does appear to be taking statements of the obvious to extremes. There is a wider point here though, and it is that a great part of the curriculum in advanced hospitality management courses emphasizes the 'people aspects' of the sector – employment, guest satisfaction, customer relationship management and so on. One industry colleague, a vice president with an international branded hotel company who understandably wished to remain anonymous, told me:

There is still a tendency for hotel schools to push the touchy-feely aspects of the industry to the exclusion of teaching how to make money. Finance teaching in hotel schools is dreadful. We are not part of the tourism or heritage industry or some quaint afternoon cream tea outfit. Sure, customer and guest satisfaction is important ... it's rhetoric ... but for hotels the customer's satisfaction is much less significant than their ability and willingness to pay – and on time!

This has the appearance of an extreme view but it is echoed elsewhere. The industry analyst Slattery (2002: 21) notes that: 'It is inaccurate and misleading to assume that in the hospitality business the critical relationship is between host and guest. Hotels, restaurants, bars and the other hospitality venues are businesses where the critical relationship is between sellers and buyers. The buyers are not guests, they are customers. The relationship is not philanthropic it is economic.'

In this chapter, we examine certain aspects of higher hospitality management education. To include discussion of education in a textbook is somewhat unusual. Educators are always a little wary of having education exposed to the scrutiny of those they teach. However, in many societies, education is at the heart of multiple ideological and political struggles. In countries where education is becoming more market driven (e.g. the UK) and students are required to contribute significantly to the cost of that education, the question of the extent to which higher education can and should be accountable to students, their parents and wider society is both legitimate and relevant. There are also specific reasons why the study of higher hospitality management education is important. Hospitality educators have always trumpeted their closeness to the industry and consistently stressed the industry 'relevance' of their education programmes. In (frequent) contrast to this, industry figures complain of the lack of relevance of educational curricula. An examination of this tension reveals much about the origins and nature of many of the management practices that we have encountered in previous chapters. Similarly, understanding the history of higher hospitality education – how it has evolved – informs our understanding of how hospitality has been viewed more widely within the higher education system.

A Brief History of Hospitality Education

There can be no reasonably well attuned hospitality academic who has not encountered the astonishment of the uninitiated in comments of the 'You teach students to be waiters – in a university?' kind. (Brotherton and Wood, 2008a: 10-11)

As one of the few growth areas of the UK economy, it is ironic, therefore that those who work in restaurants still garner little respect. How many parents want their children to become chefs? Some, maybe. Restaurant or catering managers? Perhaps. Serving staff? Not likely. (Harris, 2012a: 30)

Sociologically speaking, snobbery is a little-researched phenomenon yet as Brotherton and Wood's comment above suggests, higher hospitality education faces its fair share of the phenomenon, not least from within the system of which it is a part (if an eminent academic sociologist can describe low-paid employment in hospitality and other sectors as 'McJobs' – see Chapter 3 – without being overly criticized, then this should not come as a surprise). Although the quality of this snobbery varies considerably in the Anglosphere (and elsewhere) the historical association of hospitality with (domestic) service, servants, servility and servitude persists, as hinted at in the above quotation from Harris. Though the existence of snobbery is difficult to document empirically (and, of course, equally difficult to refute), it is a phenomenon to which we should remain alert (see Wood, 2014).

In 2000, England's then Chief Inspector of Schools Chris Woodhead criticized 'vacuous' university courses that he identified as including, *inter alia*, golf course management (http://news.bbc.co.uk/1/hi/education/878600.stm, last accessed 05.04.13). In 2003, the then UK government minister responsible for the higher education sector made similar remarks (http://news.bbc.co.uk/1/hi/education/2655127.stm, last accessed 08.05.14). In 2007, a UK organization called the TaxPayers' Alliance, which campaigns for lower taxes and against government 'waste', published a report labelling many university tourism and hospitality management programmes as 'non-courses' – defined as 'university degrees that lend the respectability of scholarly qualifications to non-academic subjects' (TaxPayers' Alliance, 2007: 1). Interestingly this report does not now appear to be available on their website although it is alluded to in another article (see http://www.taxpayersalliance.com/waste/2007/08/the-non-courses.html, last accessed 03.06.12).

Many governments around the world have sought in recent decades to increase the 'relevance' of education, relevance usually being defined in terms of obtaining gainful employment and generating economic wealth. Despite complying, if sometimes reluctantly, with this vision, higher education institutions have often been criticized for doing too little by politicians and policy makers. When we consider the remarks reported above, we are not analysing some rational position but rather the passing off of beliefs, values, prejudices and ideologies as meaningful insights. In brief defence of golf management courses, while it is reasonable to suppose that the demand for golf course managers is not infinite then there is little question that, globally, the golf 'industry' contributes substantially to national economies not only in the provision of venues for playing the game but in the industries supported (e.g. equipment – see http://www.golf-research-group.com/start.html, last accessed 01.02.13). One inference that might be drawn from Chris Woodhead's remark is that British universities are oversupplied with undergraduate degrees in golf management – in fact consultation of several popular university study websites reveals no more than half a dozen references to bachelor's programmes in the field including the University of Birmingham's prestigious course in association with the Professional Golfers' Association (PGA) (see http://www.birmingham.ac.uk/schools/sport-exercise/our-students/agms-students.aspx, last accessed 03.04.14). Similarly, although members of the tourism and hospitality industries might, as we have asserted (see Chapter 2), be inclined to overstate the importance of the sectors, there is little doubt that these industries are an important component of most economies and, as it is hoped that this book has so far shown, of sufficient complexity as to require an appropriately intelligent and indeed, *intellectual* approach to their study and management.

There is a long tradition of negativity in the UK, and, variably, in other parts of the world, towards the study and practice of certain 'vocational' knowledge and skills. Some vocational subjects – notably medicine and law – are highly valued. Others are less so. Societies may, perfectly reasonably, place different values on different vocations. The amount and quality of knowledge that an individual needs to acquire and practise their vocation may vary significantly between subjects. One would normally prefer a qualified and experienced surgeon to perform a life-threatening operation over a qualified and experienced chef de cuisine. Subjects may thus be variably academic, but (as the Taxpayers' Alliance would have us believe) non-academic? If hospitality and tourism management courses are non-courses and they are, in essence, an applied extension of business and management courses, does this make the latter non-courses too? The poverty of the criticisms outlined above should not disguise the fact, as we noted in Chapter 1, that business and management as subject areas lack intellectual coherence. However, the content and value of education, vocational or otherwise, is unlikely to be enhanced by juvenile name calling.

The development of higher hospitality management education

Hospitality management education is that form of post-school educational provision preparing people for management careers in the hospitality industry as opposed to careers in any of the mainly functional occupational specializations of the sector (for example, those of engineer and chef). Initial education in hospitality management is increasingly at the 'first degree', bachelor's level, although this is not invariably the case. Those who graduate from courses in hospitality management and remain and develop within the industry may in time reasonably expect to achieve unit manager and/or strategic management positions, or become specialized in some key functional management role, for example human resources, sales and marketing. (Wood, 2013a: 63-64)

The origins of higher level hospitality education lie in vocational programmes designed to train front line workers (principally chefs, cooks and waiters), although the two oldest schools in the world (Lausanne in Switzerland, established 1893 and the School of Hotel Administration of Cornell University, USA, established 1922) more or less from their beginning focused on how best to *manage* hotels. In Britain, the Scottish Hotel School, established in Glasgow in 1944, was a courageous attempt to fuse emerging theoretical treatments of management with the practical emphasis found in the Lausanne curriculum (Gee, 1994). But in the UK and much of the rest of the English-speaking world it was the latter years of the twentieth century that saw the growth of hotel schools in institutes of higher education offering bachelor's degrees and higher level qualifications. Barrows (1999: 10) notes that at the end of the last century, four-year university programmes in hospitality management in the USA numbered around 175, the majority having been started during the 1970s and 1980s. Prior to this, around 10 to 12 hospitality management programmes dominated American university provision. A similar situation prevailed in the UK (Gee, 1994). In the 1960s, Britain had only three university level hotel management schools: the Scottish Hotel School (by now incorporated within the then new Strathclyde University in Glasgow); Surrey University near London (itself forged from a College of Advanced Technology that housed a reputable hotel school); and Cardiff University in Wales. Further degree level development of hospitality education took place from the 1970s onwards in the polytechnics created by the 1964–1970 UK governments, the majority of which became universities in 1992.

Growing international provision of higher level hospitality management education has come to follow one of two broad models (Brotherton and Wood, 2008a). Whether in the private or public sector, the first is where a hotel management school is part of a larger educational organization, usually a university. Emphasis here is placed on the expectation that academic personnel are conducting both teaching and academic research even though the latter may be somewhat limited. This model is found extensively in the UK, Australia and New Zealand where there are (relatively) few private schools of hospitality and the majority of higher education institutions are funded by government (in America, provision is distributed over a range of institutions including public and private universities and colleges, see Barrows, 1999). The second model of delivery is principally where hotel management schools are stand-alone entities, essentially 'monotechnics' (Baum, 2012), that is, offering only hospitality and closely related subjects like tourism and events management. In these establishments little emphasis is placed on the value of producing academic research and academic personnel are teaching focused. This model is found almost exclusively in the large private sector with hotel schools often partnering foreign universities and colleges who validate their diploma and degree programmes. The UK has relatively little private provision whereas in Switzerland it is extensive (and where, it is worth noting in passing – see the discussion in Chapter 1 – the term 'hospitality' has been most actively excluded from the names of these schools). Other countries, Malaysia and India among them, evidence 'mixed' provision. Elsewhere, hospitality education has been largely excluded from traditional universities, viewed and confined as a subject to be taught in vocational colleges (whether private or public) below university level (as in France, see Lominé, 2003; Wood, 2013a) or in universities of applied science (as in the Netherlands and Germany).

In an age when international higher education is obsessed with rankings, the reputations of a number of hotel schools remain high with both other educators and with industry. For many, a single country, Switzerland, with its myriad number of (mainly private) hotel schools, is believed, whether accurately or not, to represent a benchmark for excellence in international hospitality education and Swiss schools regularly figure in anecdotal discourse as among the 'best'. Globally, higher hospitality management education appears in general to be thriving, and indeed to offer the prospect of expansion in both the public and private sector (see Barrows and Johan, 2008; also Wood, 2004a, 2004b). Public sector provision of higher hospitality management education generally remains the norm in much of continental Europe although it tends to be confined to vocational rather than traditional universities in a region where distinctions of this nature are fairly rigidly maintained, or located in non-university institutions of higher education. Private sector provision grows apace in many developing economies where the state does not have the resources to radically expand public sector education (for example India; see Gupta and Wood, 2008). In recent years, the entrance of international corporations into the higher education market has had significant impact on hospitality higher education, as private sector hotel management schools have proved attractive acquisitions to such businesses.

The Current Situation – the Case of the UK

At the same time, in the UK, higher hospitality management education (normally found in public sector universities) appears to be contracting with the termination of (or merger into other) schools in many establishments, the most high profile casualty of which was the Scottish Hotel School, closed in its 65th year by Strathclyde University in 2009. A report for the UK Council for Hospitality Management Education (CHME) by Walmsley (2011: 36) hinted at a possible decline in the number of enrolments on hospitality management related programmes. A noticeable decline in the number of students studying for sub-degree qualifications was evident as was an increase in popularity of master's level courses. In point of fact, UK higher hospitality management education has always experienced difficulties within the wider higher education system, enjoying periodic booms as well as busts. Underlying this variability, however, have been persistent problems of credibility. As Lynch (2010: 3) notes, 'Hospitality has long laboured with problems of perception in terms of its occupational status so it is perhaps inevitable that its academic status should suffer too.' It is certainly fair to say that in terms of credibility, UK higher hospitality education has failed to command both the systematic support of the industry it is intended to serve and the respect and support of the wider academic community in which it functions. Brotherton and Wood (2008a) and Baum (2012) identify several dimensions to this issue, the latter in a concise and insightful, if ultimately depressing, summary of the perceived shortcomings of hospitality management education that he describes as a 'post-mortem'. These are discussed here under four headings: the operational bias of hospitality management courses and the readiness of hospitality graduates; isolationism; the perceived 'relevance' of the curriculum to industry and academic audiences; and the quality of research in hospitality management.

Operational but not ready

First, for much of the history of hospitality management education the view has been taken by educators and endorsed by many employers, that programmes of study should have a pronounced operational bias. This has manifested itself (and continues so to do) in two ways – a curriculum emphasizing practical skills, particularly in food preparation and service, and a general orientation towards unit management in the hospitality industry as the ceiling of ambition for students. The practical elements of the curriculum have usually been met via hotel management schools operating training restaurants and kitchens as part of their facilities. In constrained funding circumstances the provision of such facilities has often been seen by publicly funded UK higher education institutions as an undesirable expense (this attitude can be contrasted to that of Hong Kong Polytechnic University which recently opened its own learning and training hotel, and to various US universities which operate hotels as part of their educational offering – for example at the Kemmons Wilson School of Hospitality and Resort Management, University of Memphis). Alternative models have been employed to ensure that 'training' components can be delivered. Thus, practical training can be acquired (a) during internships rather than in school; (b) during in-service training in facilities like staff dining rooms; and (c) in the training facilities of other, vocational or technical, colleges (see Dutton and Farbrother, 2005; Alexander, 2007, 2008; Alexander et al., 2009). These alternative models have become the norm in some programmes where the universities of which they are part have withdrawn funding for dedicated facilities.

Of course, the provision of specialist hospitality learning facilities and the philosophies they reflect are legitimate matters for debate in terms of learning and teaching. More important from the political point of view, however, is that despite training kitchens and restaurants being regarded as a 'must' by the industry, the same industry has rarely been satisfied with the outcome of the educative process. Hospitality industry employers – and not only in the UK – have a long history of complaining about the fitness for purpose of higher hospitality education. In translation, this usually means that (a) educational institutions are not graduating enough people who can operationally multi-task over long work shifts for limited (in the short-term) reward; and/or (b) students are not sufficiently competent in the (generally) lower level skills. Peacock (2012) reported that the hotel chain Malmaison and Hotel du Vin 'has joined the growing list of employers warning that UK job applicants are unemployable because they lack basic skills, with most of its jobs taken by foreign workers'. The company's spokesman is further quoted as saying: 'Often UK applicants don't want to take up the challenge because it's hard work and unsociable hours and that tends to put people off', and 'A lot of people don't want to join at entry level and work their way up.' The spokesman continued, noting that they (the company) had 108 vacancies it was struggling to fill. 'The trends we've noticed from applicants, especially from the UK, is that people don't see our industry as a career choice. Typically it's seen more as a stop gap between studies or employment.' Going even further, he warned that British teenagers were too influenced by celebrity culture chasing after an unrealistic dream of being a pop singer rather than putting the hard graft in for jobs. One can only sympathize with this spokesman: how is it possible that the attraction of a successful career as a wealthy pop star scores over the virtues of a minimum-wage job in the hospitality industry? Occasionally, criticism of hospitality education is not concerned with whether expensively trained graduates can wait table, but rather bemoans the absence of higher level skills. In the discussion on security in Chapter 4 we recorded the comments of Paul Moxness, Vice President, Corporate Safety and Security with the Carlson Rezidor hotel group on the lack of preparedness of hospitality graduates with regard to risk management knowledge and skills. A longer-standing critic has particularly focused on the failure of educational programmes to prepare graduates for corporate level management. Slattery (1997, 2010) criticizes the operational bias of hospitality management courses and the failure to teach corporate management skills, noting that very few hospitality graduates are represented in the most senior corporate positions. Both of these commentators articulate plausible criticisms of hospitality education and educators find themselves squeezed between the famously clichéd rock and a hard place – the demand for higher level skills being met by the demand for 'business as usual' in terms of providing graduates as operational cannon-fodder.

It is little surprise that many hospitality educators in the UK feel that the hospitality industry's principal role in education is the proffering of unhelpful criticism. In the United States, the culture of educational and industry philanthropy and engagement with higher education is generally perceived as more supportive, extending formal arrangements including endowments for faculty positions, research and more prosaic but no less important 'bricks and mortar' projects (Barrows, 1999) (at the time of writing there is not a single hotel school in the UK named or endowed for a significant entrepreneur in the industry or publicly supported by a major hospitality company). In summarizing much of what has been discussed in this section we can turn to Raybould and Wilkins (2005: 211), who write: 'There continues to be a distinction between industry and student perceptions of what skills and roles are appropriate for graduates entering the industry. Students have been criticised for having unrealistic expectations of the types of responsibilities they may be given and consequently the types of skills they will be expected to exercise on entering the industry.' Raybould and Wilkins continue by noting that employers 'tend to discount students' formal qualifications on the grounds of lack of experience and frequently we hear the complaint that students are "over-qualified but under-experienced" for even entry level management positions'. In their own study of the skills that managers believed to be important in hospitality managers, Raybould and Wilkins (2005: 211–212) found that interpersonal, problem solving and self-management skills were ranked but skills related to the conceptual and analytical domain tended to be dismissed. None of this is surprising, there is a strong current of anti-intellectualism in the UK hospitality industry and, rather than welcoming graduates into the industry, managers are dismissive of their qualifications and sceptical about their lack of experience. The myth of lack of competence needs to be put to rest however. There is hardly any aspect of a junior manager's job in hospitality with which an averagely intelligent graduate cannot cope given a reasonable amount of support and mentoring – hospitality management most definitely is *not* rocket science.

Isolationism

Secondly, a parallel phenomenon to that of the operational bias of higher hospitality education is identified by Baum (2012). This is the issue of isolationism: hospitality management education has traditionally had separate, dedicated provision in educational institutions, separate from business schools. Indeed, there is a long tradition in UK higher education of hotel school personnel arguing that the industry is so different, even unique, when compared to other industries and other manifestations of management practice that separateness from wider business education is essential. We noted the existence of this phenomenon of exceptionalism in the Preface to this text. For Baum (and, it should be said, many others) there are no rational reasons for this isolationism save that as a model it preserves the power of the hospitality industry to influence and sustain the operationally biased 'practical and skills-based training culture' education model in the field (Baum, 2012: 53). As we noted in Chapter 7 and elsewhere, and as reasserted by Baum (2012: 55), the current model of higher hospitality education prepares students for relatively low level entry positions on graduation and leads to relatively few hospitality management graduates playing 'true leadership or innovator roles in the contemporary global industry'. More than this though, the chicken of isolationism has come home to roost with a vengeance and in retrospect the efforts of UK hotel schools to maintain their separate identities looks, in the light of the aforementioned closures and mergers, very much a case of turkeys voting for Christmas.

Perceived relevance of the curriculum

Thirdly, the boastful claims of hotel schools that their courses are designed to meet the needs of industry not only falter on their frequent rejection by industry as noted earlier, but on two assumptions that underlie the assertion. The first of these is that the prime function of education is to prepare people for employment as opposed to, say, instilling a love of learning, providing a basis for living an examined life and laying down knowledge that while of no immediate value may be tempered in the future by experience thereby creating worthy citizens. If some forms of education are only about employability then it is difficult to see how they differ from training, and training need not be paid for by the state in expensive universities, but by those desirous of employees with that training. Consider the following example. The UK Institute of Hospitality runs an 'academic partner' scheme (providing marketing and educational support for members) and in a 2013 report on its implementation at University College Birmingham quotes the Dean of the Hospitality and Events School as stating (Walker, 2013b: 11, emphasis added): 'One of the key reasons behind becoming an Academic Partner is to ensure that we are responding to industry when delivering and creating hospitality programmes. We aim to produce graduates who can add *immediate* value to an organization.' This seems (indeed, in the current climate, is) entirely plausible and sensible. However, recalling the criticisms dealt with at the beginning of this section, one of the difficulties facing 'hospitality management', particularly within the higher education establishment, is the perception that it is merely a specialized form of (fairly low level) training rather than an instance of education. How will this impression be overcome if hospitality education focuses only on operational training imperatives alone?

The other assumption underlying boastfulness about the relevance of hospitality curricula to 'the industry' is that 'the industry' is not some homogeneous sector with an agreed list of its skill needs. There is a remarkable lack of evidence in the public domain as to what the industry's needs really are beyond, as we saw in Chapters 3 and 7, people who are prepared to work (at least in the early part of their careers) for long hours, low pay and with a great deal of self-sacrifice. In the Preface we noted Mars et al.'s (1979) view that students are 'prepared' for this by socialization experienced while on internships, where they absorb the industry's (low) cultural expectations of them. As Baum (2012) again perceptively and rather more acidly points out, a curriculum oriented towards operational skills means that a hospitality student's internship programme often consists of low level operative roles in restaurants. It is unsurprising that many educators find enthusiasm among students for career employment in the industry drops dramatically after their first internship.

The quality of hospitality research

A final reason why the credibility of hospitality as a subject suffers within higher education relates to research. A central issue, especially in the English-speaking academic world where research as a measure of performance has become an obsession, is the claim by fellow academics that the measured (on the basis of often questionable criteria, it must be noted) quantity and quality of hospitality research output is inferior to that of other, related subjects – and in particular 'general' management and business studies. In the UK where the periodic national assessment of research quality has governmental funding as well as reputational implications for universities and other higher education institutions, the quality of hospitality and tourism research has been found wanting. The panel assessing hospitality research in the 2001 Research Assessment Exercise noted:

> Hospitality is less mature as a sub-area, and there is little work of international quality, with around half rated at below national level. Much of the output published in hospitality journals comprises conceptual work, extended literature reviews, and reports of small pilot studies. The sub-area relies heavily on theory developed in the management field, with only application to the hospitality industry, and in some cases work lags a number of years behind theory development in mainstream management. (http://www.rae.ac.uk/2001/overview/, last accessed 22.11.14)

These somewhat damning remarks repay careful dissection. Hospitality management is indeed, in the UK at least, a relatively young ('less mature') subject area in higher education. The growth of higher hospitality education, and subsequently of research to support it, can most accurately be dated to the mid-1980s, a period of development of around 30 years. That most provision began in vocational education institutions (principally polytechnics) that were not 'upgraded' to universities until the early 1990s (and until then had no governmental requirement to undertake research) combined with the fact that even with growth of the field, the extent of provision remained relatively low compared to other subjects, mean that the hospitality research base began, and has remained, quite small (according to Walmsley (2011: 36), drawing on official statistics, in 2008-2009 only 23% of hospitality academics had doctoral degrees). In a young, developing and relatively underresourced field, one might therefore expect that published research output might reasonably focus on 'conceptual work, extended literature reviews, and reports of small pilot studies' and while possibly agreeing with the RAE panel's views about the second and third in this list, it is not made clear what is exactly wrong with 'conceptual work', which is essential to both theory building and accurate empirical research. Conceptual work is at the heart – or should be – of any serious research endeavour. One must similarly be sceptical of the apparent negative attached to the observation that hospitality research 'relies heavily on theory developed in the management field, with only application to the hospitality industry'. As we saw in Chapter 1, a 'management' paradigm has and remains dominant in hospitality higher education – if this paradigm does not thus draw on general management theory in its research, what is it to draw on – black magic?

The most generous observation one can make on the remarks of the RAE panel is that they are entirely consistent – as one would expect – with those who think that current, mainstream, management knowledge and research enjoy some privileged position in terms of inherent philosophy, quality and insight. As we saw in Chapter 1, however, we cannot be confident about this. The irony of the RAE panel's comments on hospitality management research is that their analysis could be applied equally to a significant proportion of general management research. That it is not is almost certainly evidence of the political rather than intellectual basis to the very concept of research evaluation. This has continued to evolve in the UK and other countries. Now, academic journals in the business and management field are graded by professional organizations, the most prominent of which is that of the Association of Business Schools (motto: 'Innovative, involved, international and impactful' – maybe they should have added 'immodest', see http://www.associationofbusinessschools. org/, last accessed 22.11.14). Academics in business and management subjects are encouraged to publish in higher rated journals but clearly not all can do so. From the point of view of hospitality, Lynch (2010: 3) observes that journal grading systems generally rate hospitality journals poorly, 'the highest graded journals barely reach the target for being deemed of an acceptable quality. In consequence, this approach effectively negates any such hospitality journal as an approved research publication outlet.'

The dog eats dog culture of research and publishing in the academic world – and specifically the business and management field – might matter more if even the majority of research output (a) was indeed impactful and had a truly genuine and positive effect on the way business performs, or (b) performed an important, socially critical role in warning of the opportunities and dangers of business activity. In both instances only a small proportion of research arguably does so and, with some irony, this is equally true of hospitality management research where a young field has struggled to play the research game without the historic intellectual capital to do so overly successfully. In a 2013 interview with the *Financial Times* newspaper, Larry Zicklin, former Chairman of Neuberger Berman, a leading Wall Street investment company, committed several acts of apostasy by claiming that most people do not understand business research; that research primarily validates the academic reward system; that there is relatively little demand from business for research; and that teaching ability should be the number one criterion for appointing business school faculty (Wylie, 2013).

Not Dead Yet – A Wider Picture

Opposition to the idea of hospitality management as an academic and intellectual endeavour has come from an industry obsessed with retaining a ready-trained no-cost supply of operational managers; and from an academic establishment obsessed with 'research'. In public sector higher education, with a research-oriented culture the future does not look good for hospitality management. The question thus arises what, if anything, can be done?

In terms of the fate of hospitality management as a subject in public sector higher education, there is some concern that Australia is moving in the same direction as Britain (O'Mahony, 2009). Barrows and Johan (2008) are more optimistic about the potential for higher hospitality education in the USA. In many other countries, the issues facing the UK have little salience because hospitality education is not located within the traditional (university) higher education sector but confined to a sub-stratum of strictly 'vocational' institutions. One of the most interesting developments in hospitality higher education in the last 10 years has been the growth of the private sector. This is not overly surprising. The hospitality industry's demand for future managers has not gone away and indeed in the so-called developing and emerging economies may actually be increasing. Any continuing decline of higher hospitality management education provision within traditional public universities and similar institutions will probably stimulate private provision if demand for student places remains unchanged or increases. In the developing world, in emerging economies, and in certain developed countries with large youthful populations, the traditional public sector is too small to meet the demand for university places, especially in countries that have seen a rapid growth of the middle classes. Furthermore, there is a significant preference among emergent economy middle classes for their children to hold at least a first degree irrespective of the subjects studied thus presaging a future in which all formally educated entrants to the industry will be graduates.

In the past, there has been a high concentration of independent private hospitality education in Switzerland, which as we have already noted, but for reasons that often appear mysterious to many, has a reputation as the 'natural' home of hospitality. This situation is changing rapidly however as growth in demand stimulates the creation of private sector institutions in countries that would previously educate their potential hospitality managers overseas. Many developing and emerging economies enjoy cost advantages over mature economies that may in the long term lead to a decline in demand for hospitality management education in the latter. A further addition to the mix is the presence of the aforementioned private international 'for-profit' (as well as 'not-for-profit') education companies including Laureate International Universities (with 74 schools globally, see http://www.laureate.net/OurNetwork, last accessed 04.04.14), Kaplan (http://www.kaplan.com/, last accessed 04.04.14) and Apollo (http://www.apollo.edu/, last accessed 04.04.14).

Many people see advantages to this expansion of private sector education. It can offer opportunities for degree study that would not otherwise be available in many countries. Because most providers charge (often substantial) fees it is possible that courses in hospitality might attract students with a higher level of motivation to remain with the industry upon graduation (a long-standing issue in the UK and other Anglosphere countries being that graduates soon leave the industry in large numbers for apparently greener pastures). Because in most private higher education institutes there is no requirement or impetus to undertake research it is possible that resources can be more effectively targeted on learning, teaching and graduate career placement. *Contra* these points, there have been expressions of concern about the motivation and quality of many private schools, not least those associated with for-profit corporations and others besides. Some criticisms have come from teaching unions, which have something of a vested interest in state funded education (see, for example, University and College Union, 2010), but a US Congress report of 2012 was also highly critical of private providers (see Crotty, 2012, and the web page of Senator Tom Harkin who chaired the committee, http://www.harkin.senate.gov/help/forprofitcolleges.cfm, last accessed 04.04.14). It is certainly a matter of concern that many private providers of higher education might escape application of those quality assurance mechanisms present in many countries and with which state colleges are required to comply. Further, the absence of a research culture in private sector establishments increases the onus on those delivering courses to ensure that curriculum knowledge and teaching scholarship is as up-to-date as possible, something that is not always possible when a private college's business model relies heavily on part-time staff/adjunct faculty with many other commitments.

Concluding Remarks

In this chapter we have briefly reviewed the history of hospitality higher education and some of the current challenges and opportunities it faces. In the UK and many other countries it is at present highly unfashionable to contest the idea that education is simply about meeting the needs of particular vocations, professions or industries. Many in the academic world cling to this view however, and with considerable reason. It surely cannot be sufficient that a subject relies solely for its existence on the justification that it prepares people for careers in a particular vocation or industry. Some academic 'bottom' is required. This can be in the form of intrinsic specialist knowledge as opposed to being a simple instance of the application of some other field(s) of knowledge, or it can be in terms of the leverage of knowledge within a curriculum to furnish future graduates with the intellectual and technical skills to meet long-term future challenges, many of which may as yet be ill-defined if known at all.

Further Reading

Barrows, C W (1999) 'Introduction to hospitality education', in C W Barrows and R H Bosselman (Eds) *Hospitality Management Education*, Binghamton: The Haworth Press, 1–20.

Barrows, C W and Johan, N (2008) 'Hospitality management education', in B Brotherton and R C Wood (Eds) *The Sage Handbook of Hospitality Management*, London: Sage, 146–162.

Brotherton, B and Wood, R C (2008) 'Editorial introduction', in B Brotherton and R C Wood (Eds) *The Sage Handbook of Hospitality Management*, London: Sage, 1–34.

Wood, R C (2013) 'Hospitality management education', in R C Wood (Ed) *Key Concepts in Hospitality Management*, London: Sage, 63–67.

9

CONCLUSION –
THE PROOF OF THE PUDDING?

> After reading this chapter, you should:
>
> (a) be able to relate the content of Chapters 1-8 more clearly to the themes introduced in the Author's Preface;
>
> (b) be able to appreciate the scope and dangers of innovation in a hospitality industry that is inherently conservative; and
>
> (c) be ready to develop your own critical evaluation of the core premises of the book by reference to the conclusions drawn and the evidence considered.

Through a Glass Darkly

In the Preface to this book, five groups of themes that recur in the analysis of hospitality and the hospitality industry were identified. These were: (1) the contested nature of hospitality and management; (2) the general economic significance of the industry at global, national and local levels; (3) the role of people as employees in hospitality services; (4) the characteristics of the hospitality product and service mix; and (5) the conservatism, exceptionalism and operational bias that permeates values and practise in hospitality management.

In respect of the first of these, the contested nature of hospitality and management itself, in Chapter 1 we examined both various ways in which the study of hospitality and the hospitality industry has been approached, academically, while additionally reflecting on the uncertainties of management knowledge. In Chapter 2, an attempt was made to make some assessment of the general economic and business importance of the hospitality industry. That parts of it are significant in our everyday lives goes without saying but upon close inspection we find an industry dominated by small and medium sized enterprises often operating at the economic margins. In the corporate sector, many hotel companies are not, in ownership terms, in the hotel business anymore but in the business of strategic and operational brand management. As part of the wider industrial landscape, only 10 companies in travel, leisure, tourism and hospitality feature in the Financial Times Global 500 (Chapter 2, Table 2.1). The general sense is of a risk-averse industry particularly intent on the avoidance of ownership of physical assets. We also noted in Chapter 2 that hospitality is often a capital intensive business which led us in Chapter 3 to question whether the 'people industry' tag normally attached to the sector is especially appropriate, not least in the light of the industry's increasingly negative global reputation for people management, not least in the field of reward. We gave some consideration to the nature of people management practices in examining managers' roles and their education in Chapters 7 and 8. Throughout the text we have touched, often indirectly, on numerous manifestations of the hospitality product and service mix. The core issue here is that though frequently classified as 'just' a service industry, the sector clearly engages in both selling services and products.

The final theme considered in the Preface, the conservatism, exceptionalism and operational bias that was asserted as permeating the industry, is perhaps the most telling. Although the sector can claim occasional modest (but rarely radical) innovations, the fundamental nature, relative to human needs, of the core hospitality products and the practices of hospitality management has changed, where it has changed at all, only very slowly. Almost certainly the most radical change in the hotel sector in recent decades has been the (gradual) adoption of the asset light model of business operation, which can be construed as a conservative strategy offering, as we have previously noted, potentially substantial reductions in business risk. The industry's representative and advocacy bodies have regularly lobbied government and other authorities for exceptional treatment in a variety of economic and policy areas, most of which are underpinned by a simple desire to furnish operators with opportunities to add to their bottom line. At the same time, the macro-economic importance of tourism and hospitality in many countries means that the sectors benefit from a range of hidden promotional activities undertaken on their behalf by governments. The operational bias of management in the industry has been illustrated at numerous points in the text. Indeed, once again, as far as both the branded chain hotel and restaurant sectors are concerned, the arm's length method of management and growth, whether through franchises or management contracts, and the concomitant growth of specialist management companies could be seen as having the effect of reinforcing the sector's existing operational bias, the most obvious consequence of which is seen in its effect on management and management practices. As we saw in Chapter 7, commentators have pointed to the 'being there' style of management, especially in hotels, which emphasizes a culture of 'presenteeism' among managers and other workers, encouraging managers to 'trade down' (engage in non-managerial activities or activities that could be delegated) and thus effectively discouraging strategic thought and reflection. This culture is reinforced by hospitality education, where these behaviours are embedded in the curriculum and thus condition students' expectations of their future roles (Chapter 8).

This, then, is a summary of some of the main issues considered in this book. From the point of view of managing hospitality organizations, it is necessary to recognize two key points. First, whereas the operational bias of hospitality management may have certain deleterious effects on management practice and the career scope of managers, a pragmatic view recognizes that this soon becomes self-evident to those engaged in the field. Reactions against the (often physical) hard work, occasional ethical ambivalence and absence of work–life balance in the hospitality industry frequently occur during education, many hospitality students as a result never joining the industry. Of course, there are substantial cultural variations in this phenomenon. Secondly, to some extent, academic research into hospitality management has not yet caught up with the changes that have been taking place in recent decades in terms of the growth of asset light models. Indeed, in some parts of the world, the industry itself, in what it demands of hospitality management graduates, has not caught up with this change. Whereas there is undoubted breadth to hospitality management degrees in terms, for example, of providing education in marketing and strategic management, it may make more sense to replace these relatively little-used knowledge and skill domains (in chain hotels and restaurants at least) with education in franchise concepts; management contract content and negotiation; risk assessment and management; and the forms and provision of multi-brand management 'from a distance', as reflected in the demand for hotel asset management companies. All are skills of a largely strategic quality (though with clear operational applications) increasingly in demand and likely to remain so in the future – and it is to the future that we now turn.

Visions in a Crystal Ball

In the business world, the future is inevitably bound up with the demand for creativity and innovation: creativity and innovation are seen as a driver of future competitive advantage and both are widely touted as the panacea for all the ills of the economy. It was ever thus. August Escoffier, one of the fathers of the modern hospitality industry, summarized the problem of culinary creativity and innovation more than a hundred years ago when he wrote:

> But novelty is the universal cry – novelty by hook or by crook! It is an exceedingly commWon mania among people of inordinate wealth to exact incessantly new or so-called new dishes … . Novelty! It is the prevailing cry; it is imperiously demanded by everyone. (http://www.escoffier-online.com/complete-guide-to-the-art-of-modern-cookery, last accessed 22.11.14)

Scholars of food studies will be no stranger to the above quotation but may be less familiar with what Escoffier goes on to say:

> For all that, the number of alimentary substances is comparatively small, the number of their combinations is not infinite, and the amount of raw material placed either by art or by nature at the disposal of a cook does not grow in proportion to the whims of the public.

What feats of ingenuity have we not been forced to perform, at times, in order to meet our customers' wishes [?] Personally, I have ceased counting the nights spent in the attempt to discover new combinations, when, completely broken with the fatigue of a heavy day, my body ought to have been at rest. (http://www.escoffier-online.com/complete-guide-to-the-art-of-modern-cookery)

Escoffier's observations have a far more wide-ranging application than cookery. If creativity and innovation are terms to have any real meaning this can only be in the sense of reference to something comparatively rare and 'game-changing'. Walker (2012b: 20) reports that the 2011 UK innovation survey of 14,000 manufacturing and service enterprises found that a mere 25% of hotels and restaurants were innovative (only retail, on 23%, was lower) defined as having used 'new and improved products and processes or made changes in their business structures or management and marketing practices during the previous two years'. This is an exemplary instance of a meaningless low level definition of innovation – relying on 'something' being 'used'. A hospitality industry forum held by the UK Institute of Hospitality (Walker, 2012b) generated a far from original list of industry 'innovations', most of which we have touched upon in this book: the creation of new markets; management strategies; newly improved processes; various forms of modular construction; software to manage stock, recipes and menus; and budget hotel accommodation (which had created new markets).

With regular monotony there are periodic conjectures as to the likely future for the hospitality industry. Futurology is often a largely meaningless activity, even when based on detailed extrapolation of data, but one which nevertheless makes large sums of money for consultants. Very short-term predictions about the future can enjoy a degree of accuracy simply by virtue that they *are* so short-term as to be really statements concerning what is about to happen or already happening. Simon Calder (2013) visiting the Sleep 2013 exhibition in London reported that: 'Hotel reception staff and bell-hops are endangered species. Guests at the hotel of the future will bypass the front desk, wheel their own bags – and open their room door with a code sent to their smartphone.' With the possible exception of the last, all these are in play to one degree or another. Other predictions mentioned in the same article could describe swathes of the industry as it currently is: smaller rooms (already got them); the elimination of human-performed and other services that are 'unimportant' to guests (an ongoing process in some sectors for the last 50 years or more); and the death of the budget hotel as customers seek 'affordable luxury' in well-designed hotels (see Chapters 2 and 6). A typical strategy in futurology literature is to claim that overwhelming changes in customer orientation are 'forcing' an industry or a sector to reorient its behaviour. Waldthausen and Oehmichen (2013: 1) marshal impressive evidence from industry luminaries to make this point. Michael Tiedy, Senior Vice President, Brand Design and Innovation at Starwood, is recorded as saying that modern hotel guests would rather 'participate than flaunt'. Sara Kearney, Senior Vice President of Brands at Hyatt Hotels and Resorts, comments of hotel guests: 'They are ready to explore and crave a sense of economy and also yearn for real social interaction'. Waldthausen and Oehmichen's report is driven by the assumption that hotel guests are in search of experiences over expressions of status. We must, in hope, assume that the narrative projections of senior corporate marketing and brand officers are based on at least some evidence although the suspicion lingers that such narratives are more expressions of what corporations want to believe, or to attain, rather than what is actually going on. Indeed, as we have both stated and implied at various points in this text (see especially Chapter 4) there is so much wrong with the basic design and configuration of many hotel and other hospitality products that senior managements might be better directed towards improving and maintaining the basic elements of their offerings rather than focusing on gnomic marketing and management pronouncements that address peripheral issues.

Moving on, virtual tourism and hospitality have attracted some attention but according to Johnson and Dodd (2010: 47), citing a study by Book (2003), virtual worlds are not as yet a realistic substitute for a genuine holiday trip although the potential for information and communication technology to support and mediate touristic and hospitality experiences in the future is something that needs to be carefully monitored. An interesting and altogether more 'low-tech' development in recent years but one having considerable impact on the hospitality industry is the growth of the 'sharing economy' whereby people rent underused assets directly from each other via dedicated internet websites. Companies such as Airbnb offer what is essentially an extension of the 'home stay' concept allowing people to rent out rooms in the homes of others. It is, in essence, an example of 'reverse innovation' in the sense that it is redolent of pre-industrial hospitality where homeowners were bound by social and religious obligation to offer travellers (then a relatively rare phenomenon) shelter and protection. Airbnb was established in San Francisco in 2008; the company claims to have had 11 million users and is reputedly valued at more than all but the top four international hotel brands (*The Economist*, 2014b, 2014c; Kurtz, 2014). As we saw in Chapter 4 with the rise of internet-based hotel rating and review sites, when the hotel industry is threatened its first response is to cry foul. So it has been with Airbnb. *The Economist* (2014b) reported that the Hotel Association of New York was lobbying for stricter enforcement of regulations that prevent absent owners from letting their apartments for fewer than 30 days, which would, apparently, render most of Airbnb's listings illegal. *The Economist* (2014b) noted a Boston University report suggesting that where Airbnb had established a significant presence (Texas was the locus of the research) it failed to have impact on business and luxury hotels but cut the revenues of budget hotels by 5% in two years. It commented:

> If Airbnb were to keep growing at its current rate − its listings are doubling every year − the Texas study suggests that by 2016 the dent in budget hotels' takings will be 10%. With their high fixed costs, that could push many of them into the red. Of course, Airbnb may hit the limits of either supply or demand

before then, but smaller hotels are already blaming it for their woes. 'I see a direct correlation between our revenues going down and [Airbnb's] going up,' says Vijay Dandapani, the president of Apple Core Hotels in New York. 'We had continued growth until Airbnb.'

Reasons to be Cheerful?

In all its myriad forms, the hospitality industry will undoubtedly continue to play an important role in the lives of many. The corporate sector will extend its influence further round the globe. While Asia will continue to see development in international and local chain hotels, Africa is likely to be the market battleground of the future. According to Ward (2013: 34–35) there are 29 hotel chains with 90,000 rooms operating in Africa, 48,000 in the north and 41,000 in sub-Saharan Africa. Around 40,000 further rooms are in the pipeline with Hilton, Radisson Blue and the Accor brands Novotel and Ibis the leading developers but other international brands active as well (including Marriott and Kempinski). This is good news for job creation but improving and/or maintaining the quality of jobs is another issue. Countries that are welcoming to hotel development will, if the experience of the American, British and certain other national hospitality industries is anything to go by, have to be vigilant in insisting on high standards in employment practice. As we have seen in this book, many 'poor' labour practices in hospitality persist because they can – resistance from employees if it takes any form at all assumes the character of take it – then quickly leave it. All this said, there is at least *some* diversity in the management approaches that hospitality organizations adopt towards their employees and there are many good employers. It remains an industry in which, for the most part, seniority, and the rewards that seniority brings, can be attained quite quickly. Just as the industry will continue to develop, so too will hospitality education although it is to be hoped that in the curriculum and research, more critical approaches are taken. Much hospitality education is still rooted in an outdated model that fails to take account of the industry's diversity. Most hospitality research is largely ignored by the industry, and in general, the 'managerial' bias of researchers does not lend itself to either critical or innovative output: a great deal of hospitality research, particularly in the fields of strategy, marketing and consumption, comprises small-scale studies of frequently trivial topics, poorly executed, often using inappropriate quantitative techniques. Here, hospitality researchers can learn an important lesson from their cousins in tourism, namely that a field or sub-field cannot meaningfully progress in research without even minimally poor theoretical reference points.

Hospitality and the hospitality industry are fascinating subjects for research and of course they are fascinating to experience. This book has sought to scratch the surface in understanding these phenomena, which represent and play to basic human needs in a way that is often taken for granted. If the text goes a very small way to emboldening students, academic colleagues and the general reader to question and reflect upon this fundamental area of economic and social life then it will have fulfilled a positive, if limited, service.

Further Reading

Economist, The (2013) 'A short history of hotels: be my guest', 21 December, retrieved from http://www.economist.com/news/christmas-specials/21591743-be-my-guest, last accessed 07.05.14.

Economist, The (2014) 'The sharing economy: boom and backlash', 26 April, retrieved from http://www.economist.com/news/business/21601254-consumers-and-investors-are-delighted-startups-offering-spare-rooms-or-rides-across-town, last accessed 10.05.14.

Economist, The (2014) 'Airbnb versus hotels: room for all, for now', 26 April, retrieved from http://www.economist.com/news/business/21601259-there-are-signs-sharing-site-starting-threaten-budget-hotels-room-all, last accessed 10.05.14.

WEB RESOURCES AND APPLICATIONS

As might be imagined, there are numerous resources available on the internet and elsewhere that provide a wealth of information on the hospitality industry. Care always needs to be exercised as far as possible in verifying the data they provide (and, often, the claims made for data, or claims made more generally). For the financially/ economically competent or for those willing to spend a little time acquiring such competence, two 'apps' are also useful additions to anyone's tablet device. They are Bloomberg and Yahoo! Finance both of which can be customized in a variety of ways to reflect interests in stock market performance. Both also provide a useful financial news service. Websites of particular interest are listed below.

Websites

- Big Hospitality (http://www.bighospitality.co.uk/) is a UK-based news service with several useful sections and a number of free downloads, including news-letters, available upon (free) subscription.

- The British Hospitality Association (BHA) (http://www.bha.org.uk/) is the industry representative organization in Great Britain. Membership is required to access the full range of services but there is a useful and free news page and occasional free reports.

- The Council for Hospitality Management Education (CHME) (http://www. chme.org.uk/) is a UK-based organization representing educational institutions offering higher hospitality education. It offers limited downloads but the website as a whole offers a range of useful information including reports on the organiza-tion's annual research conference.

- ehotelier (http://ehotelier.com/) is a vital source of news, comment, career opportunities and diverse other topics allowing free registration for various news-letters and other materials.

- The European Foundation for the Improvement of Living and Working Conditions (Eurofound) (http://www.eurofound.europa.eu/index.htm) is an agency of the European Union providing knowledge 'in the area of social and work-related policies'. Its website offers a wide range of information and reports, the latter mainly free. A strength of this service is that many of the site's resources are avail-able in the multiple languages of the European Union.

- FM Link (http://www.fmlink.com/) is one of the facilities-management profession's main websites and though covering all aspects of facilities management contains a number of useful resources that have applications to hospitality.

- FnB News (http://www.fnbnews.com/) or Food and Beverage News is an Indian-based and -focused website that offers useful insights into the state of the sector in that country.

- FoodBev (http://www.foodbev.com/) is a UK-based news website with aspirations to a more global reach.

- Horizons (http://www.hrzns.com/) is an extremely useful food and food service industry oriented website with some free downloads; helpful for obtaining trend data.

- Hotel Business (http://www.hotelbusiness.com/main.php) is a specialist new service (US-based but global in scope); to access many services a free subscription is required.

- Hotel Marketing (http://www.hotelmarketing.com/) is as its name suggests a news website with an emphasis on marketing; it offers a free subscription newsletter and other services.

- Hotel News Now (http://www.hotelnewsnow.com/) is a US-based, but global in scope, specialist news service covering a range of topics and with a particularly useful news line for forecasting.

- Hotel News Resource (http://www.hotelnewsresource.com/) – as with ehotelier (see above) this is an essential for all those interested in the business of hotels. This website continues to grow in scope and importance and has material on development, marketing, environment and technology among other topics.

- HOTREC (http://www.hotrec.eu/) styles itself as 'the umbrella association of national trade associations representing the hotels, restaurants, cafés and similar establishments in Europe' claiming to act 'as the representative of the hospitality businesses vis-à-vis the EU institutions'. Its website covers a wide range of policy issues relating to hospitality in Europe (including tourism, food, hospitality, consumer affairs, taxation, sustainability, hotel classification schemes, competition and enterprise) and offers many free downloads.

- HVS (www.hvs.com/Library/Articles) is a globally leading consultancy in hospitality covering a variety of services including hotel valuation. Registration (no charge) allows access to its library which offers a plethora of free downloads, numerous paid items and the option of receiving regular newsletters on various topics.

- Informe Design (http://www.informedesign.org/) is an excellent research-oriented website on design matters that offers a wide range of free downloads, many of value to those associated with the hospitality industry.

- The Institute of Hospitality (https://www.instituteofhospitality.org/) is a UK-based organization of hospitality professionals; paid membership is required to access its best resources.

- The International Labour Organization (ILO) (http://www.ilo.org/global/lang--en/index.htm) is a United Nations specialized agency. Its website has a wealth of statistical data.

- The National Restaurant Association (NRA) (http://www.restaurant.org/Home) is America's leading membership organization in the field and has a useful website offering a wealth of largely free information.

- The Office for National Statistics (ONS) (UK) (http://www.ons.gov.uk/ons/index.html) is an invaluable source of official data on a wide range of topics including employment-related statistics. Many of the data supplied are, if not quite published in real time, highly contemporaneous for those requiring up-to-date information.

- People 1st (http://www.people1st.co.uk/) is a UK body which, in its own words, is 'the skills and workforce development charity for employers in the hospitality, tourism, leisure, travel, passenger transport and retail industries focusing on transforming skills in the sector through the development of effective recruitment, training and talent management solutions'. It regularly produces a number of free trend reports on employment and skills in the industries covered and on a variety of other related subjects.

- WageIndicator (wageindicator.com) is a website dedicated to achieving global coverage of fundamental employment concepts and data on wages as they apply at the world, regional and country level.

REFERENCES

Adamo, A P (1999) 'Hotel engineering and maintenance', in C S Verginis and R C Wood (Eds) *Accommodation Management: Perspectives for the International Hotel Industry*, London: International Thomson Business Press, 128-149.

Alexander, M (2007) 'Purple rinses and pseudo-Escoffierian menus: the problem with training restaurants', *The Hospitality Review*, 9, 3: 29-36.

Alexander, M (2008) 'Reflecting on changes in operational training in UK hospitality management degree programmes', *International Journal of Contemporary Hospitality Management*, 19, 3: 211-220.

Alexander, M, Lynch, P and Murray, R (2009) 'Reassessing the core of hospitality management education: the continuing importance of training restaurants', *Journal of Hospitality, Leisure, Sport and Tourism Education*, 8, 1: 55-69.

Aliouche, E H and Schlentrich, U (2013) 'Franchising', in R C Wood (Ed) *Key Concepts in Hospitality Management*, Sage: London, 41-45.

Aliouche, E H, Kaen, F and Schlentrich, U (2012) 'The market performance of franchise stock portfolios', *International Journal of Contemporary Hospitality Management*, 24, 5: 791-809.

Alon, I, Ni, L and Wang, Y (2012) 'Examining the determinants of hotel chain expansion through international franchising', *International Journal of Hospitality Management*, 31, 2: 379-386.

Alvesson, M, Bridgman, T and Willmott, H (2009) 'Introduction', in M Alvesson, T Bridgman and H Willmott (Eds) *The Oxford Handbook of Critical Management Studies*, Oxford: Oxford University Press, 1-26.

Anon (1992) 'Report finds word of mouth sells covers', *Caterer and Hotelkeeper*, 30 April: 14.

Anon (1998) 'Dining by numbers', *Caterer and Hotelkeeper*, 26 March: 60-62.

Anon (2013) 'Accessibility – the bottom line', *Hospitality*, Issue 30: 11.

Arnaldo, M J (1981) 'Hotel general managers: a profile', *Cornell Hotel and Restaurant Administration Quarterly*, 22, 3: 53-56.

Assaf, G, Josiassenc, A and Knezevic Cvelbara, L (2012) 'Does triple bottom line reporting improve hotel performance?', *International Journal of Hospitality Management*, 31, 2: 596-600.

Auty, S (1992) 'Consumer choice and segmentation in the restaurant industry', *Service Industries Journal*, 12, 3: 324-339.

Baggini, J (2014) *The Virtues of the Table: How to Eat and Think*, London: Granta.

Baker, S, Huyton, J and Bradley, P (2000) *Principles of Hotel Front Office Operations*, London: Continuum, 2nd Ed.

Balekjian, C and Sarheim, L (2011) *Boutique Hotels Segment: The Challenge of Standing out from the Crowd*, London: HVS, retrieved from http://www.hvs.com/Content/3171.pdf, last accessed 27.04.14.

Ball, S, Jones, P, Kirk, D and Lockwood, A (2003) *Hospitality Operations: A Systems Approach*, London: Continuum.

Banerjee, P (2013) 'Hotels and security', in R C Wood (Ed) *Key Concepts in Hospitality Management*, London: Sage, 77–81.

Bañuls, A L and Ramón Rodríguez, A B (2005) 'Returns on education in the Spanish tourism labour market', *Tourism Economics*, 11, 1: 119–132.

Barrows, C W (1999) 'Introduction to hospitality education', in C W Barrows and R H Bosselman (Eds) *Hospitality Management Education*, Binghamton: The Haworth Press, 1–20.

Barrows, C W and Johan, N (2008) 'Hospitality management education', in B Brotherton and R C Wood (Eds) *The Sage Handbook of Hospitality Management*, London: Sage, 146–162.

Barrows, C W, Lattuca, F P and Bosselman, R H (1989) 'Influence of restaurant reviews upon consumers', *FIU Hospitality Review*, 7, 2: 84–92.

Baum, T (1989) 'Managing hotels in Ireland: research and development for change', *International Journal of Hospitality Management*, 8, 2: 131–144.

Baum, T (Ed) (1993) *Human Resource Issues in International Tourism*, Oxford: Butterworth-Heinemann.

Baum, T (1995) *Managing Human Resources in the European Tourism and Hospitality Industry: A Strategic Approach*, London: Chapman and Hall.

Baum, T (2006) *Managing People in International Tourism, Hospitality and Leisure*, London: Thomson.

Baum, T (2008) 'The social construction of skills: a hospitality sector perspective', *European Journal of Vocational Training*, 44, 2: 74–88.

Baum, T (2012) 'Picking o'er the bones: a postmortem on hospitality management education (DoB 1893)', in *Proceedings of the CAUTHE Conference 2012: The New Golden Age of Tourism and Hospitality, Book 2*, Melbourne: CAUTHE, 53–56.

Bauman, Z (1990) *Thinking Sociologically*, Oxford: Blackwell.

Beardsworth, A and Keil, T (1997) *Sociology on the Menu: An Invitation to the Study of Food and Society*, London: Routledge.

Beechey, V (1982) 'The sexual division of labour and the labour process: a critical assessment of Braverman', in S Wood (Ed) *The Degradation of Work? Skill, Deskilling and the Labour Process*, London: Hutchinson, 54–73.

Bell, D (1973) *The Coming of Post-industrial Society*, London: Heinemann.

Bell, D (2007) 'The hospitable city: social relations in commercial spaces', *Progress in Human Geography*, 31, 1: 7–22.

Bell, D, Deighton, J, Reinartz, W J, Rust, R T and Swartz, G (2002) 'Seven barriers to customer equity management', *Journal of Service Research*, 5, 1: 77–85.

Bell, S and Henry, J F (2001) 'Hospitality versus exchange: the limits of monetary economics', *Review of Social Economy*, 59, 2: 203-228.

Berger, F and Ferguson, D H (1986) 'Myriad management methods: restaurant managers tell all', *Cornell Hotel and Restaurant Administration Quarterly*, 26, 4: 16-24.

Berkeley Scott (2013) *Hospitality and Leisure Salary Survey 2013*, retrieved from http://www.berkeley-scott.co.uk/2013-hospitality-and-leisure-salary-survey, last accessed 03.04.13.

Bernini, C and Guizzardi, A (2012) 'Accommodation industry or accommodation industries? Evidence from the analysis of production processes', *Anatolia – An International Journal of Tourism and Hospitality Research*, 23, 1: 4-16.

Bernstein, J and Ellison, J (2011) 'Hotel confidential', *Newsweek*, 18 June: 46-49, retrieved from http://www.thedailybeast.com/newsweek/2011/06/05/hotel-confidential.html, last accessed 30.05.12.

Bhasin, K (2011) 'The 10 industries with the most loyal customers', retrieved from http://www.businessinsider.com/industries-customer-loyalty-2011-9?op=1, last accessed 24.05.14.

Birdir, K (2002) 'General manager turnover and root causes', *International Journal of Contemporary Hospitality Management*, 14, 1: 43-47.

Bolat, T and Yılmaz, O (2009) 'The relationship between outsourcing and organizational performance: Is it myth or reality for the hotel sector?', *International Journal of Contemporary Hospitality Management*, 21, 1: 7-23.

Bolton, S (2005) *Emotion Management in the Workplace*, London: Palgrave.

Book, B (2003) 'Travelling through cyberspace: tourism and photography in virtual worlds', in *Tourism Photography: Still Visions – Changing Lives Conference*, Sheffield, UK, 20-23 July, page 3.

Boone, J, Houran, J, Veller, T, Keith, M, Kefgen, K and Nikolaeva, K (2013) 'Rethinking a glass ceiling in the hospitality industry', Mineola, NY: HVS, retrieved from http://www.4hoteliers.com/features/article/7890, last accessed 18.04.14.

Boston Consulting Group (1970) *The Product Portfolio*, retrieved from http://www.bcg.com/expertise_impact/publications/PublicationDetails.aspx?id=tcm:12-13257, last accessed 18.06.14.

Bowen, J (2008) 'Marketing and consumer behaviour in hospitality', in B Brotherton and R C Wood (Eds) *The Sage Handbook of Hospitality Management*, London: Sage, 302-315.

Bowey, A (1976) *The Sociology of Organizations*, London: Hodder and Stoughton.

Boyne, S (2010) 'Leadership research in hospitality: a critical review', in *British Academy of Management (BAM) Conference*, University of Sheffield, 14-16 September, retrieved from http://aalborg.academia.edu/StevenBoyne/Papers, last accessed 17.04.14.

Braverman, H (1974) *Labour and Monopoly Capital*, New York: Monthly Review Press.

British Hospitality Association (2010) *Creating Jobs in Britain – A Hospitality Economy Proposition*, retrieved from http://www.bha.org.uk/wp-content/uploads/2010/11/BHA-Economic-Report-Nov2010FINAL.pdf, last accessed 03.04.13.

Brookes, M and Roper, A (2012) 'Realising plural-form benefits in international hotel chains', *Tourism Management*, 33, 3: 580-591.

Brotherton, B (1999) 'Towards a definitive view of the nature of hospitality and hospitality management', *International Journal of Contemporary Hospitality Management*, 11, 4: 165-173.

Brotherton, B and Wood, R C (2000) 'Hospitality and hospitality management', in C Lashley and A Morrison (Eds) *In Search of Hospitality*, Oxford: Butterworth-Heinemann, 135-156.

Brotherton, B and Wood, R C (2008a) 'Editorial introduction', in B Brotherton and R C Wood (Eds) *The Sage Handbook of Hospitality Management*, London: Sage, 1-34.

Brotherton, R and Wood, R C (2008b) 'The nature and meanings of hospitality', in B Brotherton and R C Wood (Eds) *The Sage Handbook of Hospitality Management*, London: Sage, 37-61.

Brownell, J (1993) 'Communicating with credibility: the gender gap', *Cornell Hotel and Restaurant Administration Quarterly*, 34, 2: 52-54.

Brownell, J (1994) 'Women in hospitality management: general managers' perceptions of factors related to career development', *International Journal of Hospitality Management*, 13, 2: 101-117.

Brownell, J (2013) 'Women, gender and hospitality employment', in R C Wood (Ed) *Key Concepts in Hospitality Management*, London: Sage, 157-162.

Brûlé, T (2010) 'Inn focus – global', *Monocle*, Issue 30, February: 35-36.

Burgess, J (1982) 'Perspectives on gift exchange and hospitable behaviour', *International Journal of Hospitality Management*, 1, 1: 49-57.

Burrell, G (2009) 'Handbooks, swarms and living dangerously', in M Alvesson, T Bridgman and H Willmott (Eds) *The Oxford Handbook of Critical Management Studies*, Oxford: Oxford University Press, 551-562.

Calder, S (2013) 'Shape of things to come? A glimpse into the hotel experience a decade ahead', *The Independent*, retrieved from http://www.independent.co.uk/travel/news-and-advice/shapes-of-things-to-come-a-glimpse-into-the-hotel-experience-a-decade-ahead-8952561.html, last accessed 23.01.14.

Campbell-Smith, G (1967) *The Marketing of the Meal Experience*, Guildford: University of Surrey Press.

Campbell-Smith, G (1970) 'Marketing the meal experience', *Cornell Hotel and Restaurant Administration Quarterly*, 11, 1: 73-102.

Campos Blanco, A, Oehmichen, A and Frood, S (2010) *Branded Budget Hotels in Europe: A Development Guide*, London and Manchester: HVS and Davis Langdon, retrieved from http://www.hvs.com/Content/3044.pdf, last accessed 01.05.14.

Chan, E S W (2011) 'Implementing environmental management systems in small- and medium-sized hotels: obstacles', *Journal of Hospitality and Tourism Research*, 35, 1: 3-23.

Chan, E S W and Lam, D (2013) 'Hotel safety and security systems: bridging the gap between managers and guests', *International Journal of Hospitality Management*, 32: 202-216.

Chareanpunsirikul, S and Wood, R C (2002) 'Mintzberg, managers and methodology: some observations from a study of hotel general managers', *Tourism Management*, 23, 3: 551-556.

Chia, R and Holt, R (2008) 'The nature of knowledge in business schools', *Academy of Management Learning and Education*, 7, 4: 471–486.

Choa, S, Woods, R H, Jang, S and Erdem, M (2006) 'Measuring the impact of human resource management practices on hospitality firms' performances', *International Journal of Hospitality Management*, 25, 2: 262–277.

Christensen Hughes, J (2008) 'Human resource management in the hospitality industry', in B Brotherton and R C Wood (Eds) *The Sage Handbook of Hospitality Management*, London: Sage, 273–301.

Cleveland, J N, O'Neill, J W, Himelright, J L, Harrison, M M, Crouter, A C and Drago, R (2007) 'Work and family issues in the hospitality industry: perspectives of entrants, managers, and spouses', *Journal of Hospitality and Tourism Research*, 31, 3: 275–298.

Commission on Industrial Relations (1971) *The Hotel and Catering Industry, Part 1: Hotels and Restaurants*, London: HMSO.

Commission for Racial Equality (2006) *Factfile 1: Employment and Ethnicity*, London: Commission for Racial Equality.

Corrigan, C (2002) 'An introduction to hotel engineering', retrieved from http://www.maintenanceresources.com/referencelibrary/ezine/hoteleng.html, last accessed 26.05.14.

Craige, B J (Ed) (2010) *Relativism in the Arts*, Athens, GA: University of Georgia Press.

Cross, R G (1997) 'Launching the revenue rocket: how revenue management can work for your business', *Cornell Hotel and Restaurant Administration Quarterly*, 38, 2: 32–43.

Crotty, J M (2012) 'For-profit colleges thrashed in congressional report', retrieved from http://www.forbes.com/sites/jamesmarshallcrotty/2012/08/02/for-profit-colleges-thrashed-in-congressional-report/, last accessed 04.04.14.

Cullen, J and McLaughlin, A (2006) 'What drives the persistence of presenteeism as a managerial value in hotels? Observations noted during an Irish work–life balance research project', *International Journal of Hospitality Management*, 25, 3: 510–516.

Cunill, O M and Forteza, C M (2010) 'The franchise contract in hotel chains: a study of hotel chain growth and market concentrations', *Tourism Economics*, 16, 3: 493–515.

Curtin, D W (1992) 'Food/body/person', in D W Curtin and L M Heldke (Eds) *Cooking, Eating, Thinking: Transformative Philosophies of Food*, Bloomington and Indianapolis: Indiana University Press, 3–22.

Davidson, M C G, Timo, N and Wang, Y (2010) 'How much does labour turnover cost? A case study of Australian four- and five-star hotels', *International Journal of Contemporary Hospitality Management*, 22, 4: 451–466.

Davis, N Z (2000) *The Gift in Sixteenth Century France*, Oxford: Oxford University Press.

Delves Broughton, P (2012a) *Life's A Pitch: What the World's Best Sales People Can Teach Us All*, New York: Penguin.

Delves Broughton, P (2012b) 'Selling deserves a corner office', *Financial Times*, 30 April, retrieved from http://www.ft.com/intl/cms/s/0/bb59f2b4-908e-11e1-8adc-00144feab49a.html?siteedition=intl#axzz30pCW5hCU, last accessed 05.05.14.

Derrida, J (2000) *Of Hospitality*, Stanford, CA: Stanford University Press.

Dev, C, Brown, J R and Zhou, K Z (2008) 'Global brand expansion: how to select a market entry strategy', *Cornell Hotel and Restaurant Administration Quarterly*, 48, 1: 13-27.

Dev, C, Buschman, J D and Bowen, J T (2010) 'Hospitality marketing: a retrospective analysis (1960-2010) and predictions (2010-2020)', *Cornell Hospitality Quarterly*, 51, 4: 459-469.

deRoos, J A (2010) 'Hotel management contracts – past and present', *Cornell Hospitality Quarterly*, 51, 1: 68-80.

DESTASIS (2013) 'Labour costs in Germany 32% higher than the EU average in 2012', retrieved from https://www.destatis.de/EN/PressServices/Press/pr/2013/03/PE13_116_624.html, last accessed 03.04.13.

Detlefsen, H and Glodz, M (2013) *Historical Trends: Hotel Management Contracts*, Chicago: HVS.

Dion, K, Berscheid, E and Walster, E (1972) 'What is beautiful is good', *Journal of Personality and Social Psychology*, 24, 3: 285-290.

DiPietro, R and Pizam, A (2007) 'Employee alienation in the quick service restaurant industry', *Journal of Hospitality and Tourism Research*, 32, 1: 22-39.

Driver, C (1983) *The British at Table 1940–1980*, London: Chatto and Windus.

Duncan, T, Scott, D G and Baum, T (2013) 'The mobilities of hospitality work: an exploration of issues and debates', *Annals of Tourism Research*, 41: 1-19.

Durand, T and Dameron, S (2011) 'Where have all the business schools gone?', *British Journal of Management*, 22, 3: 559-563.

Durie, A (2011) 'Review of K D Gorman "The Origins of Hospitality and Tourism"', Oxford: Goodfellow Publishers', *Hospitality and Society*, 1, 1: 91-92.

Dutton, C and Farbrother, C (2005) 'Responding to change in higher education hospitality provision: two universities' approaches', *Link*, 12: 10-11.

Economist, The (2009) 'Schumpeter: the pedagogy of the privileged', 26 September: 72, retrieved from http://www.economist.com/node/14493183, last accessed 08.05.14.

Economist, The (2010a) 'Who's writing the poor reviews?', 14 May, retrieved from http://www.economist.com/blogs/gulliver/2010/.../reviews_travel_websites, last accessed 30.05.12.

Economist, The (2010b) 'Asset-light or asset-right?', 13 November: 71-72.

Economist, The (2011a) 'The art of selling: the death of the salesman has been greatly exaggerated', 22 October, retrieved from http://www.economist.com/node/21533371, last accessed 05.05.14.

Economist, The (2011b) 'Starwood asks guests to share opinions in-house', 26 October, retrieved from http://www.economist.com/blogs/gulliver/2011/10/hotel-reviews, last accessed 02.06.12.

Economist, The (2012) 'Salesmanship: ice to the Eskimos. Can the dubious art of selling become more scientific?', 7 April, retrieved from http://www.economist.com/node/21552189, last accessed 05.05.14.

Economist, The (2013a) 'Global hotel rates: pricey nights', 6 February, retrieved from http://www.economist.com/blogs/gulliver/2013/02/global-hotel-rates, last accessed 09.03.13.

Economist, The (2013b) 'McDonald's University: fries with that? A degree in burgerology – and a job, too', 27 April, retrieved from http://www.economist.com/news/international/21576656-degree-burgerologyand-job-too-fries, last accessed 11.01.14.

Economist, The (2013c) 'Importing them by the shipload', 23 November, retrieved from http://www.economist.com/news/britain/21590558-attracting-tourists-britains-regions-will-get-tougher-economy-grows-importing-them, last accessed 25.11.13.

Economist, The (2013d) 'A short history of hotels: be my guest', 21 December, retrieved from http://www.economist.com/news/christmas-specials/21591743-be-my-guest, last accessed 07.05.14.

Economist, The (2014a) 'Schumpeter: those who can't, teach', 6 February, retrieved from http://www.economist.com/news/business/21595929-business-schools-are-better-analysing-disruptive-innovation-dealing-it-those-who, last accessed 09.03.14.

Economist, The (2014b) 'The sharing economy: boom and backlash', 26 April, retrieved from http://www.economist.com/news/business/21601254-consumers-and-investors-are-delighted-startups-offering-spare-rooms-or-rides-across-town, last accessed 10.05.14.

Economist, The (2014c) 'Airbnb versus hotels: room for all, for now', 26 April, retrieved from http://www.economist.com/news/business/21601259-there-are-signs-sharing-site-starting-threaten-budget-hotels-room-all, last accessed 10.05.14.

Education and Training Advisory Council (ETAC) (1983) *Hotel and Catering Skills – Now and in the Future, Part II: Jobs and Skills*, Wembley: HCITB.

Egencia (2012) *Business Travel by Business Travellers*, retrieved from https://www.egencia.co.uk/public/uk/media/pdfs/UK_Business_Traveller_Report.pdf, last accessed 02.06.12.

Ellis, R C and Stipanuk, D M (1999) *Security and Loss Prevention Management*, East Lansing, MI: American Hotel and Lodging Association, 2nd Ed.

Elmer, E M and Houran, J (2008) *Physical Attractiveness in the Workplace: Customers Do Judge Books by their Covers*, Mineola, NY: 20/20 Skills, retrieved from http://www.2020skills.com/asts/PhysicalAttractivenessintheWorkplace.pdf, last accessed 27.03.14.

Enz, C A (2001) 'What keeps you up at night?', *Cornell Hotel and Restaurant Administration Quarterly* 42, 2: 38-45.

Enz, C A (2009) 'Human resource management: a troubling issue for the global hotel industry', *Cornell Hospitality Quarterly*, 50, 4: 578-583.

Ernst and Young (2013) *Global Hospitality Insights:Top Thoughts for 2013*, retrieved from http://www.ey.com/Publication/vwLUAssets/Top_thoughts_for_2013/$FILE/Top_thoughts_for_2013.pdf, last accessed 26.01.14.

Erviani, N K (2014) 'Province badly needs hotel moratorium: Association', *The Jakarta Post*, 3 January: 5.

European Foundation for the Improvement of Living and Working Conditions (Eurofound) (2004) *EU Hotel and Restaurant Sector: Work and Employment Conditions*, retrieved from http://www.eurofound.europa.eu/pubdocs/2003/98/en/1/ef0398en.pdf, last accessed 15.09.13.

European Foundation for the Improvement of Living and Working Conditions (Eurofound) (2009) *Hotels and Restaurants Factsheet*, retrieved from http://www.eurofound.europa.eu/publications/htmlfiles/ef08144.htm, last accessed 03.04.13.

Falbo, B (1999) 'Room cleanliness remains key to garnering repeat business', *Hotel and Motel Management*, 214, 15: 60-61.

Feickert, J, Verma, R, Plaschka, G and Dev, C S (2006) 'Safeguarding your customers: the guest's view of hotel security', *Cornell Hotel and Restaurant Administration Quarterly*, 47, 3: 224-244.

Ferguson, D H and Berger, F (1984) 'Restaurant managers: what do they really do?', *Cornell Hotel and Restaurant Administration Quarterly*, 25: 26-36.

Fineman, S (2012) *Work: A Very Short Introduction*, Oxford: Oxford University Press.

Finkelstein, J (1989) *Dining Out: A Sociology of Modern Manners*, Cambridge: Polity Press.

Fitzhugh, K and Piercy, N (2010) 'Improving the relationship between sales and marketing', *European Business Review*, 22, 3: 287-305.

F.L.C. (2000) 'Travellers value cleanliness above all', *Cornell Hotel and Restaurant Administration Quarterly*, 41, 5: 6.

Frapin-Beaugé, A J M, Verginis, C and Wood, R C (2008) 'Accommodation and facilities management', in B Brotherton and R C Wood (Eds) *The Sage Handbook of Hospitality Management*, London: Sage, 383-399.

Frisbee, W R and Madeira, K (1986) 'Restaurant meals – convenience goods or luxuries?', *Service Industries Journal*, 6, 2: 172-192.

Gabriel, Y (1987) *Working Lives in Catering*, London: Routledge and Kegan Paul.

Gannon, J, Roper, A and Doherty, L (2010) 'The impact of hotel management contracting on IHRM practices: understanding the bricks and brains split', *International Journal of Contemporary Hospitality Management*, 22, 5: 638-658.

Gee, D A C (1994) 'The Scottish Hotel School – the first fifty years', in A V Seaton, C L Jenkins, R C Wood, P U C Dieke, M M Bennett, L R MacLellan and R Smith (Eds) *Tourism: The State of the Art*, Chichester: John Wiley, xvi-xxiii.

Gershuny, J (1978) *After Industrial Society: The Emerging Self-Service Economy*, London: Macmillan.

Gershuny, J (1979) 'The informal economy: its role in post-industrial society', *Futures*, 11, 1: 3-15.

Ghoshal, S (2005) 'Bad management theories are destroying good management practices', *Academy of Management Learning and Education*, 4, 1: 75–91.

Gilling, A (1996) 'Where there's Mc there's brass', *Times Higher Education Supplement*, 19 August: 24, retrieved from http://www.timeshighereducation.co.uk/books/where-theres-mc-theres-brass/162237.article, last accessed 26.03.14.

Go, F and Pine, R (1995) *Globalization Strategy in the Hotel Industry*, London: Routledge.

Goff, B (2007) 'Hospitality design that meets a hierarchy of needs', *Implications*, 5, 7, retrieved from http://www.informedesign.org/NewsletterArchive.aspx, last accessed 13.04.13.

Golding, C (1998) 'Hotels must update attitudes to women', *Caterer and Hotelkeeper*, 10 September: 18.

Goldsmith, A L, Nickson, D P, Sloan, D H and Wood, R C (1997) *Human Resource Management for Hospitality Services*, London: International Thomson Business Press.

Goldstein, K A (2012) *A Phased Approach to Investing in Hotel Environmental Performance*, retrieved from http://www.hvs.com/Content/3250.pdf, last accessed 18.09.13.

Goldstein, K A and Primlani, R V (2012) 'Current trends and opportunities in hotel sustainability', retrieved from http://www.hvs.com/article/5655/current-trends-and-opportunities-in-hotel-sustainability/, last accessed 18.09.13.

Gould, A M (2010) 'Working at McDonalds: some redeeming features of McJobs', *Work Employment and Society*, 24, 4: 780–802.

Greenfield, H I (2002) 'A note on the goods/services dichotomy', *Service Industries Journal*, 22, 4: 19–21.

Griseri, P, Schipper, F, Laurie, N and Diben, M (2010) 'Real knowledge managers', *The Philosophers' Magazine*, Issue 49: 77–80.

Gronroos, C (2007) *Service Management and Marketing: Customer Management in Service*, Chichester: John Wiley, 3rd Ed.

Guerrier, Y (1986) 'Hotel manager: an unsuitable job for a woman?', *Service Industries Journal*, 6, 2: 227–240.

Guerrier, Y (1987) 'Hotel managers' careers and their impact on hotels in Britain', *International Journal of Hospitality Management*, 6, 3: 121–130.

Guerrier, Y (1999) *Organizational Behaviour in Hotels: An International Perspective*, Chichester: John Wiley.

Guerrier, Y (2008) 'Organisation studies and hospitality management', in B Brotherton and R C Wood (Eds) *The Sage Handbook of Hospitality Management*, London: Sage, 257–272.

Guerrier, Y and Adib, A S (2000) ' "No, we don't provide that service":The harassment of hotel employees by customers', *Work, Employment and Society*, 14, 4: 689–705.

Guerrier, Y and Lockwood, A (1989) 'Developing hotel managers – a reappraisal', *International Journal of Hospitality Management*, 8, 2: 82–89.

Guillet, B D and Mattila, A (2010) 'A descriptive examination of corporate governance in the hospitality industry', *International Journal of Hospitality Management*, 29, 4: 677–684.

Gunn, J (2003) 'Third party politics', *Caterer and Hotelkeeper*, 6 February: 30–32.

Gupta, S and Wood, R C (2008) 'Human resource challenges in the Indian hotel sector', *Asian Journal of Tourism and Hospitality Research*, 2, 2: 87–96.

Gustafsson, I-B, Öström, Å, Johansson, J and Mossberg, L (2006) 'The Five Aspects Meal Model: a tool for developing meal services in restaurants', *Journal of Foodservice*, 17, 2: 84–93.

Hackett, C (1981) 'The woman food and beverage manager', *Cornell Hotel and Restaurant Administration Quarterly*, 22, 3: 79–85.

Hales, C and Nightingale, M (1986) 'What are unit managers supposed to do? A contingent methodology for investigating managerial role requirements', *International Journal of Hospitality Management*, 5, 1: 3–11.

Hall, J (2013) 'They won't be lovin' it: McDonald's admits 90% of employees are on zero-hours contracts without guaranteed work or a stable income', *The Independent*, 6 August, retrieved from http://www.independent.co.uk/news/uk/home-news/they-wont-be-lovin-it-mcdonalds-admits-90-of-employees-are-on-zerohours-contracts-without-guaranteed-work-or-a-stable-income-8747986.html, last accessed 12.04.14.

Handy, C (2007) *Myself and Other More Important Matters*, London: Arrow.

Harlow, K (2014) 'Hotels try to create female friendly experiences', *SharpHeels*, 26 February, retrieved from http://sharpheels.com/2014/02/female-friendly-hotels/, last accessed 24.05.14.

Harper, S, Brown, C and Irvine, W (2005) 'Qualifications: a fast-track to hotel general manager?', *International Journal of Contemporary Hospitality Management*, 17, 1: 51–64.

Harris, C and Small, J (2013) 'Obesity and hotel staffing: are hotels guilty of "lookism"?', *Hospitality and Society*, 3, 2: 111–127.

Harris, C, Tregidga, H and Williamson, D (2011) 'Cinderella in Babylon: the representation of housekeeping and housekeepers in the UK television series *Hotel Babylon*', *Hospitality and Society*, 1, 1: 47–66.

Harris, D (2012a) 'The waiting game', *Hospitality*, Issue 26: 30–33.

Harris, D (2012b) 'The true cost of refurbishment', *Hospitality*, Issue 27: 32–34.

Harris, D (2013) 'UK hotels attract new owners', *Hospitality*, Issue 30: 26–29.

Harris, K J (2008) 'Calculating ROI for training in the lodging industry: where is the bottom line?', *International Journal of Hospitality Management*, 26, 2: 485–498.

Harris, K J and Bonn, M A (2000) 'Training techniques and tools: evidence from the foodservice industry', *Journal of Hospitality and Tourism Research*, 24, 3: 320–335.

Hartley, J, Potts, J, Cunningham, S, Flew, T, Keane, M and Banks, J (2013) *Key Concepts in Creative Industries*, London: Sage.

Hassanien, A and Losekoot, E (2002) 'The application of facilities management expertise to the hotel renovation process', *Facilities*, 20, 7–8: 230–238.

Hayes, D K and Huffman, L (1985) 'Menu analysis: a better way', *Cornell Hotel and Restaurant Administration Quarterly*, 24, 4: 64–70.

Heal, F (1990) *Hospitality in Early Modern England*, Oxford: Clarendon Press.

Heller, L (2011) 'More business failures expected for hospitality SMEs', retrieved from http://www.bighospitality.co.uk/Trends-Reports/More-business-failures-expected-for-hospitality-SMEs, last accessed 11.05.14.

Hemmington, N (2007) 'From service to experience: understanding and defining the hospitality business', *Service Industries Journal*, 27, 6: 747–755.

Henson, S (2011) 'Survey shows bed bug pandemic is growing, even in large commercial facilities', FM Link, retrieved from http://www.fmlink.com/article.cgi?type=News&archive=false&title=Survey%20shows%20bed%20bug%20pandemic%20is%20growing%2C%20even%20in%20large%20commercial%20facilities&mode=source&catid=&display=article&id=42095, last accessed 21.04.14.

Hermans, O (2013) 'Customer relationship management', in R C Wood (Ed) *Key Concepts in Hospitality Management*, London: Sage, 18–22.

Heskett, J (2005) *Design: A Very Short Introduction*, Oxford: Oxford University Press.

Hickman, M (2010) 'Hoteliers to take their revenge on TripAdvisor's critiques in court', *The Independent*, 11 September, retrieved from http://www.independent.co.uk/travel/news-and-advice/hoteliers-to-take-their-revenge-on-tripadvisors-critiques-in-court-2076417.html, last accessed 30.05.12.

Hickman, M, Usborne, S and Grice, A (2008) 'Revealed: how the restaurant chains pocket your tips', *The Independent*, 15 July, retrieved from http://www.independent.co.uk./news/uk/home-news/revealed-how-the-restaurant-chains-pocket-your-tips-867634.html, last accessed 15.09.13.

Hinkin, T R and Tracey, J B (2000) 'The cost of turnover: putting a price on the learning curve', *Cornell Hotel and Restaurant Administration Quarterly*, 41, 3: 14–21.

Hochschild, A (1983) *The Managed Heart*, Berkeley: University of California Press.

Hodgkinson, G P and Starkey, K (2011) 'Not simply returning to the same answer over and over again: reframing relevance', *British Journal of Management*, 22, 3: 355–369.

Horizons (2011) 'Market structure and trends: key highlights from 2011', retrieved from http://www.hrzns.com/mint/pepper/tillkruess/downloads/tracker.php?url=http://www.hrzns.com/files/Market_Structure_and_Trends_Key_Highlights_From_2011.pdf&force&inline, last accessed 05.06.14.

Horizons (2012a) 'Does the US lead?', retrieved from http://www.hrzns.com/mint/pepper/tillkruess/downloads/tracker.php?url=http://www.hrzns.com/files/Does_the_US_lead.pdf&force&inline, last accessed 05.06.14.

Horizons (2012b) 'Consumer eating out trends: 10 things you need to know ... and what they mean', retrieved from http://www.hrzns.com/mint/pepper/tillkruess/downloads/tracker.php?url=http://www.hrzns.com/files/Consumer_eating_out_trends_10_things_you_need_to_know.pdf&force&inline, last accessed 06.06.14.

Horizons (2014) 'UK foodservice industry in 2013', retrieved from http://www.hrzns.com/mint/pepper/tillkruess/downloads/tracker.php?url=http://www.hrzns.com/files/UK_Foodservice_Industry_in_2013.pdf&force&inline, last accessed 06.06.14.

Hosany, S and Witham, M (2010) 'Dimensions of cruisers' experiences, satisfaction and intention to recommend', *Journal of Travel Research*, 49, 3: 351–364.

Hotel and Catering Industry Training Board (HCITB) (1984) *Women's Path to Management in the Hotel and Catering Industry*, London: HCITB.

Hsu, L-T, Jang, S and Canter, D D (2010) 'Factors affecting franchise decisions in the restaurant industry', *Journal of Hospitality and Tourism Research*, 34, 4: 440-454.

Huelin, A and Jones, P (1990) 'Thinking about catering systems', *International Journal of Operations and Production Management*, 10, 8: 42-52.

Hunter Powell, P and Watson, D (2006) 'Service unseen: the hotel room attendant at work', *International Journal of Hospitality Management*, 25, 2: 297-312.

Hyman, R (2006) 'Marxist thought and the analysis of work', in M Korczynski, R Hodson and P Edwards (Eds) *Social Theory at Work*, Oxford: Oxford University Press, 26-55.

Ibrahim, U (2012) 'Less is more', *Hospitality*, Issue 25: 28-29.

Ielacqua, L and Smith, T (2012) 'Hotel contracts – to lease or not to lease?', London: HVS, retrieved from http://www.hvs.com/article/5925/hotel-contracts-to-lease-or-not-to-lease/, last accessed 15.05.14.

IHS Global Insight (2014) *Franchise Business Economic Outlook for 2014*, retrieved from http://franchiseeconomy.com/wpcontent/uploads/2014/01/Franchise_Business_Outlook_January_2014-1-13-13.pdf, last accessed 08.06.14.

Institute of Hospitality (2010) 'Is security ever compromised by investment decisions?', *Hospitality*, Issue 20: 12.

Institute of Hospitality (2011) 'Risk management increases profits', *Hospitality*, Issue 24: 10-11.

International Labour Organization (ILO) (1965) *Tripartite Technical Meeting on Hotels, Restaurants and Similar Establishments, Report 1: Review of the Social and Economic Problems of Employees in Hotels, Restaurants and Similar Establishments*, Geneva: International Labour Office.

International Labour Organization (ILO) (1974) *Second Tripartite Technical Meeting for Hotels, Restaurants and Similar Establishments: Conditions of Work and Life of Migrant and Seasonal Workers Employed in Hotels, Restaurants and Similar Establishments*, Geneva: International Labour Office.

International Labour Organization (ILO) (1980) *Employment in the Hotel and Catering Industry*, Geneva: International Labour Office.

International Labour Organization (ILO) (2001) *Human Resources Development, Employment and Globalization in the Hotel, Catering and Tourism Sector: Report for Discussion at the Tripartite Meeting on the Human Resources Development, Employment and Globalization in the Hotel, Catering and Tourism Sector*, Geneva: International Labour Office, retrieved from http://www.turismdurabil.ro/literatura/csr/additional_documents/ILO-report%20tourism.pdf, last accessed 24.05.14.

International Labour Organization (ILO) (2010) *Developments and Challenges in the Hospitality and Tourism Sector*, Geneva: International Labour Office, retrieved from http://www.ilo.org/wcmsp5/groups/public/@ed_norm/@relconf/documents/meetingdocument/wcms_166938.pdf, last accessed 07.03.14.

International Labour Organization (ILO) (2014) *Employment in the Tourism Sector (Hotels and Restaurants as a Proxy)*, retrieved from http://www.ilo.org/wcmsp5/groups/public/---ed_dialogue/---sector/documents/publication/wcms_235636.pdf, last accessed 10.06.14.

JNA and HVS Design (2013) *2013 Hotel Cost Estimating Guide*, Washington, DC: JNA and HVS, retrieved from http://hvsdesignservices.com/wp-content/uploads/2014/04/2013-Cost-Estimating-Guide-.pdf, last accessed 23.05.14.

Johns, N and Jones, P (1999a) 'Systems and management: mind over matter', *The Hospitality Review*, 1, 3: 43-48.

Johns, N and Jones, P (1999b) 'Systems and management: the principles of performance', *The Hospitality Review*, 1, 4: 40-44.

Johns, N and Jones, P (2000) 'Systems and management: understanding the real world', *The Hospitality Review*, 2, 1: 47-52.

Johns, N and Pine, R (2002) 'Consumer behaviour in the food service industry: a review', *International Journal of Hospitality Management*, 21, 2: 119-134.

Johns, N, Tyas, P, Ingold, T and Hopkinson, S (1996) 'Investigation of the perceived components of the meal experience using perceptual gap methodology', *Progress in Tourism and Hospitality Research*, 2, 1: 15-26.

Johnson, K (1985) 'Labour turnover in hotels – revisited', *Service Industries Journal*, 5, 2: 135-152.

Johnson, K and Dodd, L (2010) 'Virtually real tourism', *The Hospitality Review*, 12, 1: 45-52.

Johnson, T S (2011) 'Business education is no more than vocational jibber-jabber', letter in *The Financial Times*, 2 May: 10.

Jolson, M A and Bushman, F A (1978) 'Third-party consumer information systems: the case of the food critic', *Journal of Retailing*, 54, 4: 63-79.

Jones, P (1993) 'A taxonomy of foodservice operations', in *2nd Annual CHME Research Conference*, Manchester, April.

Jones, P (1994) 'Foodservice operations', in P Jones and P Merricks (Eds) *The Management of Foodservice Operations*, London: Cassell, 3-17.

Jones, P and Lockwood, A (2008) 'Researching hospitality management: it's OK to use the "m" word', *The Hospitality Review*, 10, 3: 26-30.

Josephi, S (2013) 'Revenue management', in R C Wood (Ed) *Key Concepts in Hospitality Management*, London: Sage, 140-144.

Kappa, M M, Nitschke, A and Schappert, P B (1997) *Managing Housekeeping Operations*, Lansing, MI: Educational Institute of the AH&LA, 2nd Ed.

Kasavana, M L and Smith, D I (1982) *Menu Engineering*, Victoria: Hospitality Publications.

Kattara, H (2005) 'Career challenges for female managers in Egyptian hotels', *International Journal of Contemporary Hospitality Management*, 17, 3: 238-251.

Kerr, W R (2003) *Tourism Public Policy, and the Strategic Management of Failure*, London: Routledge.

Kerr, W R and Wood, R C (2000) 'Political values of tourism and hospitality industry professionals: a Scottish case study', *Tourism Management*, 21, 4: 323-330.

Kimes, S E (1989) 'The basics of yield management', *Cornell Hotel and Restaurant Administration Quarterly*, 30, 3: 14-19.

Kirk, D (2000) 'The value of systems in hospitality management', *The Hospitality Review*, 2, 2: 55-56.

Kline, S and Harris, K (2008) 'ROI is MIA: why are hoteliers failing to demand the ROI of training?', *International Journal of Contemporary Hospitality Management*, 20, 1: 45–59.

Knox, A (2010) '"Lost in translation": an analysis of temporary work agency employment in hotels', *Work, Employment and Society*, 24, 3: 449–467.

Kociatkiewicz, J and Kostera, M (2009) 'Experiencing the shadow: organizational exclusion and denial within experience economy', *Organization*, 17, 2: 257–282.

Kooi, S (2013) 'Front office management', in R C Wood (Ed) *Key Concepts in Hospitality Management*, London: Sage, 46–50.

Korczynski, M and Ott, U (2006) 'The menu in society: mediating structures of power and enchanting myths of individual sovereignty', *Sociology*, 40, 5: 911–928.

Kotler, P, Bowen, J and Makens, J (2009) *Hospitality and Tourism Marketing*, London: Pearson, 5th Ed.

Kumar, K (1978) *Prophecy and Progress*, Harmondsworth: Penguin.

Kumar, K (2004) *From Post-industrial to Post-modern Society: New Theories of the Contemporary World*, London: Wiley Blackwell.

Kurtz, M (2014) 'Airbnb's inroads into the hotel industry', retrieved from http://www.hvs.com/article/6952/in-focus-airbnbs-inroads-into-the-hotel-industry/?campaign=email, last accessed 25.06.14.

Ladkin, A (2002) 'Career analysis: a case study of hotel general managers in Australia', *Tourism Management*, 23, 4: 379–388.

Ladkin, A and Juwaheer, T D (2000) 'The career paths of hotel general managers in Mauritius', *International Journal of Contemporary Hospitality Management*, 12, 2: 119–125.

Ladkin, A. and Riley, M (1996) 'Mobility and structure in the career paths of UK hotel general managers: a labour market hybrid of the bureaucratic model?', *Tourism Management*, 17, 6: 443–452.

Lai, J H K (2013) 'An analysis of maintenance demand, manpower, and performance of hotel engineering facilities', *Journal of Hospitality and Tourism Research*, 37, 3: 426–444.

Lai, J H K and Yik, F W H (2012) 'Hotel engineering facilities: a case study of maintenance performance', *International Journal of Hospitality Management*, 31, 1: 229–235.

Lamminmaki, D (2011) 'An examination of factors motivating hotel outsourcing', *International Journal of Hospitality Management*, 30, 4: 963–973.

Lander, N (2006) 'The man behind Ping Pong', retrieved from http://www.nicklander.com/bodytext__.php?text=ping.txt&set=r_lo_ch, last accessed 27.03.14.

Lane, C (2010) 'The Michelin-starred restaurant sector as a cultural industry: a cross-national comparison of restaurants in the UK and Germany', *Food, Culture and Society*, 13, 4: 493–519.

Langston, J and Livingstone, B (2010) 'Riding the cycle', 30 years of *Hospitality* Magazine, UK Institute of Hospitality, 14–15.

Lanz, L, Fischhof, B and Lee, R (2010) *How are Hotels Embracing Social Media in 2010?*, Mineola, NY: HVS, retrieved from http://www.hvs.com/staticcontent/library/nyu2010/Journal/articles/SocialMediaIn2010.pdf, last accessed 19.04.14.

Lashley, C (2000) *Hospitality Retail Management: A Unit Manager's Guide*, Oxford: Butterworth-Heinemann.

Lashley, C (2007a) 'Studying hospitality: beyond the envelope', *International Journal of Culture, Tourism and Hospitality Research*, 1, 3: 185–188.

Lashley, C (2007b) 'Discovering hospitality: observations from recent research', *International Journal of Culture, Tourism and Hospitality Research*, 1, 3: 214–226.

Lashley, C (2008) 'Studying hospitality: insights from social sciences', *Scandinavian Journal of Hospitality and Tourism*, 8, 1: 69–84.

Lashley, C and Morrison, A J (Eds) (2000) *In Search of Hospitality: Historical and Sociological Perspectives*, Oxford: Butterworth-Heinemann.

Legrand, W, Simons-Kaufman, C and Sloan, P (2012) *Sustainable Hospitality and Tourism as Motors for Development: Case Studies from Developing Regions of the World*, London: Routledge.

Leiper, N (2008) 'Why "the tourism industry" is misleading as a generic expression: the case for the plural variation, "tourism industries" ', *Tourism Management*, 29, 2: 237–251.

Levere, J L (2010) 'Take our guests – Please! Comedy is just one tool used to educate staff', *Financial Times*, 8 September: 20.

Levitt, T (1972) 'Production line approach to service', *Harvard Business Review*, Sept.-Oct.: 41–52.

Ley, D A (1980) 'The effective General Manager: leader or entrepreneur?', *Cornell Hotel and Restaurant Administration Quarterly*, 21, 3: 66–67.

Li, L and Wang Leung, R (2001) 'Female managers in Asian hotels: profile and career challenges', *International Journal of Contemporary Hospitality Management*, 13, 4: 189–196.

Lin, I Y and Namasivayam, K (2011) 'Understanding restaurant tipping systems: a human resources perspective', *International Journal of Contemporary Hospitality Management*, 23, 7: 923–940.

Littler, C R (1982) *The Development of the Labour Process in Capitalist Societies*, London: Heinemann.

Liu, S, Xu, Q and Tao, T (2014) 'Analysis of development trend and operation models for midscale hotels in China', Guangzhou: HVS, retrieved from http://www.hvs.com/article/6866/analysis-of-development-trend-and-operation-models-for/, last accessed 25.04.14.

Lominé, L L (2003) 'Hospitality, leisure, sport and tourism in higher education in France', *Journal of Hospitality, Leisure, Sport and Tourism Education*, 2, 1: 105–112.

Lucas, R (1995) *Managing Employee Relations in the Hotel and Catering Industry*, London: Cassell.

Lucas, R (2004) *Employment Relations in the Hospitality and Tourism Industries*, London: Routledge.

Lugosi, P (2009) 'The production of hospitable space: commercial propositions and consumer co-creation in a bar operation', *Space and Culture*, 12, 4: 396–411.

Lugosi, P, Lynch, P and Morrison, A (2009) 'Critical hospitality management research', *Service Industries Journal*, 29, 10: 1465–1478.

Lupton, D (1996) *Food, the Body and the Self*, London: Sage.

Lynch, P A (2010) 'Publishing first-rate hospitality research', *The Hospitality Review*, 12, 3: 3-5.

Lyon, P, Taylor, S and Smith, S (1994) 'McDonaldization: a reply to Ritzer's thesis', *International Journal of Hospitality Management*, 13, 2: 95-99.

Lyon, P, Taylor, S and Smith, S (1995) 'Is Big Mac the big threat? A rejoinder to Silverstone and Wood', *International Journal of Hospitality Management*, 14, 2: 119-122.

McBride, K (2012) 'Is hospitality really a low-pay sector?', *Hospitality*, Issue 28: 19.

McNulty, E (2013) 'Let's just stop calling them leaders', *Strategy and Business*, Issue 73: 17-18, retrieved from http://www.strategy-business.com/blog/Lets-Just-Stop-Calling-Them-Leaders?gko=d1a76, last accessed 18.04.14.

Magnini, V and Honeycutt Jr, E D (2003) 'Learning orientation and the hotel expatriate manager experience', *International Journal of Hospitality Management*, 22, 3: 267-280.

Mansbach, D (2010) 'Hotel restaurant solutions – turning a headache into an opportunity', retrieved from http://www.hotelnewsresource.com/article45482.html, last accessed 31.03.14.

Marchante, A J, Ortega, B and Pagán, R (2007) 'An analysis of educational mismatch and labour mobility in the hospitality industry', *Journal of Hospitality and Tourism Research*, 31, 3: 299-320.

Marée, G (2013) 'Design for hotels', in R C Wood (Ed) *Key Concepts in Hospitality Management*, London: Sage, 23-27.

Mars, G and Nicod, M (1984) *The World of Waiters*, London: George Allen and Unwin.

Mars, G, Bryant, D and Mitchell, P (1979) *Manpower Problems in the Hotel and Catering Industry*, Farnborough: Gower.

Mauss, M (2000 [1924]) *The Gift*, London: Routledge.

Mazurkiewicz, R (1983) 'Gender and social consumption', *Service Industries Journal*, 3, 1: 49-62.

Melissen, F (2013a) 'Hotels, hospitality and sustainability', in R C Wood (Ed) *Key Concepts in Hospitality Management*, London: Sage, 68-72.

Melissen, F (2013b) 'Sustainable hospitality: a meaningful notion?', *Journal of Sustainable Tourism*, 21, 6: 810-824.

Mennell, S (1985) *All Manners of Food: Eating and Taste in England and France from the Middle Ages to the Present*, Oxford: Basil Blackwell.

Mesure, S and Blagoeva, E (2013) 'Hotels call time on the minibar: they're too much hassle to maintain and too expensive to police', *The Independent*, 31 March, retrieved from http://www.independent.co.uk/travel/hotels/hotels-call-time-on-the-minibar-theyre-too-much-hassle-to-maintain-and-too-expensive-to-police-8555237.html, last accessed 03.04.13.

Meudell, K and Rodham, K (1998) 'Money isn't everything … or is it? A preliminary research study into money as a motivator in the licensed house sector', *International Journal of Contemporary Hospitality Management*, 10, 4: 128-132.

Meyer, D (2006) *Setting the Table: The Transforming Power of Hospitality in Business*, New York: Harper.

Miles, S (2001) *Social Theory in the Real World*, London: Sage.

Miller, J E (1980) *Menu Pricing and Strategy*, New York: Van Nostrand Reinhold, 2nd Ed.

Mintzberg, H (2004) *Managers Not MBAs*, London: Financial Times/Prentice Hall.

Mintzberg, H (2012) 'Managing the myths of health care', *World Hospitals and Health Services*, 48, 3: 4-7.

Molz, J G and Gibson, S (Eds) (2007) *Mobilizing Hospitality: The Ethics of Social Relations in a Mobile World*, Aldershot: Ashgate.

Mooney, S (1994) 'Planning and developing the menu', in P Jones and P Merricks (Eds) *The Management of Foodservice Operations*, London: Cassell, 45-58.

Moorhead, G and Griffin, R W (1989) *Organizational Behaviour*, Princeton, NJ: Houghton-Mifflin.

Morrison, A and O'Gorman, K (2008) 'Hospitality studies and hospitality management: a symbiotic relationship', *International Journal of Hospitality Management*, 27, 2: 214-221.

Morrison, A J and O'Mahoney, B (2003) 'The liberation of hospitality management education', *International Journal of Contemporary Hospitality Management*, 15, 1: 38-44.

Mount, F (2013) *The New Few or a Very British Oligarchy*, London: Simon and Schuster.

Muhlmann, W E (1932) 'Hospitality', in E R A Seligmann (Ed) *Encyclopaedia of the Social Sciences*, Vol. 7, New York: Macmillan, 462-464.

Muston, S (2011) 'Not just gin and crisps: raising the (mini) bar', *The Independent*, 16 November, retrieved from http://www.independent.co.uk/travel/news-and-advice/not-just-gin-and--crisps-raising-the-mini-bar-6262608.html, last accessed 03.04.13.

Muston, S (2013) 'Room service: the final call on a luxury that is just not profitable', *The Independent*, 4 June, retrieved from http://www.independent.co.uk/travel/hotels/room-service-the-final-call-on-a-luxury-that-is-just-not-profitable-8644598.html, last accessed 05.09.13.

Nailon, P (1968) *A Study of Management Activities in Units of an Hotel Group*, unpublished M.Phil thesis, University of Surrey.

Nebel, E, Braunlich, C and Zhang, Y (1994) 'Hotel food and beverage directors' career paths in American luxury hotels', *International Journal of Contemporary Hospitality Management*, 6, 6: 3-10.

Ng, C W and Pine, R (2003) 'Women and men in hotel management in Hong Kong: perceptions of gender and career development issues', *International Journal of Hospitality Management*, 22, 1: 85-102.

Nicholls, L (2013) 'The gastropub revolution: pub-restaurants begin to dominate eating-out market', retrieved from http://www.bighospitality.co.uk/Trends-Reports/The-gastropub-revolution-Pub-restaurants-begin-to-dominate-eating-out-market, last accessed 07.06.13.

Nicholls, S and Kang, S (2012) 'Green initiatives in the lodging sector: are properties putting their principles into practice?', *International Journal of Hospitality Management*, 31, 2: 609-611.

Nickson, D and Warhurst, C (2007) 'Opening Pandora's Box: aesthetic labour and hospitality', in C Lashley, A Morrison and P Lynch (Eds) *Hospitality: A Social Lens*, London: Elsevier, 155-171.

NTC/Bacon and Woodrow (1995) *Pay and Benefits Pocket Book*, Henley: NTC Publications Ltd.

Office for National Statistics (2012) *Annual Survey of Hours and Earnings, 2012 Provisional Results*, retrieved from http://www.ons.gov.uk/ons/rel/ashe/annual-survey-of-hours-and-earnings/2012-provisional-results/stb-ashe-statistical-bulletin-2012.html, last accessed 28.03.13.

Office for National Statistics (2013) *Labour Market Statistics, September 2013*, retrieved from http://www.ons.gov.uk/ons/rel/lms/labour-market-statistics/september2013/statistical-bulletin.html, last accessed 14.09.13.

O'Gorman, K (2006) 'Jacques Derrida's philosophy of hospitality', *The Hospitality Review*, 8, 4: 50-57.

O'Mahony, B (2009) 'University kitchen nightmares enter a new ERA', *The Hospitality Review*, 11, 4: 5-7.

O'Neill, J W and Matilla, A S (2010) 'Hotel brand strategy', *Cornell Hospitality Quarterly*, 51, 1: 27-34.

Palmer, A (2007) *Principles of Services Marketing*, London: McGraw-Hill, 5th Ed.

Panvisavas, V and Taylor, J S (2006) 'The use of management contracts by international hotel firms in Thailand', *International Journal of Contemporary Hospitality Management*, 18, 3: 231-245.

Paraskevas, A (2013) 'Aligning strategy to threat: a baseline anti-terrorism strategy for hotels', *International Journal of Contemporary Hospitality Management*, 25, 1: 140-162.

Parsa, H G, Self, J T, Njite, D and King, T (2005) 'Why restaurants fail', *Cornell Hotel and Restaurant Administration Quarterly*, 46, 3: 304-322.

Pavesic, D V (1983) 'Cost/margin analysis: a third approach to menu pricing and design', *International Journal of Hospitality Management*, 2, 3: 127-134.

Pavesic, D V (1985) 'Prime members: finding your menu's strengths', *Cornell Hotel and Restaurant Administration Quarterly*, 26, 3: 71-77.

Pavesic, D V (1989) 'Psychological aspects of menu pricing', *International Journal of Hospitality Management*, 8, 1: 43-49.

Payne, L and Perret, S (2014) '2014 hotel franchising in Europe', retrieved from http://www.hvs.com/article/6934/hotel-franchising-in-europe-2014/, last accessed 20.06.14.

Peacock, L (2012) 'Hotel chain "can't find UK staff" as foreign workers take most jobs', *The Telegraph*, retrieved from http://www.telegraph.co.uk/finance/jobs/9113424/Hotel-chain-cant-find-UK-staff-as-foreign-workers-take-most-jobs.html, last accessed 07.03.13.

People 1st (2010) *The Hospitality, Leisure, Travel and Tourism Sector: Key Facts and Figures*, retrieved from http://www.people1st.co.uk/getattachment/Research-policy/

Research-reports/State-of-the-Nation-Hospitality-Tourism/State_of_the_ Nation_2010_Executive_Summary.pdf.aspx, last accessed 22.11.14.

People 1st (2014) *State of the Nation Report 2013*, retrieved from http://www. people1st.co.uk/getattachment/Research-policy/Research-reports/State- of-the-NationHospitalityTourism/SOTN_2013_final.pdf.aspx, last accessed 09.07.14.

Pfeffer, J and Sutton, R L (2006) *Hard Facts, Dangerous Half-Truths and Total Nonsense: Profiting from Evidence-based Management*, Boston: Harvard Business Press.

Pickworth, J R (1988) 'Service delivery systems in the food service industry', *International Journal of Hospitality Management*, 7, 1: 43-62.

Pickworth, J R and Fletcher, E L (1980) 'The role of today's food service manager', *Cornell Hotel and Restaurant Administration Quarterly*, 21, 3: 68-72.

Piercy, N (2012) 'Letter', *Financial Times*, 8 May: 10.

Pine, J and Gilmore, J (1999) *The Experience Economy*, Boston: Harvard Business School Press.

Pizam, A and Shani, A (2009) 'The nature of the hospitality industry: present and future managers' perspectives', *Anatolia – An International Journal of Tourism and Hospitality Research*, 20, 1: 134-150.

Polizzi, O (2012) 'Hotel pet hates: from towel art to bath butler service', *The Telegraph*, retrieved from http://www.telegraph.co.uk/travel/9477339/Hotel-pet-hates- from-towel-art-to-bath-butler-service.html, last accessed 07.03.13.

Pritchard, A and Morgan, N (2006) 'Hotel Babylon? Exploring hotels as liminal sites of transition and transgression', *Tourism Management*, 27, 5: 762-772.

Purcell, K (1993) 'Equal opportunities in the hospitality industry: custom and credentials', *International Journal of Hospitality Management*, 12, 2: 127-140.

Pyper, D and McGuinness, F (2014) 'Zero-hours contracts', Standard Note SN/BT/6553, London: House of Commons Library, retrieved from http://www.parliament.uk/ briefing-papers/SN06553/zerohours-contracts, last accessed 12.04.14.

Qu, X and O'Neill, J W (2010) 'Work–family balance as a potential strategic advantage: a hotel general manager perspective', *Journal of Hospitality and Tourism Research*, 34, 4: 415-439.

Rahman, N (2010) 'Toward a theory of restaurant décor: an empirical examination of Italian restaurants in Manhattan', *Journal of Hospitality and Tourism Research*, 34, 3: 330-340.

Rahmana, I, Reynolds, D and Svarena, S (2012) 'How "green" are North American hotels? An exploration of low-cost adoption practices', *International Journal of Hospitality Management*, 31, 3: 720-727.

Rawstron, C (1999) 'Housekeeping management in the contemporary hotel industry', in C S Verginis and R C Wood (Eds) *Accommodation Management: Perspectives for the International Hotel Industry*, London: International Thomson Business Press, 114-127.

Raybould, M and Wilkins, H (2005) 'Over qualified and under experienced: turning graduates into hospitality managers', *International Journal of Contemporary Hospitality Management*, 17, 3: 203-216.

Riley, M (1984) 'Hotels and group identity', *Tourism Management*, 3, 2: 102-109.

Riley, M (2000) 'Can hotel restaurants ever be profitable? Short- and long-term perspectives', in R C Wood (Ed) *Strategic Questions in Food and Beverage Management*, Oxford: Butterworth-Heinemann, 112-118.

Riley, M (2005) 'Food and beverage management: a review of change', *International Journal of Contemporary Hospitality Management*, 17, 1: 88-93.

Riley, M and Turam, K (1988) 'The career paths of hotel managers: a developmental approach', in *Proceedings of the International Association of Hotel Management Schools Symposium*, Leeds, UK, November.

Riley, M, Ladkin, A and Szivas, E (2002) *Tourism Employment: Analysis and Planning*, Bristol: Channel View Publications.

Ritzer, G (1993) *The McDonaldization of Society*, Beverley Hills: Pine Forge Press.

Rivera, M (2013) 'A 7-step strategy to manage hotel online guest reviews', San Francisco: HVS, retrieved from http://www.hvs.com/article/6283/a-7-step-strategy-to-manage-hotel-online-guest-reviews/, last accessed 19.04.14.

Robbins, S P (1992) *Essentials of Organizational Behaviour*, London: Prentice-Hall, 3rd Ed.

Robbins, T (2012) 'Prefab rooms and linen by Frette', *Financial Times (Life and Arts)*, 14/15 July: 7.

Roberts, J (2005) 'The Ritzerization of knowledge', *Critical Perspectives on International Business*, 1, 1: 56-63.

Robinson, R N S (2008) 'Revisiting hospitality's marginal worker thesis: a mono-occupational perspective', *International Journal of Hospitality Management*, 27, 3: 403-413.

Robson, S and Pullman, M (2005) 'Hotels: differentiating with design', *Implications*, retrieved from http://www.informedesign.org/_news/june_v03r-p.pdf, last accessed 04.04.13.

Rodgers, S (2005a) 'Selecting a food service system: a review', *International Journal of Contemporary Hospitality Management*, 17, 2: 157-169.

Rodgers, S (2005b) 'Applied research and educational needs in food service management', *International Journal of Contemporary Hospitality Management*, 17, 4: 302-314.

Rodgers, S (2007) 'Innovation in food service technology and its strategic role', *International Journal of Hospitality Management*, 26, 4: 899-912.

Rodgers, S (2009) 'The state of technological sophistication and the need for new specialised tertiary degrees in food services', *International Journal of Hospitality Management*, 28, 1: 71-77.

Roper, A (2013) 'All change: the new competitive landscape of multinational hotel companies', press release, University of West London, retrieved from http://www.uwl.ac.uk/sites/default/files/Academic-schools/London-School-of-Hospitality%20and%20Tourism/Campaigns-andevents/PDF/All_Change_lecture_abstract_Angela_Roper.pdf, last accessed 15.05.14.

Rose, M (1988) *Industrial Behaviour*, Harmondsworth: Penguin, 2nd Ed.

Rosenberg, P and Choufany, H M (2009) 'Spiritual lodging – the Sharia-compliant hotel concept', Dubai: HVS Global Hospitality Services, retrieved from http://

www.hvs.com/article/3894/spiritual-lodging-the-sharia-compliant-hotel-concept/, last accessed 26.09.13.

Rushmore, S (2003) 'How can hotels make money on F&B?', *Hotels*, April: 30, retrieved from http://www.hvs.com/article/51/how-can-hotels-make-money-on-f-b/, last accessed 11.01.14.

Saunders, K C (1981) *Social Stigma of Occupations*, Farnborough: Gower.

Schiller, B (2011) 'Academia strives for relevance' *Financial Times* online, 25 April, retrieved from http://www.ft.com/intl/cms/s/2/4eeab7d4-6c37-11e0-a049-00144feab49a.html#axzz, last accessed 17.04.14.

Schneider, M, Tucker, G and Scoviak, M (1999) *The Professional Housekeeper*, New York: John Wiley, 4th Ed.

Seed, J (2010) *Marx: A Guide for the Perplexed*, London: Continuum.

Seul Ki, L and SooCheong, J (2012) 'Re-examining the overcapacity of the US lodging industry', *International Journal of Hospitality Management*, 31, 4: 1050-1058.

Shamir, B (1978) 'Between bureaucracy and hospitality – some organizational characteristics of hotels', *Journal of Management Studies*, 15, 3: 285-307.

Shamir, B (1981) 'The workplace as a community: the case of British hotels', *Industrial Relations Journal*, 12, 6: 45-56.

Simpson, M and Rossiter, P (2012) 'Join the linen room lockdown', *Hospitality*, Issue 26: 18.

Singh, A (2010) 'Environment responsive solutions for hospitality', retrieved from http://www.hvs.com/article/4592/environment-responsive-solutions-for-hospitality/, last accessed 18.09.13.

Singh, A J, Kline, R D, Ma, Q and Beals, P (2012) 'Evolution of hotel asset management: the historical context and current profile of the profession', *Cornell Hospitality Quarterly*, 53, 4: 326-338.

Slattery, P (1997) 'Management – are we heading for mediocrity?', *Hospitality*, July/August: 24-25.

Slattery, P (2002) 'Finding the hospitality industry', *Journal of Hospitality, Leisure, Sport and Tourism Education*, 1, 1: 19-28.

Slattery, P (2010) 'The rise of global corporations', 30 Years of *Hospitality* Magazine, UK Institute of Hospitality, 10-12.

Sloan, P, Legrand, W and Chen, J C (2011) *Sustainability in the Hospitality Industry*, London: Routledge.

Smith, M, MacLeod, N and Hart Robertson, M (2010) *Key Concepts in Tourist Studies*, London: Sage.

Smith, O (2012) 'Travellers fleeced by hotel Wi-Fi charges', *The Telegraph*, retrieved from http://www.telegraph.co.uk/travel/travelnews/9116022/Travellers-fleeced-by-hotel-Wi-Fi-charges.html, last accessed 09.03.13.

Smith, S L J (2006) 'How big? How many? Enterprise size distributions in tourism and other industries', *Journal of Travel Research*, 45, 1: 53-58.

Sohn, J, Tang, C-H and Jang, S (2013) 'Does the asset-light and fee-oriented strategy create value?', *International Journal of Hospitality Management*, 32: 270-277.

Soltani, E and Wilkinson, A (2010) 'What is happening to flexible workers in the supply chain partnerships between hotel housekeeping departments and their partner employment agencies?', *International Journal of Hospitality Management*, 29, 1: 108-119.

Stalcup, L D and Pearson, T A (2001) 'A model of the causes of management turnover in hotels', *Journal of Hospitality and Tourism Research*, 25, 1: 17-30.

Stewart, M (2009) *The Management Myth: Why the Experts Keep Getting it Wrong*, New York: Norton.

Stierand, M and Lynch, P (2008) 'The art of creating culinary innovations', *Tourism and Hospitality Research*, 8, 4: 337-350.

Stierand, M and Wood, R C (2012) 'Reconceptualising the commercial meal experience in the hospitality industry', *Journal of Hospitality and Tourism Management*, 19, 1: 143-148.

Strannegård, L and Strannegård, M (2012) 'Works of art: aesthetic ambitions in design hotels', *Annals of Tourism Research*, 39, 4: 1995-2012.

Sturman, M C (2001) 'The compensation conundrum: does the hospitality industry shortchange its employees – and itself?', *Cornell Hotel and Restaurant Administration Quarterly*, 42, 4: 70-76.

Tadajewski, M, MacLaran, P, Parsons, E and Parker, M (2011) *Key Concepts in Critical Management Studies*, London: Sage.

Taylor, J, Reynolds, D and Brown, D M (2009) 'Multi-factor menu analysis using data envelopment analysis', *International Journal of Contemporary Hospitality Management*, 21, 2: 213-225.

Telfer, E (1996) *Food For Thought: Philosophy and Food*, London: Routledge.

Thadani, M and Mobar, J S (2013) 'Critical challenges faced by hotel owners in India', Gurgaon: HVS, retrieved from http://www.hvs.com/article/6568/critical-challenges-faced-by-hotel-owners-in-india/, last accessed 22.04.14.

Thomas, R, Shaw, G and Page, S J (2011) 'Understanding small firms in tourism: a perspective on research trends and challenges', *Tourism Management*, 32, 5: 963-976.

Thompson, P (1989) *The Nature of Work: An Introduction to Debates on the Labour Process*, London: Macmillan.

Thrane, C (2010) 'Education and earnings in the tourism industry – the role of sheepskin effects', *Tourism Economics*, 16, 3: 549-563.

Timo, N and Littler, C (1996) 'The routinisation of services: the McDonaldization of service work?', in *The Globalization of Production and the Regulation of Labour Conference*, Warwick, September.

Tomsky, J (2012) *Heads in Beds: A Reckless Memoir of Hotels, Hustles and So-Called Hospitality*, New York: Anchor Books.

Travolution (2013) 'GenY travel staff get on due to digital skills but not loyal', retrieved from http://www.travolution.co.uk/articles/2013/04/19/6657/gen-y-travel-staff-get-on-due-to-digital-skills-but-not-loyal.html, last accessed 06.03.14.

Tresidder, R (2011) 'Reading hospitality: the semiotics of Le Manoir aux Quat'Saisons', *Hospitality and Society*, 1, 1: 167-184.

UK Cabinet Office (2008) *Food: An Analysis of the Issues*, retrieved from http://
webarchive.nationalarchives.gov.uk/+/http:/www.cabinetoffice.gov.uk/media/
cabinetoffice/strategy/assets/food/food_analysis.pdf, last accessed 10.06.14.

Umbreit, W T (1986) 'Developing behaviourally-anchored scales for evaluating job
performance of hotel managers', *International Journal of Hospitality Management*,
5, 2: 55–61.

Umbreit, W T and Eder, R W (1987) 'Linking hotel manager behaviour with
outcome measures of effectiveness', *International Journal of Hospitality Management*,
6, 3: 139–147.

UN Department of Safety and Security (2006) *Be Safe Be Secure: Security Guidelines for Women*, retrieved from http://www.ilo.org/wcmsp5/groups/public/---
dgreports/---gender/documents/instructionalmaterial/wcms_083929.pdf,   last
accessed 10.04.13.

Underhill, P (2011) 'Should I stay or should I go?', in *What Women Want: The Science
of Female Shopping*, New York: Simon and Schuster, 71–88.

University and College Union (2010) *Subprime Education? A Report on the Growth of
Private Providers and the Crisis of UK Higher Education*, London: UCU, retrieved
from http://www.ucu.org.uk/media/pdf/k/l/ucu_subprimeed_briefing_sep10.
pdf, last accessed 08.03.14.

Unvala, C and Donaldson, J (1988) 'The service sector: some unresolved issues',
Service Industries Journal, 8, 4: 459–69.

van Ginneken, R (2011) 'Expert attitudes to management contracts in the Dutch
hotel industry: a DELPHI approach', *Journal of Hospitality and Tourism Management*,
18, 1: 140–146.

Vardharajan, K and Mobar, J S (2013) 'Hotels in India: trends and opportunities
2013', Gurgaon: HVS, retrieved from http://www.hvs.com/article/6499/2013-
hotels-in-india-trends-opportunities/, last accessed 25.04.14.

Veller, T (2007) 'Bellboy to general manager – how long is the road?', Hotel
News Resource, retrieved from http://www.hvs.com/article/2664/bellboy-to-
general-manager-how-long-is-the-road/, last accessed 03.04.13.

Venison, P (1983) *Managing Hotels*, Oxford: Butterworth-Heinemann.

Venison, P (2005) *100 Tips for Hoteliers: What Every Successful Hotel Professional Needs
to Know and Do*, Lincoln, NE: iUniverse.

Waldthausen, V and Oehmichen, A (2013) 'A new breed of traveller: how consumers
are driving change in the hotel industry', London: HVS, retrieved from http://
www.hvs.com/article/6675/a-new-breed-of-traveller-%E2%80%93-how-
consumers-are-driving-change/, last accessed 18.06.14.

Walker, B (2010) 'Paying for it', *Hospitality*, Issue 19: 40–43.

Walker, B (2011) 'Housekeeping, the heart of hotels', *Hospitality*, Issue 23: 18–22.

Walker, B (2012a) 'Don't keep security a secret', *Hospitality*, Issue 26: 22–25.

Walker, B (2012b) 'Business innovation', *Hospitality*, Issue 28: 20–24.

Walker, B (2013a) 'Stretching the boundaries', *Hospitality*, Issue 29: 12–13.

Walker, B (2013b) 'Institute launches new Academic Partner scheme', *Hospitality*,
Issue 31: 11.

Walker, B and Mielisch, A (2010) 'Dutch courage', *Hospitality*, Issue 20: 42–45.

Waller, K (1996) *Improving Food and Beverage Performance*, Oxford: Butterworth-Heinemann.

Walmsley, A (2011) *CHME Report on Hospitality Higher Education in the UK, 2011*, Leeds: Council for Hospitality Management Education, retrieved from http://www.chme.org.uk/download/files/Publications/CHME_Report_on_Hospitality_Higher_Education_UK_2011.pdf, last accessed 03.04.13.

Ward, T (2013) 'Checking into Africa', *Hospitality*, Issue 30: 34–36.

Warde, A and Martens L (1998) 'Eating out and the commercialisation of mental life', *British Food Journal*, 100, 3: 147-153.

Warde, A and Martens, L (1999) 'Eating out: reflections on the experience of consumers in England', in J Germov and L Williams (Eds) *A Sociology of Food and Nutrition: The Social Appetite*, Oxford: Oxford University Press, 116-134.

Warde, A and Martens, L (2000) *Eating Out: Social Differentiation, Consumption and Pleasure*, Cambridge: Cambridge University Press.

Warhurst, C and Nickson, D (2007) 'Employee experience of aesthetic labour in retail and hospitality', *Work, Employment and Society*, 21, 1: 103-120.

Waryszak, R and King, B (2001) 'Managerial attitudes towards work activities in the hospitality and service industries', *International Journal of Contemporary Hospitality Management*, 13, 4: 197-203.

Weiss, R, Feinstein, R, Hale, A and Dalbor, M (2004) 'Customer satisfaction of theme restaurant attributes and their influence on return intent', *Journal of Foodservice Business Research*, 7, 1: 23-41.

White, M (2012) 'Hotels target upgrades', *Portfolio*, Issue 74, February (published for Emirates Airlines by Motivate Publishing, Dubai).

Whitla, P, Walters, P G P and Davies, H (2007) 'Global strategies in the international hotel industry', *International Journal of Hospitality Management*, 26, 4: 777-792.

Williams, A (2002) *Understanding the Hospitality Consumer*, Oxford: Butterworth-Heinemann.

Williams, S, Adam-Smith, D and Norris, G (2004) 'Remuneration practices in the UK hospitality industry in the age of the National Minimum Wage', *Service Industries Journal*, 24, 1: 171-186.

Williams-Knight, E (2014) 'Catering to women: hotel design and amenities', retrieved from http://hotelexecutive.com/business_review/3512/catering-to-women-hotel-design-and amenities, last accessed 24.05.14.

Williamson, D, Harris, C, Matthews, S and Parker J (2012) 'Golden opportunities: a decade of exit interviews and turnover in the New Zealand hotel industry', in *Proceedings of the CAUTHE Conference 2012: The New Golden Age of Tourism and Hospitality, Book 2*, Melbourne: CAUTHE, 675-684.

Withnall, A (2014) 'London overtakes Paris to become world's most popular destination for foreign tourists', *The Independent*, 8 May, retrieved from http://www.independent.co.uk/news/uk/home-news/london-overtakes-paris-to-become-worlds-most-popular-destination-for-foreign-tourists-9340154.html, last accessed 12.05.14.

Wood, R C (1992) 'Deviants and misfits: hotel and catering labour and the marginal worker thesis', *International Journal of Hospitality Management*, 11, 3: 179–182.

Wood, R C (1994a) 'Hotel culture and social control', *Annals of Tourism Research*, 21, 1: 65–80.

Wood, R C (1994b) *Organizational Behaviour for Hospitality Management*, Oxford: Butterworth-Heinemann.

Wood, R C (1995a) 'Wages Council abolition: doing labour a favour?', *Renewal*, 3, 1: 72–81.

Wood, R C (1995b) *The Sociology of the Meal*, Edinburgh: Edinburgh University Press.

Wood, R C (1996) 'The last feather-bedded industry? Government, politics and the hospitality industry during and after the 1992 General Election', *Tourism Management*, 17, 8: 583–592.

Wood, R C (1997) *Working in Hotels and Catering*, London: International Thomson Business Press, 2nd Ed.

Wood, R C (1998) 'New wine in old bottles: critical limitations of the McDonaldization thesis – the case of hospitality services', in M Alfino, JS Caputo and R Wynyard (Eds) *McDonaldization Revisited: Critical Essays on Consumer Culture*, Westport, CT: Praeger, 85–104.

Wood, R C (2000a) 'What do we really know about the requirements of food and beverage consumers? Food and beverage markets in the modern age', in R C Wood (Ed) *Strategic Questions in Food and Beverage Management*, Oxford: Butterworth-Heinemann, 10–27.

Wood, R C (2000b) 'Why are there so many celebrity chefs and cooks (and do we need them)?', in R C Wood (Ed) *Strategic Questions in Food and Beverage Management*, Oxford: Butterworth-Heinemann, 129–152.

Wood, R C (2004a) 'Hospitality education: they think it's all over … it is now', *The Hospitality Review*, 6, 2: 16–18.

Wood, R C (2004b) 'Public sorrow, private joy', *The Hospitality Review*, 6, 4: 23–27.

Wood, R C (2007) 'The future of food and beverage management research', *Journal of Hospitality and Tourism Management*, 14, 1: 6–16.

Wood, R C (2008) 'Food production and service systems theory', in B Brotherton and R C Wood (Eds) *The Sage Handbook of Hospitality Management*, London: Sage, 443–459.

Wood, R C (2011) 'Whatever happened to hotel design?', *The Hospitality Review*, 13, 4: 23–25.

Wood, R C (2013a) 'Hospitality management education', in R C Wood (Ed) *Key Concepts in Hospitality Management*, London: Sage, 63–67.

Wood, R C (2013b) 'Food production and service systems', in R C Wood (Ed) *Key Concepts in Hospitality Management*, London: Sage, 36–40.

Wood, R C (2014) 'Marxism, snobbery and the triumph of bourgeois values: a speculative analysis of implications for hospitality', *Research in Hospitality Management*, 4, 1-2: 9–12.

Worsfold, P (1989) 'Leadership and managerial effectiveness in the hospitality industry', *International Journal of Hospitality Management*, 8, 2: 145-155.

Wright, E (2013) 'The multi-branded hotel: new efficiencies through innovation', http://www.hvs.com/article/6702/the-multi-branded-hotel-new-efficiencies-through/, last accessed 15.01.14.

Wylie, I (2013) 'Research? Most people cannot understand it', *Financial Times*, 7 April, retrieved from http://www.ft.com/intl/cms/s/2/cde6163c-7f4a-11e2-97f6-00144feabdc0.html#axzz302q8ehha, last accessed 27.04.14.

Wynne-Jones, R (1996) 'They'll cook but they won't wait', *The Independent*, 23 June: 11.

Yu-Chin, H (2012) 'Hotel companies' environmental policies and practices: a content analysis of their web pages', *International Journal of Contemporary Hospitality Management*, 24, 1: 97-121.

Zampoukos, K and Ioannides, D (2011) 'The tourism labour conundrum: agenda for new research in the geography of hospitality workers', *Hospitality and Society*, 1, 1: 25-45.

INDEX

CPSIA information can be obtained
at www.ICGtesting.com
Printed in the USA
LVOW03s0912140216
475047LV00013B/380/P

9 781446 246955